FRAGILE DEMOCRACY

FRAGILE DEMOCRACY

The Use and Abuse of Power in Western Societies

Eva Etzioni-Halevy

Transaction Publishers
New Brunswick (U.S.A.) and London (U.K.)

Library of Congress Catalog Number: 88-28289
ISBN: 0-88738-270-3
Printed in the United States of America

Library of Congress Cataloging in Publication Data
Etzioni-Halevy, Eva.
Fragile democracy: on the use and abuse of power in Western societies/Eva Etzioni-Halevy.
p. cm.
Includes index.
ISBN 0-88738-270-3
1. Power (Social sciences) 2. Elite (Social sciences) 3. Democracy. I. Title.
JC330.E89 1989
321.8—dc19 88-28289
CIP

Contents

Acknowledgments

This project was initiated while I was on secondment to the Department of Sociology, Research School of Social Sciences, The Australian National University. I would like to express my gratitude to that department and its head, Professor Frank L. Jones, for affording me the opportunity to concentrate on my research and writing exempt from regular teaching duties. Further thanks are due to the Australian National University Faculties Research Fund Committee for the generous allocations of funds that have made the fieldwork included in this project possible. I would also like to take this opportunity to thank the key informants who have granted me interviews and have provided invaluable information in the course of this fieldwork. The commitment to preserve anonymity makes it impossible to mention them by name, and I must ask them to accept this general statement as an expression of personal indebtedness.

In the social sciences ideas tend to emerge as a response to other ideas and to develop as a response to critiques, and the present project is no exception. My greatest indebtedness, therefore, is not only to the theorists whose ideas have spurred this project (cited in the main body of this book), but also to the scholars who have honored it with their critical comments. Thanks for such—most helpful—comments are due in particular to the members of the following departments that have hosted work-in-progress seminars on this project: the Department of Sociology, RSSS, and the Department of Sociology, the Faculties, the Australian National University, Canberra; the Department of Sociology, La Trobe University, Melbourne, Australia; the Department of Sociology, the Ben-Gurion University, Beer Sheba; and the Department of Sociology at Bar-Ilan University, Ramat-Gan, Israel.

I am also indebted to Dr. John Braithwaite, Professor John Higley, and Professor Barry Hindess, who have read parts of this study in its various previous incarnations and reincarnations. Their critical comments have helped me greatly in the protracted process of developing, clarifying, and reformulating this book's ideas, even though the final result may not live up to their expectations.

In writing the two historical chapters included in this book I have been fortunate to have had the benefit of the counsel of the historians Dr. Iain McCalman, Mr. Christopher McGuffie, and Professor William D. Rubinstein. Special thanks for his patience are due to Professor Rubinstein, on whom I have also inflicted much of my previous work, and who has now come to my aid once again. All three scholars have offered important advice on the historical sources to be consulted and on the historical accuracy of the analysis. Perhaps even more importantly, they have also provided invaluable guidance on, and have helped me clarify to my own satisfaction, the manner in which a review of historical facts and developments may be used in an endeavor to substantiate a social-science argument. For all this I am deeply grateful to them.

I also owe a special debt of gratitude to Ms. June Adams for her patient, diligent, and most conscientious research assistance, as well as for her personal encouragement. In the acknowledgments to my previous books I have also thanked the people who have been saddled with the tedious task of typing and retyping the manuscripts. This is now no longer necessary, as I have been composing my own work on the word processor and have been introducing revisions, and revisions of revisions, as I go along. However, I would like to express my heartfelt appreciation to Ms. Jill Deck and Ms. Helen Felton for their indirect contribution to this book, through their success in teaching the craft of word processing to one as mechanically inept as I am.

Introduction: Democracy and Motherhood

In some respects democracy is like motherhood: it is unexceptionable, enjoys universal support (or so it would seem), and even those who do not practice it themselves pay lip service to it. But only those who do practice it (or write books about it) are fully aware of the many problems and difficulties it entails. And, just like support for motherhood, support for democracy has been mingled with condescension on the one hand, and idealization on the other hand.

On the one hand, many now believe that by itself motherhood is not sufficient to ensure self–fulfillment. Similarly, many now believe that by itself political democracy in its Western style—with which this book is concerned—is not sufficient to ensure social justice. In it, as in all other regimes, the lion's share inevitably goes to the lion. Others, however, continue to idealize democracy and, in their imagination, endow it with qualities that (like motherhood) it does not possess.

Some analysts—mainly Marxists and elitists—have not only denigrated Western democracy, but have gone as far as to argue that what we have today in the West is not motherhood but merely foster motherhood, not democracy, but merely pseudo-democracy: the paraphernalia of democracy, without its essence; elections that do not confer true power on the public; civil liberties that do not provide for true freedom of the individual. Some have even gone as far as to argue that this pseudo-democracy is not worth preserving, and that the civil liberties it confers may better be duplicated in a different, more equitable regime. Other analysts—particularly the theorists of pluralist democracy—have gone to the other extreme: they have expressed an overly complacent satisfaction with Western democracy, endeavoring to show, as Carole Pateman (1970, p. 16) has put it, that "the regime we ought to have is the very one that we do in fact, have."

Here, it is argued that none of these theories is sufficiently realistic and none works in the interests of democracy. The main task of this book is to make the case for a different conception, which draws on the others but is identical to none: the democratic-elite or demo-elite perspective on democracy. This perspective, it will be shown, provides an apt key for the understanding of how Western democracy evolved historically, how it functions (and malfunctions) today, and how it may change in the future. It is argued that only if we understand how democracy actually developed and how it works, only if we confront the full complexities of how power is used, abused, and countered in a democracy, only if we appreciate realistically what has (and has not) been achieved so far in limiting power and abuses of power in a democracy, can we begin to think of changes towards a better and fuller democracy in the future.

As numerous books on the topic have not failed to remind us, the word *democracy* (derived from the Greek: *demos*—the people; *kratein*—to rule) means rule by the people. Hence, if the term is taken literally, then, indeed, we have no democracy in the West. For in Western regimes the people as a whole rule no more, and minorities of power holders—or elites—rule no less than they do in other regimes. However, it will also not come as news to the reader, that in contemporary Western society the term *democracy* has altered its meaning and has come to signify rule by those whose power, or authority to rule, derives from the consent of the majority of the people as expressed through the process of free, competitive elections. Hence, the argument that what we have in the West today is not rule by the people is not synonymous with the argument that we have no democracy.

The original concept of rule by the people, though Utopian, is still important as a yardstick by which to measure the deficiencies of existing reality. For, as Oscar Wilde has correctly admonished, a world map that does not include Utopia is not worth glancing at. If present reality becomes its own yardstick, the ideological impetus for change is largely removed from the scene. But the concept becomes dangerous if we use it as a justification for (even verbally) destroying indiscriminately what we do have: the valuable together with the deficient. In this volume it is argued that (like other regimes) Western-style democracy is not short of deficiencies. But democracy also has certain institutionalized mechanisms to counter—or partly counter—its own deficiencies, and these may also form the basis for change towards a fuller democracy in the future.

The book's main argument is that democracy emerged out of a struggle over the control of resources—not (as is commonly argued) between classes as such—but between elites, including those of movements representing different social classes and genders, and it evolved through a paradoxical, combined process of the incorporation of successive elites into the establishment on the one hand, and of according more autonomy to elites on the other hand. This dual process has resulted in the development of relative autonomy of a few major elites from the state, or ruling elites; and of relative autonomy of some major elites from the elected, governing, political elite, which has come to be one of the most distinctive features of democracy as we know it in the West today. While Marxists speak of the relative autonomy of the state elites (the state apparatus) from the economic elites (the ruling class), here this argument is turned on its head, and it is argued that it is really the economic and the other elites that enjoy relative autonomy from the state elites and particularly from the governing political elite.

It is argued that the struggle between elites over the independent control of resources—which was protracted over several centuries, but culminated in the nineteenth century—manifested itself and legitimized itself as a struggle over the institutionalization of democracy, and as such led to certain democratic achievements. Thus, throughout the double historical process of incorporation and autonomization of elites, before or while they were being incorporated, and before or while they established themselves in positions of their own, some of these elites had a considerable measure of success in achieving certain civil liberties and political rights for themselves and their supporters, and these came to be (albeit imperfectly) enshrined in the principles of democracy.

Consequently, these principles, including that of the acquisition of power on the basis of free, competitive elections, and the other, complementary, principles of democracy, have been closely interrelated with the relative autonomy of elites: since they emerged out of the struggles over the incorporation and autonomization of elites, they not only spell certain political rights and liberties for the public, but concomitantly underpin, safeguard and legitimize the relative autonomy and thus the countervailing power of elites. And, indeed, therein lies a large part of those principles' value and importance.

Yet, because they underpin the relative autonomy of elites, the principles of democracy also contain an inherent contradiction. For the relative autonomy of the other elites from the elected, governing, political elite and their countervailing power as against that elite—as it emerged out of previous struggles—is of the very essence of democracy. But because the other elites normally are not elected or are elected by only part of the population, their countervailing power as against that of the generally elected, governing elite also contradicts the essence of democracy; it is crucial to democracy's most basic principles, but is also contrary to them.

The result of all this has been that in Western-style democracy today, the governing elite is limited in its power by the countervailing power of other elites, and never has full control over those other elites and over the public. Therefore, the governing elite is under constant temptation, and likely to exercise and attempt to maintain and perpetuate its power through various—at times devious—strategies of control, and frequently it produces consent for itself with the aid of manipulation and corruption. The relative autonomy of the other elites from the governing elite and the electoral and other democratic procedures that sustain it, also create the setting in which that elite's abuses of power, or manipulation and corruption, may be resisted and countered, probably more so than in other regimes.

Since, however, the relative autonomy of elites also creates a contradiction for democracy, the "rules of the game" that supposedly define and regulate that autonomy, are frequently unclear and contentious. Hence, the other elites do not necessarily have the ability to counter the abuses of power of the governing elite with the determination and success that would be required for their elimination. The relative autonomy of elites and the contradiction or dilemma this creates for democracy thus give rise to the mechanisms that counter the governing elite's abuses of power, but also render these mechanisms precarious, and they render democracy itself a fragile institutional structure. And this contradiction cannot be eliminated without eliminating democracy itself.

Looking at it from a different perspective, however, the relative autonomy of the other elites from the governing elite, and the contradiction this creates for democracy, are also important to democracy because they turn the democratic political system into an arena of perpetual and only partly institutionalized struggles, which do not necessarily lead to change, but have a greater potential than do fully institutionalized struggles of leading to change.

In particular, such struggles may be utilized in the service of change by new, nonestablished elites, knocking on the door of the establishment and struggling for incorporation on the one hand, and for autonomy on the other hand. Like their predecessors in the past, these elites, too, may well become co-opted by the establishment as they go along. But in the process, they may well do what their predecessors have done before, and achieve further rights or other changes that favor their supporters amongst the rank and file public. Thus, it is because of such counter-mechanisms, contradictions, and struggles, that Western-style democracy, though deficient, is valuable and worth preserving not only in its own right, but also as a relatively effective arena of struggle for change towards a better one.

Implied in this argument is the plea that we learn to distinguish between democracy's rectifiable flaws and its basically insoluble dilemma; between inequities that can be eliminated and the contradiction that cannot; between changes that would enhance democracy and changes that would destroy it; that greater efforts than are presently expended, be invested in seeking to do away with democracy's shortcomings, but that in the course of doing so, the fragile democratic structures themselves not be dismantled, that the baby not be discarded together with the bathwater—lest motherhood be destroyed altogether.

******

This is a dual-purpose book. Its first purpose is to present an argument on the manner in which power is used, abused and partly countered, in Western democracies. It does so from a democratic-elite or a demo-elite perspective, a well-established, but recently neglected perspective in political sociology and political science. It is intended to make the case for this perspective and contribute further towards its development. Recently, an increasing number of scholars—some of them with previous affinities to Marxism—have expressed dissatisfaction with the inadequacy of Marxist theory in conceptualizing political power, or the power of the state. Pluralist theories have been justly and increasingly accused of naïveté and have been declining in popularity now for several years. Recent elitist theories, for their part, have not caught the imagination of large numbers of scholars because of their perceived tendencies to endorse or support elite rule. All three perspectives have had difficulties in conceptualizing democracy, as will be shown below. By making the case for the demo-elite perspective, this book is intended to catch the eye of the growing number of scholars, in different disciplines, who are as dissatisfied with Marxism and elitism as they are with pluralism.

In some of its previous versions democratic-elite theory has been accused of similarity with elitism, of favoring elite rule, hence as conservative. This book is intended to show that, as it presently stands, this perspective is not vulnerable to such accusations, that it is not designed to *praise* elite rule but to *expose* its machinations in Western democracies, and that it is better equipped than other, better known, and currently still more popular theories, to do so.

The book's second purpose is to serve as a text or reading in a variety of courses in sociology and political science that are in one way or another concerned with the exercise of power in modern (especially Western) regimes: courses in contemporary political theory, including the theory of democracy, and courses in comparative politics and political sociology.

Accordingly, the book begins with a critique of the major theoretical approaches in this field. Within this broad theoretical framework the book's own central arguments are then presented. This is followed by empirical evidence—derived from historical and comparative analyses, and from some case studies (based on my own research) in support of these arguments. In presenting such evidence, the book also provides an overview of the development and present-day functioning of democracy in Western societies. The concluding chapter then brings the threads of the analysis together and endeavors to show how the analytical framework developed in previous chapters may assist in the analysis of change, and particularly of prospects for change in Western democracy.

1

Power in a Democracy: Major Theories Reconsidered

Introduction

Once upon a time social scientists believed (and Max Weber must be held at least partly responsible for this) that social and political analysis could be largely divorced from the values and ideologies of the analyst. Choice of topic, evaluation and application of results, these may be influenced by values; but the analysis itself can be kept separate from them. Today, although opinions on this topic are divided (see Horowitz, 1984, Ch. 21) it is becoming increasingly recognized that things are not that simple. While tendentious writing is justly disparaged, it still seems to be becoming increasingly recognized that even bona fide social and political theories frequently are the outgrowth of *Weltanschaungen,* and themselves have ideological implications. Theories of democracy, in particular, are widely recognized today as being prescriptive as well as descriptive, as including evaluative as well as factual statements, or as including factual statements that have normative overtones as well; and the theoretical perspective here advocated is no exception.

The evaluative component of the present perspective can best be expressed through Winston Churchill's somewhat simplistic, overquoted, but still apt statement to the effect that democracy is the worst form of government (apart from all the others that have been tried from time to time). In line with this evaluation, the present analysis explores the relationship between the power of elites in Western democracies and the manner in which such democracies not only function but also malfunction. It explores both uses and abuses of elite power in Western democracy. It explores how such power may be countered, but also the reasons for such countering being less than fully effective. It explores the shortcomings of democracy, but also its potential for change towards a more equitable system in the future. This is done in the framework of, and is intended to contribute further towards the development of a democratic-elite, or a demo-elite perspective, a well-established but recently neglected perspective in political science and political sociology.

There are other, currently more prevalent, theories that in one way or another deal with democracy—including participatory and pluralist theories of democracy, Marxist, elitist and corporatist theories. It is here considered necessary to pass them over, to single out the democratic-elite theory for reconsideration, to take it out of mothballs, dust it off, so to speak, and develop it further, for several reasons. The first reason is that the currently prevalent theories have either seen power in a democracy as more concerted and unified, or else have seen it as more widely dispersed than it actually is. The second reason is that these theories have been either excessively critical, or excessively complacent of Western democracy. Third, and in consequence of all this, these prominent theories, although they have much to contribute to the analysis of power, and although they are in some respects diametrically opposed to each other, have a common deficiency: they fail to bring into relief what is distinctive in the exercise of power in Western democracies.

This lacuna is precisely the topic on which the demo-elite perspective is focused. This theory is not designed to conceptualize and explain the exercise of power in all societies, at all times. As such, it is not a global theory, but a middle-ranging theory in the Mertonian sense. But I will endeavor to show that it has some advantages as compared to the other, currently more popular theories, in dealing with the manner in which elites have attained power and now wield power in Western, democratic regimes.

Participatory Theories of Democracy

Power in a democracy is elusive, difficult to pin down. Hence the continuing debate on where it is located and how it is exercised. Participatory theories of democracy have taken part in this debate, but have made only a slim contribution to it. While all theories of democracy are both prescriptive and descriptive, participatory theories of democracy go farthest in this respect. Both classical theories of participatory democracy such as those by Jean Jacques Rousseau and John Stuart Mill, as well as new theories of participatory democracy (e.g., Pateman, 1970; Barber, 1984; Wilson, 1984) have been recognized as *chiefly* normative and prescriptive. Or, as Sartori, (1987, p. 153) put it: "Whenever the theory is at a loss it has recourse to an *ought*." And further on (p. 161): what they claim "is nothing more than that the people *should* rule." Hence, their value lies mainly in the guidelines for social and political action they provide, rather than in their analysis of the manner in which power is actually wielded in Western-style democracies.

While the strength of participatory theories of democracy does not lie in their analysis of power in democratic regimes, some of them have been strong in their critiques of Western democracies as general social formations. According to Wilson (1984), Western, industrial societies are characterized by the ascendancy of legal-rational authority and expert dominated, formally meritocratic structures, epitomized by bureaucracy. Because of such legal-rational-bureaucratic structures, and because of their emphasis on individual material achievements, Western societies entice people away from active political participation. Hence, Western representative institutions are in decline, and there is growing political apathy and alienation amongst the public.

Whether or not one accepts this totally negative evaluation of legal-rational structures, or of bureaucracy (and it will be argued below that while bureaucracy features anti-democratic tendencies, it also plays an important role in safeguarding proper democratic procedures) in any case, this analysis raises a query. Namely, it raises the question whether Western-style democracy as a political system, as a system of gaining and exercising power, may be held accountable—even by implication—for general trends and features of modern, capitalist, industrial societies, that might well have eventuated without democracy and, indeed, would have been much more oppressive without it. It raises the question whether democracy (even in its presently imperfect form) should not rather be seen as a counter-balance to these apathy-inducing trends and tendencies of modern societies.

This question may be raised to even greater purpose with respect to the analysis of Barber, who not only disparages Western, liberal democracy for having become merely a convenient legitimizing ritual for the status quo and for manipulation by wealthy elites (1971, pp. 103–22), but also (1984) sees it as "thin" democracy because its individualist and "minimalist" values undermine the very democratic practices on which the rights of individuals rest. For in his view liberal democracy

> is concerned more to promote individual liberty than to secure public justice . . . to keep men safely apart rather than to bring them fruitfully together. As a consequence it is capable of fiercely resisting every assault on the individual—his privacy, his property, his interests and his rights—but is far less effective in resisting assaults on community or justice or citizenship or participation.(p. 4)

Individual liberty in its extreme manifestation—as stressed in liberal democracy—spells atomism, isolation, annihilation of the close social relationships in which individuality develops, hence anomie; and this may render democratic societies vulnerable to takeover by totalitarian leaders:

> The perfect liberty of theory may spell anomie in practice; perfect independence may mean defenselessness against actual bondage; perfect individuality may produce actual deracination; perfect privacy may breed an incapacity for fellowship; perfect representation may induce a paralysis of activity and a torpor of the political will. The model is perfect, but perfection can be a defect in the real world of history. "History proves" wrote Franklin Roosevelt "that dictatorships do not grow out of strong and successful governments, but out of weak and helpless ones." (p. 98)

This analysis, even more so than Wilson's analysis, is open to the question of whether it is not guilty of confusing certain traits of modern, Western society and culture in general with the traits of democracy as a political system. It may well be asked whether Barber's analysis is not holding democracy culpable for some features of Western society and culture which clearly are not rooted in it. It is true that individual and liberal values, as well as institutional arrangements to protect individual rights, are contextually interrelated with democracy. But, as has frequently been pointed out, and as will also be seen below, they have preceded rather than followed the gradual institutionalization of democracy, and therefore are certainly not its outgrowth. Advocating a change of these values and patterns by changing present day democracy into a more participatory form of democracy (and however much one may value such a democracy in its own right), seems to put the cart before the horse.

It may also be true, and has been pointed out before (see e.g., Fromm, 1960), that the excessive individualism and anomie of modern societies render them vulnerable to charismatic leaders of a totalitarian brand. But it is difficult to see how the blame for this, too, can be dumped into the lap of liberal democracy. For to do so would be to overlook the fact that in Europe totalitarian and authoritarian regimes—nazism, fascism, and communism—took over precisely where democracy was *not* developed, or had not had a chance, as yet, to take root and spawn its own traditions. In this book, too, it is being argued that democracy is fragile. But this is so because of its inherent, internal contradictions and dilemmas and not—as Barber claims—because of its vulnerability to takeovers by authoritarian or totalitarian leaders. Indeed, it is precisely in withstanding the onslaught of such leaders that—so far—Western democracies have had a pretty solid record.

Pluralist, Pluralist-Elitist, And Neo-Pluralist Theories

Another brand of democratic theories includes both older pluralist theories of democracy (e.g., Dahl, 1956; Riesman, 1961; Dahl and Lindblom, 1953) and newer pluralist theories of democracy (e.g., Polsby, 1985). These theories, while both prescriptive and descriptive, are open to a wide array of critiques on both counts. It is worth remembering that they do have some merit that—in some quarters—has been recently undervalued. It lies in showing that power in a democracy is not wholly unitary and concerted. It lies in highlighting certain linkages between power holders and members of the public in democratic societies. It lies in bringing interest groups into the orbit of political analysis. It lies in the emphasis that democratic governments are boxed in between intricately related interests that they must placate in order to survive. It lies in their highlighting the increasingly inextricable entanglement of public and private interests.

At the same time, as has now been widely recognized, pluralist theories have presented a one-sided, exaggerated, overly optimistic view of the dispersion of power in a democratic regime, as epitomized in the now-famous statement by Robert Dahl (1956, p. 137) to the effect that "all active and legitimate groups in the population can make themselves heard at some crucial stage in the process of decision." Perhaps it is true that they can all make themselves heard, but some analysts have queried whether they are all being listened to as well.

Then, too, many of the elements of the pluralist approach are geared primarily to the analysis of the American polity. And it has been queried whether they do, in fact, adequately reflect even this one system. As theorists of other schools of thought have pointed out, even in the United States (and certainly in other democratic regimes) pluralism is generally confined to secondary issues, while the most fundamental issues are under the control of central elites, or power holders. In failing to recognize this, pluralists have opened themselves to charges of naïveté, or gullibility, of looking merely at the facade rather than at the essence of what actually transpires in a democracy.

Moreover, pluralists have seen pluralism, the alleged dispersion of power among a plurality of countervailing interest groups, as promoting, indeed as one of the chief bases of, democracy. This tenet, too, has been widely queried. In this context it has been pointed out (and admitted by some pluralists themselves) that interest group leaders do not necessarily represent the interests of their rank and file members adequately, nor do the groups themselves represent all parts of the population. Various segments of the population differ greatly in the pressures they can bring to bear on, and in the responsiveness to their pressures they can elicit from the government, with the most disadvantaged groups being disadvantaged as pressure groups as well. Thus, critics continue, government deference to interest groups neither equalizes nor disperses power in a democratic fashion. It merely transfers some of it to private hands, thereby facilitating the exploitation of public policy for private benefits. By viewing it as democratic, pluralists have thus condoned and legitimized a system that actually facilitates corruption (see e.g., McConnell, 1966; Kariel, 1970; Etzioni, 1984; Schattschneider, 1960).

Some pluralists have recognized that there are elites within interest groups, and that elites are crucial even in a democracy (see e.g., Sartori, 1962; 1987; Keller, 1963; Dahl, 1967; 1970; 1971; 1982; Truman, 1971). These authors have thus moved in the direction of, or have evinced an affinity with, a democratic-elite perspective—and indeed Bachrach (1967) and Pateman (1970) (amongst others) have referred to them as democratic-elitists. But there is a litmus test which clearly identifies them as pluralists: they still view the *dispersion* of power and the competition among a *plurality* of elites as the main mechanism whereby the power of political leaders is held in check and democracy is preserved. For instance, Sartori (1987, pp. 147–8) writes of "leadership by minorities . . . characterized by a multiplicity of criss-crossing power groups engaged in coalitional maneuverings" and also: "democracies *are* characterized by diffusion of power" (p. 147). And of Dahl, Sartori (p. 154) writes that he "seeks a pluralistic diffusion . . . throughout the society as a whole, of inter elite competition." Hence, theirs may best be referred to as pluralist-elitist theories, and some of the above critiques of pluralist theories apply to their conceptions as well.

Here it is argued that while these authors are right in holding that there is a multiplicity of elites in a democracy, they have disregarded the fact that there are *elites of elites,* or elites that are significantly more powerful than other elites. For instance, they have disregarded the fact that while there are elites of ethnic groups, of consumer organizations, or even of single-parents' organizations, anti-abortion groups, and the like, these are far less powerful than the elites of government, of economic organizations or of trade unions. They have disregarded the fact that while there are many elites, there are only few major, or central, elites in Western democracies, a point to which we shall have occasion to return below.

Some of these theorists (cf. Sartori, 1987, particularly pp. 151–2) have also argued in favor of what they term a competitive-feedback theory of democracy which emphasizes competition between different political organizations and parties. This competition is seen as democratic because the public, or the majority of the public, becomes the arbiter among them, being able to bestow its electoral favors on one or the other of the contenders. Thus, through elections, the public has the power to determine not only who will rule but also to influence what rulers do once they are in office. Since elected leaders wish to maintain power, and since they can do so only by being reelected, they will ignore their electors' wishes at their own (political) peril.

Sartori (1987, p. 152) put these ideas in the following words: "The power to elect also results, in feedback fashion, in the heeding of those elected to the power of their electors. . . . Elected officials seeking reelection (in a competitive setting) are conditioned in their deciding by anticipation . . . of how electors will react to what they decide." Or, as Ippolito (1976, p. 126) formulated the idea: "the political graveyards are filled with the broken careers of politicians who failed to respond to the will of the people."

It may be suggested that while these authors are right in arguing that in Western democracies there is elite competition for which the people may serve as an arbiter, they have not sufficiently emphasized the various limitations and inadequacies of this "arbitration" process, so to speak, particularly those created by inequalities amongst various parts of the public in participation and influence, as well as those created by the (necessarily imperfect) electoral process as such—limitations that have been highlighted in particular by Marxists and elitists (see below).

Furthermore, these scholars have not sufficiently emphasized that while there is elite competition the main, and most important, competition is not inter-elite, but rather intra-elite competition, the competition between different groups or sub-elites within one elite. This includes the competition within the political elite between the elected, governing elite and the opposition, or between the leaderships of different parties; it includes the competition within the economic elite (to the extent that it has not been obviated by monopolies and cartels) among the owners and/or managers of corporations offering similar products or services; it includes the competition within the media elite among different media outlets, and so forth. Thus, the most important competition in a democracy takes place, not *between a multiplicity* of elites but *within a few* elites.

Ostensibly, this is merely a terminological quibble. In fact, however, the distinction between intra- and inter-elite relations is important, for it makes possible a certain shift of emphasis from the former to the latter, as here advocated. It is here argued that such a shift is called for, as the relations between different elites (which have been relatively neglected by the competitive theory of democracy) are no less crucial in a democracy than relations within elites. And, importantly, where the relations between, rather than within, elites are concerned, it is not elite competition, but the precarious balance of power between elites, or the relative autonomy of the other elites from the governing political elite, which lies at the crux of how power is exercised and countered in a democracy, as will be seen below.

Some erstwhile scholars of pluralism in their recent writings—also referred to as neo-pluralist (see Held, 1987, p. 201)—such as Dahl (1982, 1985) and in particular, Charles Lindblom (1977), have argued that while "a proliferation of public and private groups engaging in mutual adjustments brings a remarkably wide range of interests and considerations to bear on public policy" (p. 141), there are only two elites, or groups of leaders, that really count: political leaders and business leaders, with the latter having parity with, if not primacy over, the former. This is a combination of a pluralist conception with a quasi-Marxist tenet in pluralist parlance. The argument here developed is, that neither this pluralist conception, nor this semi-Marxist tenet adequately conceptualizes the structure of power in Western democratic regimes, that while business or economic elites are powerful in such regimes, they do not have parity with ruling, or state elites (including those of the government, its bureaucracy, the judiciary, and the armed and security forces) and that, in addition, other central elites, particularly those of trade unions and the media, must be incorporated into the analysis as well.

Some of the authors of pluralism and of pluralist-elitism (though not, to be sure, neo-pluralists such as Lindblom) have evinced an overly complacent satisfaction with existing Western democracy. They regard it, if not as the best regime in the best of all possible worlds, at least as the optimal regime in a less than perfect world. In so doing, they gloss over, and thereby lend legitimation to some of its major flaws. In view of all this, it is not surprising that while some prominent scholars continue to adhere to them, pluralist perspectives have recently declined in popularity and fallen on hard times (see e.g., Knoke, 1981; Margolis, 1983).

Recently, therefore, other theories on the exercise of power in modern society have been competing for center-stage. Although there are some overlaps between them, they may be divided into four broad paradigms. These are, first, different variants of Marxist and neo-Marxist theories, (e.g., Mandel, 1975; Poulantzas, 1975, 1978; Miliband, 1973, 1977, 1982; Zeitlin, 1980; Parenti, 1980). They include, second, what Block (1987) refers to as Marx–inspired theories, some of which have also been referred to as post-Marxist or state-centered theories (including besides Block's theory itself, those of Birnbaum and Badie, 1983; Giddens, 1977, 1981, 1982; Evans et al, 1985; Skocpol, 1979; and several others). Third, they include elite theories which, to a certain extent, follow in the footsteps of Vilfredo Pareto, Robert Michels, and C. Wright Mills (e.g., Prewitt and Stone, 1973; Dye, 1976, 1979, 1983, 1985; Dye and Zeigler, 1987; Field and Higley, 1980; Burton and Higley, 1987a and 1987b), and Marxist-influenced elite theories (e.g., Domhoff 1967, 1970, 1978, 1983; Useem, 1984). Finally, they include corporatist theories (e.g., Schmitter and Lehmbruch, 1979; Panitch, 1980, 1981; Crouch, 1979; Cawson, 1978, 1983, 1986; Jessop, 1978, 1979).

These theories have much to recommend them in that they all penetrate behind the scenes and demonstrate that (even in a democracy) the facade of pluralism really conceals a much more concerted power structure than is visible to the naked eye, that on matters that really count power is concentrated in the hands of small, interconnected groups of power holders. But some of them have been guilty of exaggeration in the opposite direction, of presenting democratic power structures as even more concerted or consensually unified than they actually are. And most of them have a common deficiency: they have failed to put their finger on the truly characteristic features of the exercise of power in a democracy.

Marxist and Marx-Inspired Theories

In several respects Marxist theories are very attractive: they show more serious concern with social inequality and exploitation than other schools of thought; they reveal the importance of class interests in social action even where such interests are not evident on the surface; they thus demystify many established ideologies and show them up for what they are: attempts to legitimize interests.

The conceptions offered by Marxists have an important drawback, however: as is becoming increasingly recognized in recent years, they are beriddled by serious problems, or even deficiencies, where the analysis of power, and particularly power in a democracy, is concerned. And although there are different schools of Marxism, and they all view the problem of power from somewhat different angles, they nonetheless share these deficiencies to a greater or lesser extent.

For, to various extents, and in multiple guises, they follow Marx's basic tenet that political struggles are reflections of socioeconomic forces, that political power is an offshoot of economic power, and that political power holders (or the state apparatus) serve basically the interests of economic power holders (or the ruling class). Some Marxists, such as Miliband, put more emphasis on the close connections of economic power holders, or capitalists—to those staffing the state apparatus—as a major factor in making the state serve capitalism. Others, e.g., Poulantzas, put more emphasis on structural factors, or the constraints of the capitalist system, in making the state apparatus an instrument of capitalism. Some put more emphasis on what they term the "relative autonomy" of the state from capitalism than others. But to the extent that they follow Marx's above tenet—even in an attenuated manner—they have failed to come to terms with the complexity of the phenomenon of power in general, and that of power in a modern, democratic society, in particular.

Not surprisingly, a growing number of Marx-inspired scholars, or scholars with previous affinities to Marxism, have become increasingly disillusioned with its inability to confront political power as a basic social factor in its own right, and with its incapacity to do justice to the crucial role of the state as the center of political power, particularly in contemporary societies. Thus, these authors—sometimes referred to as post-Marxists—have argued that the Marxist notions of determination, though only "in the last instance" of politics by the economy, and the "relative autonomy" of the state apparatus from the ruling class are inadequate or, as Hindess (1980, p. 40) put it,

> for all the diverse formulations of the idea, the precise mechanism of the supposed relationship between economic 'base' and political 'superstructure' are nowhere clearly specified. 'Determination in the last instance' and all the other slogans are little more than a gesture towards a theoretical vacancy that always remains to be filled . . . it is not merely that this theoretical vacancy is left open. The problem is that it cannot be filled: the slogans of 'relative autonomy,' 'determination in the last instance,' and all the rest, are gestural evasions of a problem that cannot be resolved. (See also Skocpol, 1979; Evans et al., 1985; and Pierson, 1984.)

And, indeed, if political power is derived from, and based on economic power, it is not at all clear what the "relative autonomy" of political power holders vis-à-vis economic power holders can possibly derive from, or be based on.

Some Marx-inspired scholars have gone further than orthodox Marxists in attempting to separate out political power from economic power, especially (but not exclusively) in capitalist societies. For instance, Block (1987) accords what he calls state managers a greater autonomy from capitalists than Marxists had generally acknowledged. He considers that there is a three-sided conflict between state managers, capitalists and the working class. Tilly (1981), Skocpol (1979), Mann (1984), and Evans et al. (1985) argue for a state-centered view, stressing the "potential autonomy" (Skocpol, 1979, p. 29) or even the actual autonomy of the state and the diverse ways in which it structures social action.

Some of these theorists also stress the political capacity of state managers and the contradictions and struggles within different branches of government. Giddens (1982), for one, emphasizes the contradictory character of the state: while constrained by capitalism, its policies are also influenced by the power of the working class, exerted through its right for the collective withdrawal of labor. Thus, he recognizes that the state has more innovative power than Marxists proper are apt to grant it (see also Plotke, Laclau, and Mouffe, 1982).

All these scholars offer valuable analyses in that they see the problem of power as more complex than Marxists proper do, and in that they thus "advance beyond reductionism" (Mann, 1984, p. 187). But even these scholars still couch their analyses broadly in terms of the parameters set out by Marx. That is to say, some of them still focus on the constraints or imperatives of the economy on the state, although they may view state managers as helping to shape these imperatives. And they still view the problem of power in terms of the degree of autonomy of the state from capitalism, from capitalists or—more broadly—from "infrastructural forms" (Mann, 1984, p. 185), or civil society, even though they may regard the state as largely or substantially autonomous from these.[1] Here, however, it is being queried whether this is indeed the most fruitful way of presenting the problem, whether a better understanding of power cannot be achieved by making the degree of autonomy of the other elites from the state elites the main focus of attention.

Marxist and similarly minded writers also have presented no clearly worked-out theory of Western democracy, and they follow Marx himself in presenting a largely ambivalent view of this brand of polity. On the one hand, Western capitalist democracy is conclusively shown to afford little (if any) choice, discretion, or power to the public. On the other hand, it is said to be preferable to all other regimes.

Marx himself denounced bourgeois democracy as nothing but a purely developed form of bourgeois rule or, as he put it, under capitalism elections merely determined "which member of the ruling class was to misrepresent the people in parliament" (1969a, p. 221). Contemporary Marxists, too, have disparaged the fact that class inequalities are translated into political inequalities, and the disproportionate leverage which the ruling or capitalist class has over the political process in capitalist democracies. They see this leverage as derived in particular from the ability of capitalists to vote not through the ballot box, but with their (corporate) feet, by shifting resources and enterprises in and out of certain economic domains or countries. They also see this leverage as derived from the capitalists' ability to finance politicians and political parties and, most importantly, through the fact that the well-being of the capitalist economies hinges on the well-being of the economic enterprises of which the capitalists have charge.

Where capitalists have so much leverage over the political system, there can be very little of that commodity left to the public. And, indeed, as modern Marxists see it, democracy in capitalist countries is basically a system that does not lend the public much power, yet is designed so as to hoodwink the public into believing that it does. The electoral system gives people the illusion that unsurmountable cleavages exist between parties, that momentous issues are at stake, and that voters, by choosing between one or the other of the political parties decide nothing less than the future of their country.

In actual fact, however, there is a basic consensus among all political parties in particular over the maintenance of the capitalist system, and thereby the preservation of the power and the privileges of the capitalists. So democracy suffers (among other things) from the Tweedledee, Tweedledum syndrome: it really makes little difference who gets elected; in any case the victor is apt to perpetuate the system no less than the vanquished opponent. It follows that Western or bourgeois democracy is but the rule of the capitalists through the instrument of free elections (see Miliband, 1973, 1982; Therborn, 1978; see also Offe, 1972).

Some Marxists and other radical writers go one step further and suggest that Western democracy in fact does not exist, or is merely an illusion, and elections are nothing but a sham (see e.g., Rotstein, 1983; Avakian, 1986). Although liberal democracy has some merits in the protection of civil rights, these are greatly outweighed by its defects, and these cannot be corrected within the present system. Therefore, we should not hesitate to abandon it altogether: "Liberal democracy's defense of civil rights should be paralleled, as it were, rather than incorporated in a theory and practice *dis*continuous with the dominant but defective and perilous tradition" (Levine, 1981, p. 206).

Marx and most contemporary Marxists or (to coin a hybrid term) the mainstream of contemporary Marxists do not go quite that far and do not dismiss democracy as totally or largely valueless. In contradiction to his previous statement, Marx admitted that democracy wrested some power, and particularly the assurance of power, out of the hands of the bourgeoisie. He went as far as to state (1969b, p. 236) that democracy was apt "to jeopardize the very foundations of bourgeois society." Major modern Marxists, too, have made it clear that they do not claim that democracy counts for nothing. Indeed, some Marxists have praised democracy as being preferable to practically all other past or present political structures, and as being capable of preventing the atrocities of fascism, Stalinism and similar regimes. In the words of Therborn (1977, p. 3): "The bitter experiences of fascism and Stalinism and the enduring legacy of the latter, have taught the firmest revolutionary opponents of capitalism that bourgeois democracy cannot be dismissed as a mere sham." (See also Miliband, 1973; Therborn, 1978.)

This view, however, raises the question of how it is that democracy, which is so innocuous, is also so effective in preventing atrocities common in many non-democratic regimes. Marxist theories supply no answer to these questions. This is not by chance or oversight. It follows from the most basic concepts and premises of Marx's and Marxist theories. For being shackled down by the central concept of the "ruling class" and by the assumption that (despite all reservations and qualifications) this class generally has the ability to shape policies to serve its own interests, Marxist theories contain no clear conception concerning the mechanisms that countervail the power of rulers and restrain both uses and abuses of power in a democracy.

This last point is extremely important, for Marx's and Marxist theories are also ideologies that have wielded great influence in the formation of the polities which now go by the name of communist regimes, and on the agendas of the bodies which now go by the name of communist parties all over the world. Marxists may correctly argue that Marx's and their own theories do not call for the dumping of democracy, do not extol the virtues of totalitarian communist regimes, and are not to blame for the aberrations and atrocities of some of those regimes, any more than Ferdinand Tönnies and Max Weber were to blame for the atrocities of nazism.

However, it must nevertheless be asked whether Marx's and Marxist theories, by putting the emphasis largely on class analysis, by undervaluing the importance of elites, and particularly of the balance, the autonomy, and the countervailing power of different elites for limiting ruling elites' power, have not inadvertently given the go-ahead to regimes where totalitarianism or authoritarianism are *not merely an aberration,* but the essence of the system. And if this is so, then communist parties in other countries, if they were to come to power, would be most likely to replicate the patterns of present communist regimes, rather than to lead to socialist democracy. In other words, the importance of the failure of Marxist theories to provide a coherent analysis of political power, or of elites, and their ambivalence with respect to democracy, may reach far beyond the level of theoretical discourse into the world of praxis, to the detriment of democracy.

The uncertainty of Marxists with respect to democracy is unhappily coupled in their conception with certainty in another respect, namely with ideological certainty. For while their theory of democracy has uncertainty built into it, their ideology of socialism does not. This, too, is a legacy Marxists have inherited from their Master, whose own ideological certitude is well described in a leading article in *The Economist* (18 February 1984, pp. 9–10) as follows:

> Marx . . . did teach that politics was a sort of science: once you knew what to do, you mixed the ingredients and got it done. Marx thought like that because he was the heir of those eighteenth-century rationalists who, having abandoned the certainty of religious belief, found themselves groping for a certainty elsewhere. Some looked to the nation state, some to science, some fatally to the sort of politics now known as ideology.

So Marx had ideological certitude because he was the heir of the enlightenment. And modern Marxists have ideological certitude because they are the heirs of Marx.

Marxist ideology espouses equality for all. Ostensibly this ideology, if widely adopted, should in fact lead to such equality. It may be argued, however, that certitude (in whatever ideology) is the antithesis of democracy and therefore also of equality. For democracy thrives on doubt, on skepticism, and on the consequent competition of ideologies. This competition of ideas is linked to the competition of elites, which, in turn, includes struggles of elites of the less advantaged, the exploited, for greater equality—more on which, below. Ideological certainty, on the other hand, or be it certainty in the ideology of equality, is the intellectual ground on which struggles, including struggles for greater equality, are likely to be eliminated.

In present capitalist-democratic systems the struggle for greater equality may be tilted in favor of the more advantaged, defending the status quo, rather than in favor of the less advantaged, calling for change—a topic that will also be resumed below. But in these struggles the disadvantaged are not completely powerless. Hence, they necessarily have better chances of leading to a lessening of inequalities than is the case in a situation in which (on the basis of ideological certainty) such political struggles for equality are legitimately suppressed.

A sign I once observed on the front door of a colleague's home aptly carried the following legend: **Beware of the Dogma.** Perhaps a similar sign ought to be erected in front of the edifice of Marxist ideology. For although this is an ideology of equality, when coupled with the dogmatic certainty with which it is propounded, it has the potential of leading to the very opposite of what it propounds, and what its supporters undoubtedly aim for, as already exemplified in the Eastern, so-called Communist bloc.

Furthermore, while greatly concerned with existing inequalities, Marxists have coined a term and developed a notion that is in itself (inadvertently) inegalitarian, or even elitist in the prescriptive or ideological sense of the term. Following Antonio Gramsci (who coined the term in the wake of Marx's own theory), many Marxists now speak of "hegemony" whereby in capitalist democracies the dominant ideology—promulgated by the ruling class—so mystifies the working class that they accept the status quo, even though it works to their disadvantage, against their interests. This concept is elitist because it assumes that not the people themselves—but rather Marxist scholars—are the ones who are competent to decide what the people's interests are (on phenomena of left-wing elitism, see also Horowitz, 1984, Ch. 17, particularly, pp 213–14).

The notion of hegemony may well have some merit in the analysis of pre- or nondemocratic societies. But its validity for the analysis of democratic societies is much more questionable. It certainly runs counter to the most elementary assumption on which both democratic theory and democratic practice are based, namely that in a democracy each (adult) person is the best judge of his or her own interests. It also begs the question of how it is that people may be so easily befuddled and duped into docility in a society where communication from a variety of sources (including that from Marxists themselves) is freely and easily available to all. Perhaps it would be an exaggeration to say with Plamenatz (as quoted in Sartori, 1987, p. 104) that

> the political vocabulary in current use is much larger than it was two hundred years ago, and most of the words and phrases added to it were invented by radicals and socialists. Indeed, many of them were either coined by Marx or else made popular by him. The language of politics, as it is spoken in Western Europe, is as much 'proletarian' as it is anything else.

Perhaps it would also be exaggerated to add with Sartori (ibid) that in continental Europe even non-Marxists have come to adopt a "pidgin Marxism" and a language of debunking rather than defending capitalism. But it is certainly true that among Western *intellectuals,* at any rate, Marxism has been quite popular for some time now, and there has been nothing to prevent those Marxist intellectuals from spreading and popularizing their ideas. Thus, the very fact that the Marxist notion of "hegemony" has become so widely accepted and popular in recent years, must itself cast doubt on its validity.

Elitist and Corporatist Theories

Elite theories and corporatist theories, too, have made only a slim contribution to the analysis of democracy. Elitists have correctly pointed out that power holders, including political elites, are universal in complex societies and that democracy is not exempt from their rule any more than other regimes are. Unlike many Marxists they have correctly understood that power holders, or elites, are not merely economic power holders, or an economically ruling class, and they have offered sophisticated analyses of elite structures, linkages and networks. But, in their own way they, too, have tended to overemphasize the interlocking or consensual unity of elites in democratic regimes, and thereby they have underemphasized the differences between elite structures in democratic and nondemocratic regimes.

Thus, C. Wright Mills, one of the fathers of modern elite theory, has posited the existence of a conglomeration of economic, political and military elites, in perpetual, though uneasy coalition with each other, which together form a concerted "power elite." Several contemporary elitists, too, have posited such a power elite or something closely akin to it, sharing a commonality of interests, an ability to impose political unity, interlocking positions, cohesiveness, or other close interrelations (see e.g., Domhoff—who may be classified as an elitist with Marxist tendencies—1967, 1970, 1974, 1978, 1983; Dye, 1976, 1979, 1983, 1985; Dye and Zeigler, 1987; Useem, 1984). Some contemporary elitists have also posited a procedural consensus between elites in stable (including stable democratic) regimes. "Elites" write Dye and Zeigler (p. 4), "share a consensus about fundamental norms underlying the social system. They agree on the 'rules of the game'" (see also Higley et al., 1979, particularly p. 11; Field and Higley, 1980; and Burton and Higley, 1987a). And while democracy may be addressed, frequently it is not the central focus of their analyses (but see Burton and Higley, 1987a).

In connection with this, some elitists have also been exceedingly critical of Western democracy. Mills, for instance, sees power in a democracy as increasingly concentrated at the top, while the masses have been becoming increasingly powerless, politically impotent, and therefore uninterested in political participation. "In many countries," grieves Mills (1959, p. 324) "they lose their will for rationally considered decision and action; they lose their sense of political belonging because they do not belong; they lose their political will, because they see no way to realize it."

More recently elitists, including for instance Dye and Zeigler (1987), as well as others (e.g., Poggi, 1978), have argued in a similar vein that the most prominent feature of Western democracy, competitive elections, forms only a very imperfect instrument of holding government elites accountable to the public. For competing elites or parties among which the public may choose in elections do not usually offer distinct policy alternatives, candidates for elections avoid, as far as possible, taking stances on issues, and even if they do, are not usually bound by their election pledges once they are elected.

Even if elites wished to give the public what it wanted, they would not be able to do so, as they cannot clearly interpret the policy mandates emanating from elections. This is so because most voters are not concerned with, and informed about policy issues, and base their electoral choices on personalities and their images rather than on such issues, and in any case frequently misinterpret candidates' policy preferences. As candidates may take positions on many different issues, they cannot know which policy position resulted in their election, hence elites do not usually have reliable knowledge on public preferences, and thus cannot shape policies to suit those preferences; elites influence the opinions of the masses more than masses influence elites.

In short, according to this view, voters can but rarely affect policy by selecting a particular candidate for office; at best, elections provide the public with an opportunity to express their opinions on the performance of past governments, but they do not provide them with an opportunity to influence the course of future events. In fact, elections serve chiefly as a symbolic exercise designed periodically to reaffirm a common belief in democracy, to give symbolic reassurance to the masses, to lend them a feeling that they do play a role in the system and thus tie the masses to the system. In other words, elections are merely a ritual, the function of which is to befuddle the public and legitimize the power of the elite ("hegemony" again, in another guise?). Or, to put it bluntly, it may not be possible to fool all of the people all of the time, but it is possible to fool many people much of the time, and in a democracy, this is enough to win, maintain, and legitimize power.

With respect to this elitist critique of democracy, as well as with respect to the Marxist critique, which similarly belittles the value of elections, one cannot do better than to reiterate (with a small variation) what Livingstone once wrote in the introduction to Gaetano Mosca's book *The Ruling Class* (1939, p. X). In response to a certain critique of Mosca's theory, Livingstone wrote that it was a very true critique; that is to say, it covered about half the truth, which is a great deal of truth for a critique to cover.

In the same vein it may be said that the above cited critiques of democracy, too, cover about half the truth; more specifically, that half which has been neglected by the pluralist-competitive theories of democracy. Thereby, it helps redress the imbalance of the overly rosy picture of democracy presented by those theories. However, it may be argued that by bringing to the fore but the other half of the truth, by focusing merely on democracy's (all too evident) shortcomings, Marxist and elitist theories not only miss out on the first half, but indeed, fail to bring into relief the intricate combination and intermeshing of both halves, which is precisely what creates the complex essence of the democratic process. It may be argued that, by failing to bring together both halves of the picture, those theories have been blinkered from perceiving an important aspect of the electoral principle, and the other principles of democracy, namely their role in sustaining a unique interplay between elites, which is of the very essence of democracy.

Corporatists—most of whom are really elite theorists in another guise—for their part, point to the close interaction between governmental, quasi-governmental, corporate and trade union elites in the making of economic policy. They correctly emphasize that such corporatist arrangements frequently short-circuit or bypass democratic institutions and procedures (although they do not supplant them). Some of them are Marxist in their leanings and convincingly point to the inordinate power of corporate, capitalist elites in Western societies. But they, too, exaggerate the extent to which different elites are in collusion with each other, and they, too, fail to bring into relief the distinctive relationship between them in a democracy.

While pluralists and pluralist elitists have thus overemphasized the dispersion of power and the multiplicity of competing elites in a democracy, Marxists, several elitists, and corporatists—in their different ways—have gone to the other extreme, overemphasizing the concerted or consensual nature of power, even in a democracy. It is here argued that a more realistic picture of the balance of power among elites in a democracy is to be gained by occupying the middle ground between these various theoretical approaches, a ground which has been left vacant by them.

A Theoretical Synthesis?

This raises the question of whether such a theoretical middle ground may best be gained by forging a synthesis of those various theories. Alford and Friedland (1985) for instance, have attempted to do just that, arguing that the three approaches: pluralism, Marxism and elitism (or managerialism) emphasize different aspects of the modern, Western capitalist state. The pluralist perspective emphasizes the democratic aspect, the managerial or elitist perspective emphasizes the bureaucratic aspect, and the class or Marxist perspective emphasizes the capitalist aspect of the modern state, and each has considerable explanatory power in its own "home" domain. Hence, a synthesis between them may be forged by integrating each approach's contribution to the explanation of its own domain, into an overall theory, which has explanatory power in all three domains.

Here, however, it is argued that the possibility of forging such a successful synthesis of the various schools of thought is severely limited by the fact that they are all based on different and largely incompatible fundamental assumptions, that they are informed by different if not opposing ideological outlooks, or *Weltanschauungen,* and that they have different and largely incongruous images of the totality of the polities, or the states, which are the objects of their analyses. Hence, the strategy here adopted is to propose not a synthesis of these perspectives, but rather the revival and further development of another approach, the democratic-elite or demo-elite perspective which in some respects agrees, but in other respects disagrees with each of these theoretical viewpoints, which draws on all three, but is identical to none. While thus taking up the middle ground between these schools of thought, the demo-elite perspective—in its present version—does so not by forcing them into a synthesis which is basically alien to them. Rather, it does so by endeavoring to establish or re-establish its own identity, or "personality" so to speak, on the shoulders of the giants who have advocated its tenets in the past.

Note

1. Even Stone (1987, p. 263) writes in terms of a "degree of autonomy" enjoyed by the elites that hold public authority.

2

Power in a Democracy: The Demo-Elite Perspective

The Arguments in a Nutshell

The identity of the demo-elite perspective, in its present version, is contained in the following assumptions and arguments, some of them in contrast, and some of them in similarity to the aforementioned theories. These are now presented in a nutshell and will be expanded upon later in the book. In contrast to the pluralist school of thought, the demo-elite perspective contains the assumption that there is not a multiplicity, but only a small number of elites that are pervasively powerful in Western societies. In contrast to the Marxist school of thought, the demo-elite perspective contains the assumption that power may be based on the control of a variety of resources, not merely economic resources and that, therefore, economic power has no primacy over other power; that in contemporary society the state acts as the main controller of resources and hence as the main center of power, and that the ruling elites, that is, the elites that have direct control of the state, are thus the central wielders of power in these societies.

However, it also contains the argument that in Western-style democracies the other elites are neither as independent from the state elites and as competitive with them as pluralists have made them out to be, nor as interlocking with them as some elitists have claimed them to be, and that even within the state itself, the various elites are neither mutually, totally independent, nor wholly interdependent and concerted in their actions. The present demo-elite perspective presents the tenet that, instead,

- there is a precarious power balance between elites, based on the relative though incomplete autonomy of the various elites from the ruling, or state elites, and on the relative autonomy of the various other elites from the governing, political elite, which is one of the most distinctive features of Western-style democracy.

Thus, while Marxists and Marx-inspired writers speak of the relative (or even complete) autonomy of the state apparatus (which is here referred to as the ruling or state elites) from the ruling class (which is here referred to as the economic elite), I argue that it is more appropriate to turn the conception upside down and speak, instead, of the relative (but incomplete) autonomy of the other elites from the ruling or state elites and of the relative (but incomplete) autonomy of the nonelected elites from the elected, governing elite, in Western democracy. But while Marxists have not furnished an adequate explanation for the alleged relative autonomy of the state elites from the economic elites, here an attempt will be made to explicate the relative autonomy of the other elites from the state and governing elites, and to derive it from the basic concepts and conceptions of the demo-elite perspective as here advocated.

- Historically, this relative autonomy of elites has come about through a power struggle of elites, resulting in a dual process of successive elites' incorporation into existing power structures on the one hand, and of successive elites' gaining increased autonomy on the other hand. This elite power struggle has also manifested itself as a struggle for the development of democracy, and the resulting relative autonomy of elites has become enshrined in and legitimized by the principles of democracy.

- Indeed—apart from whatever powers and freedoms they may grant to the public—this relative autonomy of elites is what the principles of democracy are chiefly about.

- At present, this relative autonomy of elites from the governing elite poses a contradiction, or a dilemma for democracy: it is protected by the most basic principles of democracy, particularly that of freedom of organization. However because the elites that have relative autonomy, and thus countervail the power of the elected, governing elite, are not themselves generally elected, it also contradicts the basic principles of democracy. It is thus part of the very essence of democracy yet also obviates that essence.

- Because of this contradiction, the rules that govern the relations of elites in a democracy are frequently ambiguous and controversial.

- Both the relative autonomy of elites and the unclear rules that govern their relations encourage the governing political elite to exert its power through a variety of non-coercive strategies based on its control of the state resources, and frequently through political manipulation and corruption; it also encourages the countering of such manipulation and corruption by other elites, but does not necessarily ensure that such countering will be effective.

The relative autonomy or countervailing power of elites thus provides for distinctive mechanisms to counter manipulation and corruption, but also renders those mechanisms, at times, less than adequate.

- Finally, the precarious balance of power, the relative autonomy, or the countervailing power of elites, by exacerbating—only partly institutionalized—conflicts, especially between established and non- or less established elites, also opens the prospects for change towards a more equitable democracy in the future.

On the Shoulders of Giants

In making these claims, the present version of the democratic-elite perspective does not begin *de novo*. It has its antecedents in previous democratic-elite theories, including those of Max Weber (1947, 1958, 1968); Gaetano Mosca (1939); Joseph Schumpeter (1976); and Raymond Aron (1950, 1968, 1978, 1985). Like elitists these theorists recognized that economic power was not all-pervasive and that political power had to be reckoned with as an independent factor, that elites were ubiquitous, and were to be found in democratic, no less than in nondemocratic regimes, that the elites that controlled the state were formidable, if not the most formidable elites in contemporary societies. But they differed from elitists in their recognition that elections and other democratic processes created a unique interplay among elites and between elites and the public, which distinguished democracies from other regimes. Like pluralists, these theorists recognized that elites did not form a unified "ruling class" or "power elite," and that there was a complex maneuvering among elites. But they differed from pluralists in their recognition that this maneuvering was based not on the competition between a multiplicity of power centers, but on the competition and precarious balance of power within and between a few major elites which formed a basic (though imperfect) factor sustaining democracy.

Weber, for one, emphasized the independent status of political and administrative power and authority vis-à-vis economic power, and recognized the inevitability of elites, including political and administrative elites, even in democratic societies. He further argued that representative democratic institutions provided for little control of the elected by the electors. But he thought that these institutions were nonetheless important, for they served as methods of selection and training grounds for the most qualified leaders and, more importantly, they served to keep the increasingly powerful bureaucracies in check.

Weber saw bureaucracy as a possible tool in the hands of its political master. But he was deeply concerned that the elites of the bureaucracy might themselves come to be the masters of the state and the absolute rulers over the masses in modern societies. Thus, it was up to charismatic leaders—inculcated with democratic values—to subordinate bureaucracy to a democratically elected leadership, and thereby to keep society open, or partly exempt, from such oppressive, bureaucratic rule. Even so, in the last analysis the checks politicians could put on bureaucracy were limited by its superior organization and expertise (Weber, 1947; 1958, particularly ch. 8; 1968).

Mosca, for his part, is usually considered an elitist and is generally classified together with Pareto and Michels as one of the three classical elitists. And, indeed, in some respects he may be so classified, for he made a strong case for his view that democracies, no less than other regimes, were actually ruled by minorities to which he referred as the ruling class (to be distinguished from the economically ruling class referred to in Marx's and Marxist theories). But he differed from Pareto and Michels in that in his later work (1939) he made some contributions that are especially pertinent for the democratic-elite perspective, particularly in his exploration of the relationship between the political and the bureaucratic elites in Western democracies.

Like Weber, Mosca pointed to the danger inherent in the unmitigated power of a bureaucratic elite, because of its tendency to result in an absolute, despotic, and oppressive regime. Like Weber he thus imputed a certain value to democracy for its ability to curb the power of the bureaucratic elite. But Mosca's theory is especially important for the analysis of democracy, for he also pointed to the danger inherent in the uncurbed power of an elected political elite. This danger derived from the tendency of politicians to bring about abuses of power through party-related political corruption, in the form of mutual favors and indulgences. Mosca therefore emphasized the importance of a powerful bureaucracy in curbing the corrupting power of politicians. Hence, although Mosca maintained his cynical attitude with regard to Western democracies' ability to bring about "rule by the people" or even by majorities, he nonetheless saw certain advantages in these regimes, in that they had managed to bring about a mix between bureaucratic and democratic forms of government, which led to mutual checks and balances between the various parts of the ruling class—or in our parlance, it led to a balance of power between elites—and hence to the curbing of ruling class, or elite, power.

In this respect there is a certain resemblance between Mosca and Schumpeter. For, like Mosca, Schumpeter emphasized that democracy was not rule by the people or even the majority of the people, but by elites. For Schumpeter the essence of democracy lay in the leaders' attainment of power through competition over the people's votes, and he argued that the electorate does not normally control the political leaders it has elected, except through its ability to refuse to reelect them. Political leaders, however, were forced not only to gain the majority of the people's support in an election but, in addition, were also forced to gain the support of the majority of their own parties' politicians, both inside and outside of parliament. The essence of democracy was thus an incessant struggle to gain office and stay in office. This limited the efficiency of the elected government, but by the same token it also limited its power, and therein lay its democratic essence.

There was an even greater resemblance between Mosca and Schumpeter in another respect: both recognized the importance for democracy of independent agencies and their elites in limiting the power of elected politicians, although Schumpeter conceived of such agencies and elites more broadly than did Mosca. For Schumpeter emphasized what he saw as a most important requirement for democracy: that the effective range of political decisions be limited, which implied that several types of organizations and their top position holders have a large measure of independent power as against that of the elected political leadership. And, proceeded Schumpeter, in most democracies such independence did, in fact, accrue to the judiciary, the elite of the state bureaucracy, the state bank, and to some other public agencies and commissions including, for instance, academic institutions. The independence of such agencies was of great importance, for the politicians' power to appoint the top personnel of such agencies would often suffice to corrupt them (Schumpeter, 1976).

While Weber thus brought into relief the danger for democracy that resulted from the growing power of the bureaucratic elite, Mosca and Schumpeter highlighted the other side of the coin, namely that the independent power of the bureaucratic elite (and of some other public agencies) was also a requirement for limiting the power of the governing political elite and for safeguarding the proper (non-corrupt) governmental procedures of democracy.

Aron agreed with Weber, Mosca, and Schumpeter (as well as with the elitists proper) that in any society the few (the elite) determined the lives of the many (the masses). Thus, what distinguished democratic societies from other societies, according to Aron, was not the absence of elites. Nor did Aron argue that democratic societies were distinguished from other societies in their great proliferation, or multiplicity of elites. For, although in describing democratic societies, he mentioned a "plurality of ruling categories" (1985, p. 246), he also made it very clear (1950, 1985) that in *all* modern societies there were only five groups that made up the major elites: political leaders, government administrators (or bureaucrats), economic directors, labor leaders, and military chiefs.

In Aron's view, then, the essence of democratic societies, that which distinguished them from, say, Soviet-type regimes, lay not in the great number of their elites, but in the fact that in them there was a clear differentiation between state and society. Hence, although they had only few major elite-groups, the power of those was attached to well–defined spheres of action. Democracies were also distinguished from other regimes by the fact that in them power was fought over by many claimants, by the fact that they had internally divided (rather than unified) elites, that these elites were all entitled to form organizations, that they all defended their organizations' interests, and that they therefore were in constant, free, and legitimate rivalry with each other.

Democracies, according to Aron, were further distinguished from non-democratic regimes by the fact that because of all this, the other major elites had a relative independence from the political rulers, who lacked the force to overpower them. Therefore, reasoned Aron, in a democracy, the authority of political rulers was controlled and limited (Aron, 1950, 1968, 1978, 1985). Like Mosca and Schumpeter, Aron thus emphasized the importance of the (relative) independence of other elites from the elected political elite for the curbing of that elite's power, and therefore as one of the most distinctive features of democracy.

The present version of the democratic-elite theory (or the demo-elite perspective) accepts these analyses, is based on them, and regards itself as a legitimate descendant of theirs. But although the theories of these great masters have furnished the core ideas on how democracies function, and although these ideas have furnished a better explanation on the functioning (and malfunctioning) of democracy than have the theories of other great masters, it is impossible to shirk the fact that these democratic-elite ideas have been presented in an embryonic form only, and that they require both amplification and substantiation.

Thus, it is difficult to find in these masters' writings a satisfactory explanation for the basis of that measure of independence which the other elites have been able to gain from the political elite in Western democracies, and their writings also lack an adequate exposition of the implications of this independence for the manner in which the power of elites is actually used (and abused) in Western democracies. The aim of the present analysis is to develop this conception further, to apply it to the analysis of how Western democracies have come into being, of how political power in them is exerted in both legitimate and non-legitimate ways, and of how they may change in the future.

Some Elementary Definitions and Assumptions

The main arguments of the demo-elite perspective in its present version can best be explained on the basis of some elementary definitions of the concepts of power, elites and democracy, and on the basis of some elementary assumptions pertaining to these concepts.

On Power and Elites

Partly following Weber, and partly extrapolating from some more recent theorists (e.g., Skocpol, 1979; Giddens, 1982), power is here defined as the ability to constrain or shape other people's actions, volitions, values, beliefs and life chances through control over (or having at one's disposal) resources on which these others are dependent, of which they have a need, or which may otherwise affect their lives. Resources, in turn, are here conceived of broadly, not merely in a material or economic sense, as including all (scarce) entities that may impinge on people's lives, including symbolic resources, or even resources of time and energy as will become clear below. Elites are here defined as people or groups of people who hold power and influence, that is, as people who have disproportionate control of resources (on which others are dependent, or by which they are affected) in a given sociopolitical system.[1]

In similarity to C. Wright Mills' theory, it is here assumed that there are certain positions in society, particularly in organizations, which lend their incumbents institutionalized control over resources, or power, and thus turn them into members of elites, and that people can thus gain power by getting hold of these positions. At the same time it is also the case that some people may gain control of resources without the benefit of formal positions. These persons may still be characterized as (informal) elites, or as members of (non-established, uninstitutionalized, and occasionally counter-) elites.

The present demo-elite perspective shares Weber's and some elitists' assumption that while economic power and economic class inequalities are important, political power and political inequalities are no less crucial, for political domination may be no less oppressive than economic exploitation. It assumes that in the *political* arena (with which this analysis is concerned) elites (including the economic elite) rather than classes (and particularly the "ruling class") are the main players in the field, and that they serve primarily their own, and only secondarily (if at all) broader class interests. It assumes that while the economic elite may at times utilize the political elite to serve its own interests, so, too, may the political elite utilize the economic elite to serve *its* interests.

To me it has long been a puzzling phenomenon that class analyses, concerned with economic power and exploitation, are considered progressive; but elite analyses, concerned with political power and domination, are generally considered conservative. The view that the elite which exerts political power represents the interests of the class that exerts economic power, or the ruling class, is considered avant-garde. But the view that the political elite is a separate entity which promotes primarily its own interests (particularly that of attaining and retaining power), and may even utilize the economic elite in the service of those interests, is considered status quo-oriented and therefore conservative. It will be a special task of the present analysis to demonstrate that this is not the case.

It is true that Marxist class theory—or rather ideology—includes the belief that classes can be abolished, while the demo-elite perspective in its present version does not hold out the (false) hope that elites can be abolished, as will be further argued below. But this does not imply that the demo-elite perspective endorses, legitimizes or idealizes elite rule.

In some of its earlier versions the democratic-elite perspective has been accused of doing just that. It has been dismissed by critics (e.g., Walker, 1966; Bachrach, 1967; Pateman, 1970) as elitist in the prescriptive sense, i.e., as favoring the rule of elites even in a democracy. It has also been accused of denigrating popular participation in politics as dysfunctional for democracy. And, in fact, some scholars who in previous decades have been—rightly or wrongly—classified as adherents of the democratic-elite perspective (e.g., Berelson et al., 1954; Kornhauser, 1959; Milbrath and Goel, 1965) have argued that successful democracy depends on widespread public apathy, that if the "masses" were to participate in politics in large numbers, peaceful competition amongst elites—and thus democracy—would be apt to break down.

But the demo-elite perspective in its present version makes no such claim and does not denigrate popular participation in the political arena. It does not claim that elites are desirable; it merely confronts the fact that they are there. It sets itself the task not of *praising* but of *exposing* elite rule and of analyzing the manner in which it is exercised in Western-style democracies. Although it does not include the belief that elites may be abolished, it holds out the hope that by leading to a better understanding of the elites' strategies and machinations in gaining, exercising, and maintaining power, it may also help identify the mechanisms through which the power of elites can be checked, limited and diminished.

It is here further assumed that although in contemporary societies there are a variety of elites having control of a variety of resources, most of these have control of resources that are significant only in specific contexts, or in relation to specific issues. Consequently, there are only a few elites which have control of the major resources, and thus may be considered as major or central power holders in modern societies. In line with Aron's above mentioned specification (with some variations) these major or central elites may be listed as including the following: the elected, governing political elite, the elite of the state bureaucracy, the elites of the defense and security services, and the judicial elite, here jointly referred to as the state, or ruling elites. Other major or central elites include the elites of large parties that have not been elected to office, or the opposition, the economic elite (i.e., the elite of major economic enterprises), the elite of trade and professional unions and associations, the media elite (and in some countries the church, or an equivalent religious organization), here jointly referred to as the major, or central non-ruling elites.

In contrast to these major elites, other elites—including those of a great variety of pressure groups (apart from economic organizations and trade unions), such as ethnic groups, citizens' action groups, and social-protest movements, (whose numbers have greatly proliferated in recent years) although they vary in their power from one democratic country to another—are here assumed not to equal the power of the previously mentioned major elites. Yet they may subsequently gain a greater share of power by being incorporated into the existing, central, power structures. This point will be resumed and further explicated below.

On Democracy and Elites

By contrast to the concepts of power and elites, the concept of democracy is here clarified with the aid of a more cumbersome (though by now pretty standard) definition, in which the two former concepts are incorporated. Partly following Schumpeter (1976), Lipset (1965), and Dahl (1956), democracy is here defined as a sociopolitical system in which two or more persons, groups, or organizations (such as parties) participate in the contest for government power (or for elite positions) on the strength of their past and/or their advocated policies and/or their projected images, and whereby they acquire and exercise such power on the basis of regular, free elections by all adults (whose votes have equal value) and where there are basic freedoms, including freedom from harassment, freedom of information, of speech, of association, or organization, and of participation in the contest for power, and where there are certain separations of power within the state, in accordance with general rules pertaining to those procedures and freedoms.

From the principle that all votes have equal value, it follows that the elite which becomes the governing elite, is elected by the votes of, and thus governs with a degree of consent from, the majority of the electorate. From the principles of freedom of organization and the separation of powers it follows that besides the elected, governing elite there are other relatively autonomous elites in a democracy. It is thus part of the essence of democracy that there are elites that partly countervail and limit the governing elite's power, as will be further clarified below.

For the purpose of the present analysis it is not necessary to assume that any regime fully embodies all the principles included in this definition. Rather, it is here assumed that these features have developed, and are to be found in Western-style regimes to a greater extent than is the case in other regimes. Even so, there are some marked shortfalls in their realization, as will also be seen below.

Some theories of democracy include actual public participation in politics as a basic element in the definition of democracy. In the view here presented it is *freedom* of participation in politics, and the ability of anyone wishing to do so to take part in the contest for power, that counts. For while democracy requires freedom to participate, it also requires freedom *not* to participate for anyone not wishing to do so. Hence, by the definition here suggested, freedom to participate is sufficient to qualify a regime as democratic, while the actual level of participation is best left for empirical investigation.

Some theories of democracy also include the ability of the public to influence government policy or, conversely, the responsiveness of the government, to public demands—as part of the definition of democracy. Thus, Ancker (1982, p. 218) cites May's (1978, p. 1) definition of democracy as Responsive Rule (RR), i.e., as the "necessary correspondence between acts of governance and the wishes with respect to those acts of the persons who are affected."

The view here presented is that while this element is of primary importance in a democracy, it is best to include in the definition of democracy not responsiveness as such, but rather the arrangements which at least to some extent institutionalize public influence and elite responsiveness as part of the political structure. Accordingly, the elements of influence and responsiveness are here introduced not as part of the definition but as part of a conception on the nature of democracy, while the actual degree of such influence and responsiveness are, once more, best left for empirical investigation.

On the basis of these definitions and assumptions, and before the actual arguments of the demo-elite perspective—in its present version—can be explicated, it is necessary to go over some further (rather well trodden) ground, in order to place this perspective within the spectrum of the other theories, so as to establish its own identity. In this context it is necessary to make explicit mention of the demo-elite conception that competitive elections *are* an important mechanism of democracy.

This is hardly an innovative idea, and presumably should not have to be stated at all. Except that the message now emanating from the social sciences (or rather from their Marxist and elitist contingent) is that elections do not really count, or count for very little, that they have mainly symbolic value, and serve merely as a sophisticated basis for the legitimation of the regime, as indicated before. In other words, it has now been discovered for us, that democracy is merely the system where we get to vote for the people who tell us what to do. Hence, it must be stated unequivocally that the demo-elite perspective in its present form does not share this view, but is closer to that of the pluralist and pluralist-elitist theories of democracy to the effect that elections *do* count, and certainly have more than merely symbolic value.

The efficacy of the electoral mechanism differs from one democratic country to another, and it is hereby readily granted that it contains many imperfections. It is true, as Marxists and elitists have emphasized, that elections and the other features of democracy ensure neither economic nor political equality. And, indeed, in Western democracies economic inequality is frequently converted into political inequality and vice versa. It is true that the elites from which voters can choose may not offer them a wide spectrum of policy alternatives. The political elite that holds office may not be fully informed of the public's preferences. It may not interpret electoral outcomes as intended by the public. It may be set to defend its own privileges against the wishes of the public. It may attempt to manipulate the public into believing that it is getting what it wants, or into wanting what it is getting (see below). And greater resort than is presently the case to mechanisms of public participation in decision making, such as initiatives and referenda, has the potential of creating more responsive government policies.

However, elections still play an important role. As is ostensibly self-evident—but apparently is not so to Marxists and some elitists—elections not only afford the public some (admittedly imperfect) choice of elites and projected policies, they not only confront the governing political elite with a recurring, institutionalized, threat of replacement, but, and perhaps more importantly, by doing so, elections provide a mechanism which is important in itself—and irrespective of whether the choice it offers the public is clear or fuzzy, broad or narrow—*for it forms an important component in the relative autonomy of elites in a democracy, which in turn limits the governing elite's power,* as will be argued in greater detail below.

In relation to this the demo-elite theory shares the assumption of the elitist theory to the effect that elites are inevitable and exist in democratic regimes no less than they do in other regimes. Some observers argue that this assumption is so self-evident (if not quasi-tautological) as not to deserve a mention, and certainly needs no explication. Others, however, argue that this assumption is the outgrowth of, and gives evidence of, a conservative bias. Obviously it is not possible for both arguments to be correct. If the assumption that elites are inevitable is self-evident then it must be accepted by all. If, on the other hand, it contains a conservative bias, then not all will accept it. Given this divergence of opinions, it seems worth dwelling briefly on the reasoning that lies behind the present acceptance of this assumption. It also seems worth arguing that here, at any rate, this assumption is not the outgrowth of a conservative bias.

The assumption that elites are inevitable is based on the conception of power and elites as presented before, and its application to actual reality. Power is here conceived of as based on the control of resources and in all societies (except in a utopia) resources are distributed unequally: because of preexisting (inherited) advantages, chance factors, and personal aptitudes and ambitions, some people tend to accumulate more resources than others. And even if a society came into being in which preexisting advantages were abolished, chance factors and personal aptitudes would still lead some people to accumulate more resources than others. And when resources are distributed unequally, the people who control more of the available (scarce) resources than others, can then institutionalize their own advantages, or make them part of institutional and organizational structures. They can thus constrain the actions, views, and life chances of the people who are dependent on those resources, or affected by them. And since elites are here conceived of not as "the best and the brightest" but merely as those who control a disproportionate share of resources, it follows that elites, too, are to be found in all societies and regimes.

The more specific assumption that there are elites even in a democracy follows both from the above definition of democracy and from the observation of actual reality in extant democratic regimes. If (following the literal meaning of the term) democracy were to be defined as rule by the people—the entire people—then, or course, there would be no place for elites in a democracy. But then, too, there would be no democracies to be found anywhere, the universe under discussion would be empty or, in other words, there would be nothing to analyze.

Hence, here, this utopian definition of democracy has been rejected in favor of a more realistic definition, whose centerpiece is the principle of free elections, coupled with the principle of freedom of organization. More importantly, perhaps, the electoral-organizational principle (though imperfectly implemented) is still actually the centerpiece of Western democracy as we know it today. And this principle implies an elite that gains power, or conversely loses power, through elections.

Other mechanisms of democracy designed to increase popular participation and render democracy non- or less elitist, such as referenda and initiatives, themselves also imply elites that initiate them, organize them, influence their outcomes and carry out their decisions. And even direct participation, in the form of mass demonstrations and protest movements (including those aimed at abolishing elites) are apt to bring to the fore some people who command more resources of time, motivation, and aptitude for leadership, and hence are more active and influential than others. That is, even mechanisms of direct participation are apt to generate their own (albeit informal, non-established, and at times temporary and fluid) elites, as indeed experience has shown in the past.

The Control of Resources and the Primacy of State Elites

In complex societies the major resources are accumulated in, and controlled by, organizations. It is hereby argued that (as Marxists have failed to recognize), while economic elites (which, in Western societies as we know them today, are capitalist elites) control major organizations, and hence major resources, nevertheless, in contemporary societies, the biggest accumulator and controller of resources, and the most formidable organization, is the state. And thus the elites that together have charge of the state have control of the greatest chunk of contemporary societies' resources.

For any orderly, contemporary state controls the main means or resources of coercion, which in turn lends it the ability to control a great variety of other resources, whether or not it exercises this control in actual practice. In addition, any contemporary state controls major economic resources: leaving aside communist societies where the control of the state is even more pervasive, it is the case that in practically all Western contemporary societies, the state gains control of about a third or more of gross national product through taxation; it also participates directly in the economy through government owned or partly owned enterprises.

The state, through the government, also exerts more general controls over the economy via monetary intervention (governmental influence on the quantity of money, for instance through the control of interest rates), fiscal intervention (through the government's own budget), and legal intervention (in the form of economic legislation, for instance with regard to tariffs, fair-trade practices, antitrust laws, and so forth), as well as via general policies affecting the economy.

No less important is the fact that the state—even in Western societies—also commands resources of "pure" power. Such power is backed up by coercion when all else fails, but it is not straightforward coercion. More immediately it is based on the control of structures engaged in regulatory and co-ordinatory activities (such as legislation, administration and adjudication). Power is thus a resource in its own right which, in turn, generates more power. On the basis of its control of these power structures, and on the basis of the charisma of office, the state also gains control of a variety of symbolic resources, as specified below.[2]

In the contemporary Western societies all non-state economic enterprises taken together have control of larger economic resources than does the state. But given the fact that the state has control of the coercive resources and also of co-ordinatory power structures—which private enterprises do not control—and given the fact that the state also has certain resources (monetary, fiscal and legal) of control over those private enterprises themselves, the overall balance of the control of resources is in favor of the state, even though in Western democracies (for reasons that will be clarified below) the state does not normally realize the full potential of its control in actual practice.

Economic power is here conceived of as entailing ownership and control of economic enterprises (which is in the hands of economic elites). Political power is conceived of as entailing control of the state and its institutions (which accrues to the state elites). On the basis of the previous analysis it becomes obvious that non-state economic power can be sustained only if backed up by political power, that is by control of the state, and ultimately by control of the means of coercion, over which any orderly contemporary state (largely) holds a monopoly. Hence, political power cannot be seen as derived from economic power, and, indeed, logically precedes, and to a certain extent encompasses it.

Thus, too, the elites that derive their power from the control of the state, and thus have political power, have a degree of power over the other elites, including the elites that derive their power from the control of economic enterprises, and thus have economic power. Indeed, the latter are generally dependent on the former for a variety of resources which they require in order to sustain their elite positions. For the economic elites these include, for instance, congenial economic legislation and policies, subsidies and tax exemptions, as well as contracts for a variety of goods and services. For the other elites, these include, for instance, favorable policies in other areas, a variety of forms of patronage, or even positions of power within the political establishment itself.

Lindblom (1977, esp. p. 123) has also addressed himself to the problem of which elite holds top power, and has reached a seemingly different conclusion. He has rejected the claim that the means of coercion or—as he calls them—the guns, automatically imbue state (military) elites with top power or authority, as the control over these resources can be secured only through political struggles. Instead, he has argued, top authority goes to those who have the economic resources, or the money, which is a more immediately controllable instrument of influence. Hence, in politics, it is money (and not guns) that whispers, talks, and "sometimes shouts so loud that no other messages are heard" (p. 123).

However (like Marxists whom he has increasingly come to resemble), Lindblom has not substantiated his claim—that money is more easily controllable, and therefore more influential in politics than guns—in any way, shape or form. While money does, indeed, talk in politics, it makes more sense to argue that guns can talk louder than money, and that money can talk only when the guns are silent, an argument the validity of which can be easily illustrated from a variety of nondemocratic regimes, or from cases in which democracy breaks down, as has recently happened in Fiji, for instance.

Moreover, in his analysis of the influence of money in politics, Lindblom has included money "whether from private wealth or from public funds subject to authoritative disbursement of patronage and public contracts" (p. 123). Yet, by the previously presented definition, control of public (state) funds is subsumed under political power, for it flows from the control of the institutions of the state, and accrues to state elites, rather than to economic (capitalist) elites. In fact, it is *inter alia*, precisely because of the state elites' control of public funds, which they can disburse as patronage, that economic elites are partly dependent on them.

Of course, this dependence is neither total, nor completely one-sided. As Marxists have correctly established, the elites that have control of the state, also have a certain dependence on the economic, or (presently) capitalist elites. For the "health" of the capitalist economy as we know it in Western countries today depends on the "health" of their enterprises, and the power of the state or ruling elites, in turn, depends on the well-being of that economy. To a certain extent, the dependence of these elites is thus mutual.

But if the previous analysis is correct, the elites that control the state, including the governing political elite, the elite of the state bureaucracy, the judicial elite, and the elites of the armed and security services, having control of both coercive *and* economic resources, generally have an edge of power over the elites that control only economic resources (or capitalist enterprises), even though (to reiterate), for reasons that should become clear below, in a democracy they do not always exert this power in practice.

It is true that economic elites can hold the state by the purse strings by moving their investments and enterprises out of the country, or by threatening to do so. But, once again, this can work only as long as the state elites do not make use of their coercive resources in practice as, in fact, they frequently do not, in a democracy. It is also true that the elites that jointly have control of the state, are by no means internally united; there are certainly many frictions and conflicts within and between them, as will be further argued below. But as even Marxists have recognized, neither are the economic elites (and, one may add, the other elites) united. For what Marxists refer to as the various fractions of the ruling class also have conspicuously competing and opposing interests. And the capacity of the state elites for concerted action is certainly no smaller, and possibly greater, than the capacity of the capitalists for such concerted action. Thus, it cannot be claimed that it is by virtue of their greater unity that economic elites exceed the power of the state elites.

The Relative Autonomy of Elites and the Principles of Democracy

This is not to say, however, that the ruling elites totally dominate the economic or capitalist and the other elites in a democracy. Indeed, and here I come to a central argument of the present analysis, both Marxists and elitists have failed to highlight what is one of the most distinctive features of democracy: that despite the partial interlocking of elites, and despite a certain dependence of the capitalist and other elites on the ruling, or state elites, and a (somewhat lesser) dependence of the state elites on the other major elites, in a democracy, the basis of the control of resources amongst the different elites differs to a greater extent than it does in other contemporary regimes. Hence, the sources of power of the major non–ruling elites differ from those of the ruling elites, and those of the various other elites differ from those of the governing elite to a greater extent, and they are more independent from it, than is the case in other regimes. And, through this relative independence, the other elites are able to countervail the power of the governing elite, at least in part.

It is my argument that the partial or relative autonomy of the major but non–ruling elites from the state or ruling elites, and of the non–elected elites from the elected elite, stems from the partial independence in the control of resources which today props up their power. As will be seen below, historically, this partial or relative independence was achieved through the struggles of elites for power and the control of resources, which manifested itself also as a struggle for the development and institutionalization of the principles of democracy, and its results were then enshrined in those principles. Consequently, the principles of democracy, as we know them today, are simultaneously also principles that safeguard and legitimize the relative—though incomplete—independence of elites, and thus the power of those elites to countervail, or partly countervail, the power of the governing elite. Indeed, therein lies a large part of their democratic distinctiveness and value.

This relative autonomy of elites is protected in Western, democratic regimes by various combinations of the electoral principle, in conjunction with the principles of freedom of association, or organization, and of speech, and the principle of the separation of powers within the state itself, which are part of the above definition of democracy, and which have come to be (though not necessarily perfectly) implemented in democratic regimes. Thus, the electoral principle, in conjunction with the principles of freedom of organization and speech, confront the governing political elite with a recurring, institutionalized, threat of replacement, and thereby provide the rationale, and make possible the organization and activity of the potential replacer.

Hence, as briefly indicated before, the distinctiveness of these principles lies not only in whatever influence over the political process they may lend to the public. Importantly, it also lies in providing a mechanism which underpins the existence and relative autonomy of another fraction of the political elite. It underpins the existence and autonomy, and thus confronts the governing elite with the countervailing power of the opposition, which is ever ready to replace it, and which therefore acts as a watchdog—curbing its uses and abuses of power in between elections.

The latter two principles also protect and lend legitimacy to the relative independence of the media elite, which also serves as a watchdog curbing the governing elite's uses and abuses of power. The principle of the separation of powers between the legislature, the executive and the judiciary and, within the executive, between the elected government and the appointed bureaucratic elite (however imperfectly implemented) nevertheless safeguards and legitimizes the relative autonomy of the judicial and bureaucratic elites respectively, which at times (though by no means always) have also had a certain effectiveness in countervailing and limiting the power and the abuses of power of the governing political elite.

The principle of freedom of association or organization also protects the relative autonomy of a variety of other elites. Where there is freedom of organization, and where the society is heterogeneous, actual groups, associations and organizations designed to promote sectorial interests, i.e., interest groups (including, for instance, trade unions), are apt to arise. As Dahl (1982, p. 37) put it, "because organizations are possible and advantageous, they are also inevitable."

Organizations, we have said, are accumulators of resources. Freedom of organization thus presupposes, and also protects, freedom to amass resources—including economic resources—that are, to a certain extent, exempt from state control. Since organizations can neither exist nor promote their interests without accumulating resources, as it is thus both necessary and advantageous for them to accumulate resources, they are likely to do so, and to protect them as far as possible from adverse state intervention. Freedom of organization thus entails, *inter alia,* an economy that has at least a partial immunity from state intervention.

From a demo-elite perspective it must be added that because there are elites both among and within interest groups, associations, and organizations, the most formidable of these groups and organizations (e.g., economic corporations and conglomerations and trade unions) are apt to give rise to formidable elites, which have charge of formidable, at least partly, or relatively, independent resources, and which therefore at least partly countervail the ruling elites' (and particularly the governing elite's) power. The principle of freedom of organization, or association, thus safeguards, *inter alia,* the relative autonomy of trade union and economic elites.

The Relative Autonomy of Elites and Their Divergent Interests

As is self–evident but as Marxists occasionally seem to forget, elites (like other people, or groups of people) are intent on defending and promoting their own interests. Not only power but interests, too, are linked to resources. Since elites (like other people) derive rewards from resources, it is obviously in their interest to accumulate, maintain, or increase their resources and to prevent others from increasing resources at their expense.

As is also obvious, any complex socioeconomic-political system (including a democratic one) generates large-scale resources. The resources of which the governing political elite and the other established elites have varying degrees of control are thus all based on, or derived from, the same socioeconomic-political system. As Marxists and elitists have correctly recognized, to a certain extent, their interests thus converge in the maintenance of the system on which their own dominant positions, their control of resources, and thus their personal rewards depend. Hence their tendency to be, to some extent, interlocked and to form overt or covert alliances with each other.

However, as indicated before, the principles of democracy underpin a certain differentiation in the bases of the various elites' resources. The degree to which the bases of the non-governing elites' resources are separate and independent from the control of the governing elite (and vice versa) varies to some extent in different democratic countries. But in all such countries the bases of the elites' resources are sufficiently separate from each other, for their interests to diverge at least in part.

This becomes evident, for instance, when one compares the interests of the economic, or presently, capitalist elite with those of the governing political elite. Like the governing political elite, the capitalist elite has an interest in the maintenance of the system. But—deriving its resources from property and/or profits—it also has interests that necessarily are partly different from those of the governing political elite whose main resource, power, ultimately derives from elections, and which must placate large numbers of voters, many of whose interests and ideas are diametrically opposed to those of the capitalists.

In view of all this, the Marxist argument that ultimately the state apparatus (including the governing political elite) serves the interests of the ruling class (the economic elite), begs the question of why the governing elite should so meekly and selflessly serve other people's interests. It is more realistic to perceive an area in which the elites' interests clearly converge (as Marxists have also done) and beyond it (as Marxists have not done), an area in which their interests clearly diverge. And where the interests of the various elites even partly diverge, can there be any doubt that—in the area of such divergence—each will give preference to its own interests and consign the others to oblivion?

***

The theory on the relative autonomy of the various non-governing elites from the governing elite, and on the partial divergence of interests between them in a democracy, cannot be conclusively proved on the empirical level any more than pluralist, Marxist or elite theories can be so substantiated. But it gains illustrative historical-empirical support from various sources. First, it gains support from the historical analysis provided in Chapters 3 and 4, which illustrates how the relative autonomy and countervailing power of elites developed in Western societies, and how it came to be protected by the principles of democracy.

Second, the thesis on the relative autonomy of elites gains illustrative empirical support from two previous studies of mine, the one concerned with bureaucratic elites (1985a), and the other concerned with the elites of national broadcasting corporations (which may be seen as bureaucratic and media elites at one and the same time) (1987)—both dealing with several Western democracies in a comparative perspective. Both studies have shown that there were significant differences in these respects between different democratic countries, and in all countries the bureaucratic and broadcasting elites had an obvious interest in the maintenance of the system. But, wherever closely scrutinized, bureaucratic and broadcasting elites were found to have sufficient independence from governing political elites to thwart at least some of their aims and be able to engage in some significant struggles with them. And (particularly but not exclusively where those elites also enjoyed tenure of office) they had to foresee working under governing elites of different political persuasions. For this reason they could best promote their long term interests by consolidating, increasing, and demonstrating their independence from the governing elites at any particular time.

Third, the principle of the relative autonomy of elites gives rise to certain propositions on the contradiction or dilemma of democracy and the ambivalent and controversial rules it creates, and on the manner in which the power of the governing elite is exercised in a democracy. These propositions are presented—and given illustrative empirical support—in Chapters 5,6,7, and 8. First, however, the historical development of the relative autonomy of elites in Western democracies must be illustrated. This will be done in the next two chapters.

Notes

1. By this definition, the term *elite* also encompasses the term *leaders*—the latter referring to people who first and foremost have control of symbolic resources, as in the classification below and as further clarified in Chapter 3.
2. Although these are the main resources, it is not claimed that they necessarily are the only resources controlled by the state.

3

Elite Power and the Development of Democracy (I): The Incorporation of Elites

Introduction

It is common to think of the development of democracy as a historical process in which successive social classes fought for, and gained a share of political power. First, it is held, the bourgeoisie contested the exclusive political power held by the aristocracy, and managed to gain a share of power for itself, as the franchise was extended to this property-holding class. Next, the same feat was repeated by the middle, and then the working class, and universal manhood suffrage—and democracy—was the result.

With respect to the first stage, for instance, Joseph Schumpeter (1976, p. 297) writes of the process of "political and institutional change by which the bourgeoisie reshaped, and from its own point of view rationalized, the social and political structure that preceded its ascendancy: the democratic method was the tool of this reconstruction." And Barrington Moore (1969, p. XII) writes of what he thinks "deserve to be called bourgeois revolutions . . . a necessary designation for certain violent changes that took place in English, French, and American societies on the way to becoming modern industrial democracies. . . ." With respect to the final stage, Anthony Giddens (1982, pp. 228–9) writes: "The translation of the liberal to the liberal-democratic state . . . was mainly secured through politically organized working class pressure."

With respect to all stages, however, this is true only metaphorically speaking, or as a figure of speech, if you will. Literally, the process was not one whereby entire classes struggled, pressured, and reshaped structures to suit their interests. Rather—with the possible exception of some spontaneous mass riots—the struggles were led and organized by bodies, organizations, or movements, headed by successive elites. At times these were elites that led and represented the interests of certain classes or other social groups from which they themselves originated; at times these were elites that led and represented the interests of classes other than their own (Perkin, 1969), and at times these were elites that represented no one in particular but themselves. These people—including leaders, activists, ideologues—were elites by the previously presented definition, in that they controlled a disproportionate share of resources on which social movements or other categories of people were dependent. It will be recalled, however, that resources are here defined broadly and they include, *inter alia,* time, energy, and symbolic assets such as ideologies and personal charisma, which may serve to mobilize and organize social movements.

In view of all this it may be said that the development of democracy was not the result of class struggles, but the result of elite struggles. The elites that activated these struggles could not have made much headway without popular discontent with the existing state of affairs, and without the support of certain social classes for their aims. But, conversely, the populus as a whole, or entire classes within it, could not have engaged in effective struggles without these elites to focus their discontent, and to organize their agitation. And only whenever the leaders were effective, did the struggles prove to be effective as well.

While successive, new elites organized, spearheaded, and led social struggles and movements for greater equality and democracy, they fought for, and managed to gain a share of power for themselves, most of them were incorporated into existing power structures (at times with the active connivance of established elites), while also gaining a certain degree of autonomy from or within those structures. Yet, the successive elites' struggles for democracy were not necessarily a conspiracy or a cynical ploy to deceive the masses of their supporters, and to camouflage the struggles for increased power and autonomy for themselves.

These elites' struggles found their legitimation in, and were also influenced by certain philosophies clamoring for the protection of the individual, human rights, liberty, sovereignty of the people, and, finally, democracy. Partly for this reason, they genuinely manifested themselves also as struggles for human rights, sociopolitical reforms, and eventually also for the development and implementation of the principles of democracy. In the process of gaining power and autonomy within or from the existing establishments, some of the struggling elites thus also achieved certain benefits for the classes or groups whose interests they represented, and by which they were supported.

Several of the elites did so only as long as the interests of those classes or groups coincided with their own; in some cases they subsequently abandoned or partly abandoned the interests of those classes or groups and, moreover, the achievements they provided for those groups were frequently much smaller than was initially expected. Eventually, the elites' struggles—which were protracted over several centuries, but culminated in the nineteenth century—nonetheless had some far-reaching results for those groups. They led to the reshaping of the existing political and social structures in a more egalitarian fashion (though not, of course, to the abolition of inequalities) and to the gradual development of democracy as (with all its deficiencies) we know it today.

In short, the struggles of successive elites, their attainment of a share of power, their incorporation into the establishment, the granting of a degree of autonomy to them, and their delivering of (even limited) achievements to certain classes or groups whom some of them initially represented, were all processes that led to, were manifested in, and thus were inextricably interlinked with, the development of Western democracy. Democracy thus developed out of a convergence of two processes: a process of increasing incorporation of elites, and a process of increasing autonomization, or the development of relative autonomy of elites.

Shortage of space makes it impossible to provide comprehensive support for these arguments through a historical analysis of the struggles of all elites, throughout all relevant time-spans, and by tracing the consequent development of democracy in all Western countries. But in what follows, these arguments are supported (with respect to the political elites, the elites of social and political movements, trade unions, economic, and bureaucratic elites) through a few illustrations drawn from certain historical developments of the last two centuries in two major Western countries: France and Britain. Not being a historian myself, I have no pretensions of uncovering heretofore unknown historical facts. Rather, the following analysis is intended to show how the (already well established) historical facts support the present argument.[1]

For analytical purposes this argument may be divided into two parts. The first part is that the development of democracy was a manifestation of the struggles of elites for power, a large part of which was a struggle for those elites' incorporation into existing power structures, and that these struggles also led to those elites "delivering" certain sociopolitical achievements to their supporters, and thus to advances on the road to democracy. This part of the argument is illustrated in this chapter. The second part of the argument—that the struggles of elites for power were simultaneously also struggles for the attainment of greater autonomy from, or within existing power structures, and that this, too, was inextricably interlinked with the development of democracy—is dealt with in the next chapter.

The Political Elite of the Bourgeoisie in the French Revolution and the Development of Democracy

The first part of the argument may be aptly illustrated with respect to the political elite that originated from and represented the interests of the bourgeoisie, first through the events that led up to, and also through the first stage of the French Revolution. It is widely agreed amongst historians that the discontent that led up to the Revolution was, in large part, that of the bourgeoisie that was resentful as well as morally outraged at the privileges of the aristocracy. The grievances of the bourgeoisie were spurred in particular by the fact that while it approached the aristocracy in its economic achievements it was—at least partly—blocked in its political and status achievements.

According to some historians, in the late eighteenth century, positions of top political power and distinction were practically monopolized by members of the nobility, which was actually making bourgeois access to these offices more restricted than had previously been the case. According to others, recent research has shown more de facto entry into the pre-revolution political elite by members of the bourgeoisie than had previously been thought. In any event, access to these positions was more restricted than the members of the —economically— increasingly powerful bourgeoisie would have wished, and thought justifiable, and a blocking of ambitions and aspirations was the result.

Whereas the frustration may thus have been common to the bourgeoisie in general, it was only a small elite of the bourgeoisie that took concrete action in an attempt to increase its access to political power. This was first and foremost the group of representatives of the Third Estate in the *Estates-General* summoned by the King in the spring of 1789. This body, which had last met in 1615, was made up of some 550 representatives of the First Estate, the clergy, and the Second Estate, the nobility, and 600 representatives of the Third Estate or commons (but dominated by representatives of the propertied class). The double representation of the Third Estate was unprecedented, and constituted a concession wrung from the king. In the old constitution final decisions had been made by the orders as units, so that if the Clergy and Nobility as separate houses agreed on an issue, they could carry it two to one even against the dissent of the Third Estate. However, in 1789 the representatives of the Third Estate insisted on one great assembly, to be called the National Assembly, in which they would have a majority, and which would have the power to levy taxes and draw up a constitution.

Pursuant to the king's initial opposition to this innovation, the representatives of the Third Estate met separately and vowed not to disperse until they had endowed France with a constitution. When, on another occasion, the representatives of the Third Estate were requested to withdraw, Mirabeau was said to have made his famous statement: "We are assembled here by the will of the nation. . . . " Thus, the representatives of Third Estate used the liberal idea of the sovereignty of the people ("the nation") to legitimize their own increased share of power in the French political system, to which the king was eventually forced to consent. This was not by chance. It followed from the fact that the representatives of the Third Estate in the Assembly shared the ideas of classical liberalism, as formulated by the philosophers and economists of that era.

These ideas were then most clearly set out in the famous "Declaration of the Rights of Man and of the Citizen," issued by the Assembly (which by now was dominated by representatives of the Third Estate) in August 1789. This document proclaimed that "all men are born and remain free and equal in rights," and "all citizens have the right to take part, in person or by their representatives" in the forming of the law and in voting in taxes. Yet it was careful to specify in particular those civic rights that most concretely expressed the aims of the bourgeoisie: it stressed equality of all before the law, personal freedom from arbitrary arrest or punishment, freedom of speech and of the press, but, above all, a fair distribution of the burdens of taxation and the sacredness and inviolability of private property.

The Declaration based these claims on the general doctrine that "sovereignty rests essentially in the nation" and that "law is the expression of the general will." Despite invoking the sovereignty of the people, this document was not a truly democratic manifesto. While the representatives of the bourgeoisie, who issued it, believed in constitutionalism and in civil liberties, they aimed to limit political participation to the propertied only. Consequently, the declaration included neither the principle of universal suffrage, nor that of freedom of association or organization. This became even clearer when the constitution of 1791—drawn up by the Assembly—provided suffrage only for "active," that is to say, tax-paying, or well-off citizens.

But while the drafters of the constitution were liberals rather than democrats there was enough common ground between the two for them to travel at least a certain distance along the same road. Thus, the representatives of the bourgeoisie in the National Assembly had helped increase their own political power, had helped make the elite of the bourgeoisie part of the governing elite, while simultaneously helping France to travel—albeit only a limited distance—on the road to democracy.

The storming of the Bastille in 1789 and the attack on the Tuileries in 1792 were clearly mass events, though not necessarily without their leaders. With respect to the second revolution, for instance, Palmer (1964, p. 38) writes: "With the usual aid of organizers hard to identify, the insurrection was generated at the popular level. . . . " Importantly, the next phase of the revolution, while it proceeded in the name of popular democracy, and with the active support and even pressure of the masses, it nonetheless had a relatively small number of leaders—organized in powerful "committees"—who instituted a reign of terror and a revolutionary dictatorship. And this terror-supported dictatorship, in turn, led to a further, military, dictatorship later on.

Not surprisingly, then, the Jacobin regime had driven the Revolution farther than the bourgeoisie would have wished. But the first, moderate phase of the Revolution left behind a most influential legacy: following the era of reaction and dictatorship, it was the political pattern established during this phase of the Revolution which served as a blueprint for those to be institutionalized in France itself, in Britain, and in some other European countries at least for the beginning and the middle of the nineteenth century.

The Political Elites of the Bourgeoisie and the Middle Class in the Nineteenth Century and the Development of Democracy

At the beginning of the nineteenth century, and up until 1832, the elite of the landed aristocracy or gentry—in Britain, for instance, it comprised no more than about 1,200 men—was still (Britain) or had re-established itself as (France) the chief holder of political power: it was the main component in the government and in the parliament as well. Members of the bourgeoisie were not wholly excluded. In Britain, for instance, given the corrupt nature of politics, some rich bankers, merchants, and industrialists had bought themselves seats in Parliament. Nonetheless, up until 1832, the House of Lords consisted almost entirely of great landowners. And in the House of Commons, between 1734 and 1832, three-quarters of the members were landowners or their near relations, and the rest were their friends or nominees, or else they were rich business and professional men "often with one foot on the land" (Perkin, 1969, p. 39). And in all cabinets between 1783 and 1835, peers and sons of peers formed a clear majority.[2]

This situation led to attempts to substitute more bourgeois and middle class political leadership for the traditional aristocratic one. These attempts found expression *inter alia* in the creation of middle class movements, and these broadened their appeal to include working class supporters as well. Because this was also a time of growing resentment against the repression of the impoverished, swelling, urban masses, the leaders of these movements managed to create an alliance of middle and working class interests. It resulted in two main waves of revolt: that of 1816–20, and that of 1830. They were the outgrowth of massive, widespread discontent, but were spurred by small groups of leaders and activists. Those were mainly rich (including landowners) and well educated but, particularly in Britain, also from middle class, and occasionally even working class (primarily artisan) background.

From the viewpoint of the bourgeois and middle class leaders, the main achievement of these movements came in the wake of the second wave of revolts, which in Britain led to the Reform Act of 1832, and to the incorporation of more large-scale capitalists—bankers, big industrialists—into the top ranks of power. The Whig aristocracy saw them as allies against the corrupt Tory elite, and encouraged their incorporation. Consequently, although the landed class maintained a clear majority in the House of Commons until 1885, and in the Cabinet until 1893, capitalists gained the balance of political power: they were the ones who now determined policy, mostly to suit their own interests. In France, at that time, the representatives of the *grande bourgeoisie* of bankers and big industrialists largely replaced the representatives of the nobility in the strongholds of political power. In both cases the incorporation of capitalists into the existing establishments (like the incorporation of their predecessors at the end of the eighteenth century) found its ideological basis and justification in the philosophy of liberalism and constitutionalism.

This philosophy—which became the dominant theme in European and American politics in the nineteenth century—was most fully expounded in the works of James Madison (1751–1836), Jeremy Bentham (1748–1832), and James Mill (1773–1836). While there were variations in their philosophies, their gist was the promotion of the values of freedom, reason and tolerance, and the protection of individual rights in the face of the arbitrariness of absolutism. But although they conceived of all individuals as free and equal and endowed with natural, inalienable rights, their main emphasis was on the rights of male, property owning individuals, including the inalienable right to own property.

The liberal philosophers also stressed the sovereignty of the people, the idea that government derived its legitimate power from the consent of the people, and the accountability of the governors to the governed, through the process of regular, free elections. But although the logic of their philosophy warranted universal franchise, and although they seemed to lay the philosophical basis for it, they nonetheless did not push for this measure. Bentham and Mill, for instance, even found grounds for excluding, among others, women and a large proportion of the working class from this basic democratic right, thus, in fact, limiting it to the (male) bourgeoisie and middle class.[3]

Thus backed up by the then most prevalent philosophy, it is not surprising that the Reform Act of 1832, which extended the franchise in Britain, was designed basically to increase the power of the bourgeoisie and property holders, rather than that of the people as a whole. Previously, the franchise had been limited to 40-shilling freeholders in the counties, while various unequal franchises prevailed in the boroughs, and, in fact, most town inhabitants—and thus the bulk of the bourgeoisie—were excluded from the franchise. The Reform Act retained the 40-shilling freehold qualification in the counties but replaced the traditional franchises in the boroughs with a £10 occupation franchise, thereby including city dwellers as well. But the franchise was still confined to people with property qualifications, the electorate was merely expanded from 5 to 7 percent of the adult population, in a mostly corrupt electoral system, which was therefore largely still under the influence of the wealthy. In France, too, the 1830 revolt led to reforms which somewhat lowered, but still maintained, property qualifications for the vote, and also safeguarded administrative influence over elections.

No sooner were these accomplishments put into place than the moderate liberals, representing the interests of the bourgeoisie and the middle class, moved out of the common front of opposition which they had previously shared with the radicals, representing the interests of the working class: "having gained power by the efforts of the radicals—for who else fought on the barricades?— they immediately betrayed them." (Hobsbawm, 1962, p. 148).[4] Thus, these moderate liberals would have no bar of anything as risky as full democracy and they tended to moderate their enthusiasm for further reform and even to suppress the radical left and working class revolutionaries.

Consequently, the political system put into place by major West European countries including Britain, and France at that time, was fundamentally composed of liberal institutions, based on a certain extension of voting rights but safeguarded against full democracy by property or educational qualifications for the franchise. It was in fact something very much like the institutions of the first and most moderate bourgeois phase of the French Revolution, following the model of the constitution of 1791. In this manner, elites, drawn from the bourgeoisie and the middle class and betraying their former allies from the working class, managed to attain a share of political power while also consolidating previous achievements of constitutionalism, liberalism and certain, though intentionally limited, advances towards democracy.

The Political Elite of the Working Class and the Development of Democracy

The arguments set out before can be illustrated also with respect to the more radical movements and elites representing the interests of the working class. It was seen before that the alliance of middle class and working class interests, and the revolts of 1816–20 and 1830 to which it gave rise, were exploited by the leaders representing the bourgeoisie and middle class to augment their own power, and to promote the interests of those classes. It will now be seen that, in conjunction with other working class rebellions and movements, these revolts nonetheless led to some (limited) achievements for the working class as well.

For at that time, and later in the century, there was also a development of protests and movements whose leaders (whatever their own background) more clearly represented the interests of the working class, and whose supporters came from the working class in several European countries, including Britain and France. These movements and their elites repudiated hereditary privileges, and advocated the principles of what was conceived of at the time as full democracy: equality of all before the law and universal manhood suffrage, and some (but by no means all) advocated socialism. In the face of the growing misery, discontent and disaffection among the poor—especially the urban poor—all over Western Europe, they also advocated liberation through direct action.

Despite this large-scale restlessness of the poor—and even when they relied on mass rioting and demonstrations—the proletarian movements which emerged chiefly in Britain and in France, in fact were run by small numbers of leaders and activists, and were dependent on those for their success. In the event, these leaders—drawn mainly from professionals, intellectuals, skilled craftsmen and independent artisans, small-scale domestic workers, and factory workers—were not very effective. And it is at least in part because of this lack of effectiveness of their leadership that the movements had some, but only limited achievements, and eventually broke down.

In Britain the misery of the working class gave rise to Luddism, the violent protest of skilled handworkers who felt themselves threatened by the new machinery, and by unskilled labor, and banded together to wreck machines. Aimed against the capitalists' endeavor of destroying customary trades and beating down wages it used attacks upon machinery as a means of pressuring the employers into concessions with regard to wages and other working conditions. It thus engaged in "collective bargaining by riot" (Hobsbawm, 1968, p. 7). According to Thompson (1980), although the movement found some of its expression in "spontaneous rioting" (p. 618) it generally had a "high degree of organization" (p. 604). It also had "leaders" and people who "organized" it (p. 593); "regular commanders" (p. 606); and *"provocateurs"* (p. 618) from amongst the working class.

The leaders of Luddism, however, succeeded only in organizing intermittent riots, and failed to develop it into a sustained, nationwide, working class movement. The riots originated in 1811 and spread rapidly, especially among cotton, wool and hosiery textile workers. Despite severe penalties applied by the government, Luddite riots continued intermittently until 1818. A wave of rioting and machine breaking also propagated itself among the starving farm laborers of southern and western England in 1830, and additional machine breaking in the declining hand industries—threatened by the machine—took place in 1826, in the mid-1830s and the mid-1840s, before the movement eventually disappeared.

During the same period another movement, a socialist movement—under the influence of Robert Owen—emerged, but its leadership failed to develop clear strategies and an effective organization, and the movement therefore remained weak. It organized some sporadic but futile strikes, and eventually failed and collapsed (although Owen also had a more long-range influence on the British Trade Union and co-operative movements which further developed after his death).

A more successful movement was The Movement for the People's Charter, or the Chartist Movement. In spite of its "middle class demagogues" (Perkin, 1969, p. 371), and in spite of its (albeit limited) alliance with some middle class radicals, this became an overwhelmingly working class movement. It set as its major goal the establishment of what it considered as full democracy, including universal male suffrage, paid parliamentarians, and full democratic rights for the working class, in the hope that this would also lead to an improvement of the workers' socioeconomic conditions.

The Chartists had clearly identifiable leaders as evidenced by the fact that they formed themselves into a national convention which sent delegates to London. The movement's leaders were also responsible for propaganda and for some dynamic outbursts of working class agitation, including the presentation of petitions to parliament, strikes, and riots. They instigated violent outbursts in Birmingham and Newport in 1839, and in these twenty-four workers were killed. Subsequent Chartist outbursts in 1848 reflected the general unrest throughout Europe. But thereafter the movement declined and died.

This was so largely because the movement's leaders had not been effectual organizers. "What linked even the most massive and comprehensive of their political manifestations—Chartism— . . . together was little more than a handful of radical slogans and a few powerful orators and journalists who became the voices of the poor" (Hobsbawm, 1962, p. 255). Thus, though very large, and occasionally referred to as a mass movement, Chartism, too, eventually faced defeat through the incapacity of its leaders, and its consequent inability for concerted national action.

But while these working class movements were not ultimately successful they still had some achievements at the time. Especially since they were allied with activists from the politically entrenched classes, their demands could not be ignored altogether, and they were met by some concessions. They have been held responsible for bringing about the social and political reforms encompassed in the Reform Act of 1832, including the—albeit no more than modestly effective—legislative control of factory conditions and working hours.

This was the case not so much because these movements' direct threat of violence worked, but because they increased the awareness of the upper classes to the plight of the working class and the poor, and to the long-term danger inherent in their continued repression. Hence the governing elite's willingness to introduce some—well circumscribed—reforms, so as to quiet popular discontent. These reforms "came slowly, belatedly, and only after their complete necessity had been abundantly proved. They encountered apathy and timidity, greedy self-interests and official bumbledom. . . . " (Thomson, 1966, p. 189). But they were nonetheless small steps in a general process of development without which democracy could not have come about.

In France, after the restoration, the popular basis of the regime, or in other words, the suffrage, was still very limited: from 1814 to 1830 there were only 100,000 voters, and from 1830 to 1848 there were only 200,000 voters out of a population of 30 million. The working class was denied any influence in the political system and, in protest, working class and democratic movements developed.

These movements, too, had their leaders who, initially, were mostly old-style craftsmen and journeymen. The proponents of the various brands of the new "utopian" socialism, under the influence of Saint-Simon and Fourier were uninterested in political agitation at the time, though their little groups were to act as nuclei of working class leadership and mobilizers of mass action in the revolution of 1848.

At that time there were also some more radical secret societies that combined with mob action to make democratic movements more violent than they were in Britain. As riots were suppressed by the government, this led to the further prominence of secret republican societies, some of which were under the influence of more moderate leaders—such as Louis Blanc—while others, influenced by radical leaders—such as Auguste Blanqui— were frankly communist in their aims.

Despite economic distress and unemployment among workers, the conspirators did not succeed in gaining large mass support. In the absence of such mass support, the movement remained a detached and rather weak elite, which therefore often failed, as in the attempted rising of 1839. When this uprising crumbled, several of the movement's leaders were imprisoned. Deprived of its most prominent leaders the movement fell even further out of touch with its potential supporters from the working class. Nonetheless the communist movement continued; it was joined, and later also influenced, by the ideological leadership of Karl Marx and Friedrich Engels.

As in Britain, in France, too, the working class movements that were active at the time led to some reforms, for instance the Education Act of 1833, planning to set up state-aided primary schools in every community. The fact that the act was passed in response to these movements becomes evident from its purpose as defined by chief minister Guizot —who presented the bill— as follows: "to calm and quench the people's thirst for action, as dangerous for itself as for society . . ." (Thomson, 1966, p. 190). But the economic distress of the working class continued and during the 1840s became even more acute. Hence, the most important achievement of these movements was that they led up to the revolution of 1848.

This revolution was spurred by the refusal of Louis Philippe to extend the franchise, and its result was the proclamation of the Second Republic. The revolution was spearheaded by the moderate socialist movement under the influence of Blanc and by extremist revolutionaries under the influence of Blanqui. It led to the abdication of the king and to the formation of a provisional government composed of moderate liberals, radical democrats, and socialists. This government instituted several social reforms, removing restrictions on the press and on the liberty of the citizen, and decreeing universal male suffrage, but it was soon defeated in an election.

Later in the year Paris experienced first another attempted but failed coup by the radical secret societies under the leadership of Blanqui and other revolutionary activists, and then another popular uprising. Although it had been prepared by radical agitators, in the uprising itself, no clear leaders could be seen to emerge. But the uprising was quickly quelled, and the fear of radicalism drove the government into the arms of conservativism. The new constitution made no mention of previous reforms, though it provided for universal suffrage, and the separation of powers in the state. The subsequent general election swept Louis Napoleon, and his military dictatorship, into power.

In Britain, where there had been occasional riots, but where 1848 had not brought an actual revolution, the post 1848 era saw further agitation for reform. The pressure for parliamentary reform was led by some liberal–minded Whigs, and even Conservative leaders like Disraeli responded to the popular movements by recognizing the need for parliamentary reforms. His 1867 Electoral Act introduced a household suffrage and a lodger franchise in the boroughs and established a new occupation franchise in the counties. It reduced property requirements for the vote, and in effect gave the franchise to the (male) lower middle class, while the electorate was thus increased from 7 to 16 percent of the adult population.

During that time there was also a thrust for a variety of other reforms led by activists who formed additional popular movements, associations, trade unions, and pressure groups. These applied pressure through lobbying the existing parties and playing them off against each other, through propaganda, petition and agitation. This thrust led to further reforms, including the Elementary Education Act in 1870, the establishment of the secret ballot in 1872, and the Public Health Acts, in 1872 and 1875. They also led, with Liberal acquiescence, to the election of the first two working class members of parliament, the miners' leaders Alexander Macdonald and Thomas Burt.

In France, in 1852, Louis Napoleon proclaimed himself emperor and endowed himself with quasi-monarchical powers. He endeavored to preserve the semblance of parliamentary government, but the assembly sat only three months a year and had little power. Universal male suffrage was maintained pro-forma, but in fact was made meaningless through administratively managed and manipulated elections. Yet within the next eighteen years, because universal male suffrage and parliamentary institutions did survive if only formally, and because of increasing clamor from a republican opposition, France gradually reverted to a more highly developed system of parliamentary government.

At that time the developing opposition (see below) set itself the task of promoting individual freedoms, civil liberties, and political-democratic rights for all citizens. In 1864, an opposition party leader, Thiers, presented his famous demands for five fundamental freedoms: security against personal violence and arbitrary power; freedom of the press; freedom of elections; freedom of national representation; and public (majority) opinion to direct the conduct of government.

Another leader, Leon Gambetta, was elected in a working class district on the basis of a more radical manifesto, which included besides universal suffrage, the election of all public functionaries, and free compulsory and secular primary education for all. In 1870 a new constitution was adopted and it re-established a parliamentary system somewhat similar to that of Louis Philippe. But a few weeks later, with the defeat of the French army at Sedan, the empire was overthrown and the Third Republic was proclaimed.

In 1871 the City of Paris broke into revolt. Its purpose was *inter alia* to defy the efforts of the newly elected National Assembly and the provisional government headed by Thiers to build what by then was considered a conservative regime. Power quickly fell into the hands of extremists. The lead was taken by Blanqui and his few thousand veteran revolutionary followers. Those were joined by Jacobin and socialist leaders of various brands, and together they formed a revolutionary government. After two months, in which a Paris Commune was created and terror reigned, Thiers and his forces overthrew the commune, took savage reprisals on the communards, and the revolutionary leaders were exiled or imprisoned. Thereafter the conservative Assembly proceeded to stabilize the Third Republic.

On the surface, the new regime did not differ markedly from its predecessor, but it incorporated an important difference: parliament now became the sovereign institution of the state. Also, the 1848 electoral laws were revived, and France had effective universal male suffrage from then onward. But it was only in 1879 with the granting of amnesty to their leaders that radical movements could, once again, act freely in France.

After 1871, in both Britain and France, the forces of the establishment were mostly conservative and moderate liberal elites whereas the forces of change were socialist, anarchist and communist movements and their elites, demanding complete democracy and economic reorganization. Many radical activists focused their struggles on the attainment of democracy because they expected universal suffrage to do away with all existing privileges and inequalities. Many conservatives and moderate liberals fiercely resisted democracy on precisely the same grounds. Therefore, the struggles for extension of the franchise and secrecy of the ballot were often long and fierce. They resulted in further but still limited advances on the road to democracy.

These advances found their justification in, and possibly were also spurred by the thought of the liberal-democratic philosopher John S. Mill (1806–73).

Mill, who —like his father— was a staunch defender of liberty, went further than his father and the other previous liberal philosophers in his advocacy of democracy. He favored participatory democracy to offset the dangers of an oversized and over powerful state and its corrupt practices, and also in order to foster the development of human reason and morality. He advocated individual rights, freedom of speech, of the press, and of assembly, as well as universal (including female) suffrage. But he obviated some of the thrust of his own philosophy by recommending a complex system of plural voting, so as to prevent the working classes from imposing what he considered their ignorance on the political order.

It is precisely because established leaders shared Mill's fear of full democracy, that the advances towards democracy at that time were still piecemeal and hesitant. Thus, in Britain, the 1883 Corrupt Practices Act effectively attacked the abuses that prevailed during elections and the 1884 Electoral Act extended the franchise to every man over 21 who had a home. This, however, still comprised only 28 percent of all adults, keeping the conservative and moderate liberal leadership in power.

Even so, government leaders now had to compete for popular support with more radical liberals and to face the pressures of socialist movements and labor organizations; hence they saw no choice but to institute several social and political reforms. Thus, they undertook legislation and measures that led to slow, but eventually far–reaching reforms in sanitation, working conditions and welfare provisions. This was less so in France where a prolonged struggle between republicans, monarchists and Bonapartists delayed the tackling of social problems by political leaders. Consequently, here the most effective labor regulation derived from the paternalistic bureaucracy.

This was also the time in which the socialist and communist movements were considerably strengthened and labor/socialist parties emerged or re-emerged. In Britain, a Marxist party was set up in 1883 by a wealthy eccentric: Henry Hyndman. Side by side with those parties there was also a growth of less doctrinaire socialism: in 1893, an independent Labour Party was created by Keir Hardie, rivalled by the socialist, yet rather elitist Fabian society created in 1884. In 1900 various labor and socialist groups combined with the trade union movement to found the future Labour Party, and the first members of parliament from this party were elected.

Eventually, the party's power grew: in 1906 twenty–nine Labour candidates were elected to Parliament; in 1915 the Labour Party first joined a government coalition. However, Labour was not perceived as a formidable power and a threat to the other parties until after the First World War. The Liberal party had split during the War, and was disadvantaged by the 1918 Reform Bill which enfranchised the remaining men—who overwhelmingly voted Labour—and older women (see below)—who were overwhelmingly Tory voters. Consequently, in the 1922 election, the Labour Party superseded the Liberal Party as the second great party in Britain, and in 1924 the first (minority) Labour government was formed. Since then, the Labour Party has held office intermittently, and has thus become an inextricable part of the British political establishment.

In France, from the first half of the nineteenth century and onwards, the cleavage and conflict between conservatives and liberals had been overshadowed by the appearance of the socialist movement and its parties. These, for their part, had been splintered as well: as noted, they had been divided into Blancists, Blanquists, Proudhonists and followers of other leaders, each with its own doctrines and ideologies. But despite being splintered the socialists had not been negligible in their power and influence. Their strength was revealed in both 1848 and 1871, and in both cases the liberals and conservatives were forced to unite against them.

Subsequently, the suppression of the Commune destroyed the organization of the Socialist Party for several decades. But it slowly reemerged toward the end of the century. At that time it was split into different factions which did not fuse until 1905, when they briefly combined into a unified parliamentary party, headed by Jean Jaures. Following the Russian Revolution of 1917, the party became divided again: one wing supported the Bolsheviks, while others preferred to maintain their distance from them. In 1920 this split produced the Communist Party, and it is at this time that the French party system took on its contemporary shape. From 1936 onward, the socialists have intermittently participated in government. After the liberation, the Socialist Party participated in governments that held power with communist support. From 1947, however, the Communists were eliminated from government and became a permanent opposition until they again became coalition partners in F. Mitterand's first government in 1981.

The leaders of socialist and other radical movements and parties, which were gradually strengthened after 1871, now faced a dilemma: it was their avowed purpose to overhaul the sociopolitical order in the interests of the working class. But, they faced the question of whether they could do so most effectively by gaining political power, by working within the framework of parliamentary democracy, or by standing apart, shunning compromises, and maintaining their revolutionary aims. Those who held to more extreme revolutionary doctrines, whether of Marxism, syndicalism or anarchism, chose the latter path. The communist parties, in particular, remained outsiders. They were careful to banish the suspicion that they might be turning 'bourgeois' and abandoning their aims for the sake of some immediate advantages and a share of power.

By contrast, socialists chose the path of integration into existing power structures. This created a problem, for the socialist parties were seldom the result of mass action. They were rather the work of intellectuals, political agitators, and a few individual workers. These people had something in common: as intellectuals or quasi-intellectuals they were less interested in short-term gains, more in restructuring society as a whole. As a result, the socialist parties became somewhat schizophrenic: they affirmed their allegiance to such abstract ideological aims as the class struggle and the socialization of the means of production (which were attractive mainly to intellectuals) but relegated them to the background.

Committed to seeking votes in order to gain political representation, their immediate aims and programs were more restricted, and concerned issues such as the widening of the franchise, social welfare legislation and the improvement of working conditions. With respect to the French Socialist party, for instance, Duverger (1958, p. 104) writes: "From the beginning there has been an antithesis between the revolutionary phraseology of the program and the moderate reformism of the party's activity." For this and the other socialist parties, the moment of truth came when an opportunity opened for their leaders to accept a share in government alongside non-labor parties. And in both Britain and France the socialist leaders usually took advantage of that opportunity. Consequently, they were regularly accused of betrayal.

Nonetheless, there is a wide-reaching consensus amongst historians that the growing power of organized labor movements and parties and their leaderships still had a very significant effect on sociopolitical change in the Western world. With respect to this, the attainment of a share of power by the labor and socialist leaders themselves was important. No less important was the increasing trepidation of conservative leaders, and their attempt to forestall the socialist and labor leaders gaining even greater power and engaging in even more radical, and possibly revolutionary action. Together these factors had a growing impact on a variety of reforms that occurred particularly from the latter half of the nineteenth century onwards. Thus it was both the labor elites themselves when they joined the establishment, as well as the wish of (even conservative) governing elites to safeguard their own power in the face of the growing power of those leaders, that have led to reluctant, belated, piecemeal, but in the end, still far–reaching reforms, in Western countries' working conditions, welfare measures, and political systems, including reforms towards greater democracy.

The Political Elite of Women and the Development of Democracy

At the beginning of the twentieth century there still was one major category of people that had been totally bypassed by the advances towards democracy: women. A group of their activists now organized in what came to be known as the Suffragette Campaign, demanding the vote for women. This movement was created by a small number of female activists in Manchester, in 1903. Until 1910 the movement remained small and moderate; its leaders engaged mainly in lobbying members of parliament and staging processions.

Meeting with a negative response and with ridicule, they gradually became more militant, disrupting debates in parliament, and eventually resorting to violence as well. Thus, they attempted an invasion of the Houses of Parliament and of Downing Street, where the prime minister had to be rescued by the police. Thereafter, the Suffragette Campaign was backed up by outbreaks of arson and other damage inflicted to property. Its leaders included Emmeline Pankhurst and her daughters, one of whom, Christabel Pankhurst, has been described as a rather violent and ruthless personality.

The leaders of the Liberal government at that time, though in panic, refused to give in for several years. It was only in 1918, after the war had allowed for a cooling-off period, that virtually all men in the United Kingdom, and women over the age of thirty—with certain property qualifications—were given the vote. And it was only in 1928 that the voting age for women was reduced to 21, and universal adult suffrage was thus introduced. But even then plural voting for university graduates and the holders of business premises was retained and university constituencies were still preserved. Not until 1948 were these privileges abolished, and the principle of one person-one vote was thus established.

In France, female suffrage had been proposed many times under the Third Republic, but the proposals were all knocked back by the Upper Chamber, the Senate, for fear that such suffrage would lead to an increase of political influence for the Church. Women were therefore prevented from voting until after the Second World War, and cast their ballots for the first time in 1945. In both Britain and France it was not until the beginning of the postwar era, then, that democracy in its present form (and with whatever its present deficiencies might be) was fully institutionalized.

Conclusion

The foregoing has illustrated the first part of the previously presented argument, namely that (with some minor exceptions of true mass riots) the struggles for power and improved conditions of different classes, and later of women, have been conducted not by these classes in their entirety, but by movements spearheaded by elites. And while these movements have been dependent for their success on the support of the masses of the respective classes, they have been no less dependent on the effectiveness of their leaders.

The chapter has also illustrated that, for most movements, the struggles in which they were involved have eventually resulted in the incorporation of their leaders into the existing power structures or political establishments, at times with the active cooperation of those establishments themselves. And, upon gaining a share of power, some of the leaders have been (often justifiably) accused of betraying their supporters and their supporters' causes. But in the end they have nonetheless "delivered," or else their mere presence has led to, certain improvements in the conditions of the disadvantaged classes, and advances in the establishment of Western democracy in its present form. This struggle of successive elites for power, and their gradual incorporation into existing power structures, has thus manifested itself also as the struggle for, and as advances on the road to, democracy.

Notes

1. Not being a historian, I have based the analysis in this and the following chapter on the works of prominent historians, including Anderson (1977); Hobsbawm (1962, 1972, 1975); Lefebvre (1947; 1962–1964); Lorwin (1954); Perkin (1969); Price (1975); Soboul (1977); Sowerwine (1982); Thomson (1966); Thompson (1980); and also on the works of what may be referred to as experts on developments in specific areas, e.g., on revolutions, Brinton (1939); and on political parties and elections, Ostrogorski (1902); Duverger (1958, 1964); McKenzie (1963); Leonard (1968); Macridis (1967), as well as others—cited in a further footnote and in the text itself.
2. Although titles could be purchased if there was not only cash, but also large-scale land ownership to support the claim.
3. For a concise overview of these and other ideas of liberalism, see Held (1987).
4. However, there were also some middle-class radicals (such as the Manchester Anti-Corn-Law-Leaguers) who persisted in fighting the aristocracy.

4

Elite Power and the Development of Democracy (II): The Autonomization of Elites

The second part of the argument on elites and the development of democracy is that the struggle of elites for power has also been a struggle of elites for increased autonomy, and that the elites' achievements in this respect have also been inextricably interlinked with the development of democracy. This argument may be aptly illustrated in the first place through successive elites' struggles for freedom of association or organization or, in other words, for the right to establish autonomous associations, and the actual associations (particularly trade unions) they managed to build up, chiefly throughout the nineteenth century.

Freedom of Association, Elite Autonomy, and the Development of Democracy

The instrument of association was long considered an important weapon in the struggle for reforms. In Britain, the first associations outside parliament were formed during the second part of the eighteenth century, and from then onwards associations, movements and organizations have been engaging in a variety of activities designed to achieve such reforms. As noted, these have been ranging all the way from the presentation of petitions, to strikes, demonstrations and riots.

The first of the extra-parliamentary associations in Britain was the Wilkes movement which developed into the Society for Supporting the Bill of Rights, followed by the Constitutional Society and other associations for parliamentary reform. Active during the second half of the eighteenth century, these associations subsequently declined, but soon the triumph of the French Revolution encouraged the reappearance and further development of associations or movements for parliamentary reform. Some of these were moderate, but others (such as Chartism)—composed mainly of workmen—soon became the instrument of more extreme democratic agitation in Britain.

Although freedom of association was traditionally seen as a basic right of the citizen, nonetheless the British government at first adopted a repressive policy against such associations and brought legal proceedings against their members. In 1795 the government carried a bill restricting the freedom of public meetings. The popular associations that were in existence at the time —hampered in their operations by this law—reverted to secrecy, and a network of secret societies was created. An Act further repressing associations, and in particular declaring illegal all societies the members of which had to take an oath not required by law, was passed by parliament in 1800, and any attempts of citizens to organize were severely punished.

These repressive measures were followed in 1817 by new ones placing obstacles in the way of the cooperation of various societies. Although these laws were abolished in 1825, associations, particularly workers' associations, still did not gain official recognition. At that time some associations fell into the hands of extremists. This alarmed the government and in 1831 a Royal proclamation put further restrictions on organizations. However, one of the major results of the political struggles referred to before was that freedom of association, of speech, and of meeting gradually came to assert itself, and developed further. By 1871, these freedoms had come to be accepted as legitimate in Britain.

In conjunction with gaining increased freedom, associations continued to develop and spread. One major brand of such associations was the trade unions. In Britain, these began to be formed in 1816, especially in the depressed northern counties, and attempts to link all laborers together in trade unions began in 1818. But the 1799 and 1800 laws forbidding associations had made working class organization illegal, and had laid trade unions open to charges of conspiracy. Also, at that time, their memberships were small, and they were not clearly distinguished from political movements and organizations. Their aim was political education of the people and they worked through the organization of petitions.

In the wake of the 1825 Act, accepting the legality of trade unions, these associations greatly extended their activities, new trade unions were formed and they could conduct their business more openly than had previously been the case. It was at this time that trade unions began the practice of collective bargaining for working conditions. But unions did not, as yet, gain full recognition, their scope was still limited, their leadership unstable and, consequently, they had not yet developed into firmly structured organizations. At this time, too, Robert Owen set up a Grand National Consolidated Trade

Union, intended to incorporate trade unionism into one comprehensive national organization. But the project was too ambitious and by 1834 it collapsed. Its demise came in the form of the trial and harsh punishment of a handful of laborers for taking "unlawful oaths" as members of unions.

Between 1848 and 1870, trade unions were increasingly given legal recognition by the state. Political leaders were now convinced that "labour organizations had to be recognized if they were to be tamed" (Hobsbawm, 1975, p. 113). It was thus the established political leaders' object of preventing "the emergence of labour as an independent political, and still more as revolutionary force" (ibid) which led to the granting of more freedom, and to the development of *relatively* independent labor unions. By 1871 they were given legal protection for their funds and for their methods of collective bargaining, and were protected against the charge of being conspiracies at common law. In 1876 trade unions won full legal recognition, but their rights were not fully determined until the Trades Disputes Acts of 1906 and 1913. Even thereafter some attempts were still made to suppress unions (Barbalet, unpublished); but overall such measures clearly diminished as part of the relative autonomization of their elites.

In France, trade unions had been illegal since 1791, and the Napoleonic penal code forbade all forms of economic association of workers. Louis Napoleon set up conciliation boards composed half of representatives of employers and half of representatives of the workers, with chairmen, vice chairmen, and secretaries nominated by the government. They were designed as what would now be called a corporatist arrangement to settle labor disputes, avoid strikes and promote order and discipline. But, in fact, they were often a means of improving working conditions and wages and sometimes became a focus for labor organization and agitation.

During the second half of the nineteenth century in France, too, although control over public meetings was not abandoned, it was somewhat relaxed. In 1864 the suppression of independent trade unions was partly relaxed, as the penal code which had made concerted industrial action a crime was repealed. By now trade unions were being tolerated and thereby strengthened. Even so, freedom of association and full legal rights for trade unions were not granted until 1884.

After 1871 in both Britain and France, economic expansion, in conjunction with growing freedom of association and legal recognition, brought about the expansion of trade unions. In previous decades they had been mainly craft unions, preoccupied with mutual help and mutual insurance, and had only sporadically organized strikes to reinforce their demands for higher pay and better working conditions. But at that time they tended to ally themselves more closely with political leaders, especially with radical liberal leaders:

John Brighton in Britain and the journalist Barberet in France, to enlist the masses of the less skilled workers into their ranks, and to become more active in struggling for improved working conditions.

However, in France at that time, a growing proliferation of labor movements with different political creeds, competing with one another for trade union support, divided and therefore weakened the union movement. There emerged local organizations named *bourses du traivail* which catered for a variety of the laborers' needs. In 1892 a labor leader formed them into a national federation. The Catholic church also created separate labor unions. Apart from these, socialist and communist trade unions were created and their leaders quarreled with each other and with the older liberal and the newer Catholic unions. This splintering showed the need for a national federation, which was formed in 1895. Its leaders deliberately divorced it from parliamentary politics, channeling its efforts into industrial action through collective bargaining backed by strikes.

The British union leaders followed a course of action quite different from that of their French counterparts. In 1868 the British Trades Union Congress was formed, and it proved able to hold together the old and new types of unions. In 1900 it joined the socialist societies in setting up a Labor Representation Committee to return workers' representatives to parliament. Fifteen such representatives were put up for election but only two were successful. This signaled the birth of the modern Labour Party, formally established in 1906.

In Britain as in France, towards the end and at the turn of the century, unions not only grew bigger, but also became stronger than they had ever been before. Union leaders now organized more effective industrial action, including strikes, particularly about wage claims, and those produced some achievements, although they were not necessarily as far–reaching as had initially been hoped. Concomitantly, labor unions (in conjunction with labor movements and parties) also became more effective in pressuring for legislation which would further improve working conditions and social welfare, although here, too, the achievements were never as far–reaching as the hopes and the demands that were instrumental in bringing them about.

Thus, it could be seen that the struggles for freedom of association, which were part of the struggles for democracy, and the gradually increasing achievements in this respect [1] also had far-reaching effects on trade unions and their leadership. Only when those relative freedoms were achieved could unions grow rapidly, gain mass memberships, and become powerful enough to exact improved economic conditions for their members from both employers and the state.

Interestingly, trade unions, which arose out of a mass need and enjoyed large-scale working class support, have developed into some of the most elitist, or oligarchical organizations in the Western world, as Robert Michels has clarified long ago. While some unions have developed more democratic leaderships (Lipset et al., 1956), the fact that unions have been organized by, and have worked through elites, has never been in doubt. Thus, the increased freedom of association, and the consequent greater autonomy of trade unions, has in fact spelled the greater autonomy of trade union leaders, those leaders' right and ability to "assert themselves even against the state" (Thomson, 1966, p. 273), and thereby to countervail the power of the governing elites.

Political Parties, Elite Autonomy, and the Development of Democracy

The elites' struggles for, and increasing achievement of autonomy can also be followed via the development of political parties. For parties (defined as durable organizations—with distinct political programs—competing for power through popular elections) have formed the main mechanism through which successive political elites have been able to organize in independent opposition, and as a countervailing power, to the governing elite in Western democracies. In contrast to parliamentary assemblies which are much older, political parties of this kind, with the potential for forming an organized opposition against the government, are the product of the nineteenth and twentieth centuries.

As long as Western countries were ruled by absolutist monarchs, who claimed to rule by divine right, there was little scope for the development of political parties. Such parties could develop only when rulers accepted the principle of having to legitimize their rule by popular consent, the principle of the growing power of parliamentary assemblies, and the principle of the legitimacy of opposition to their rule. Not surprisingly, this change was achieved only through protracted struggles, which were simultaneously also the struggles for the increased power of successive elites, and for the development of democracy, as mapped out before.

Once rulers and governing elites had accepted the legitimacy (or perhaps the inevitability) of political parties, they gradually came to utilize them to mobilize popular support for themselves, just as potential alternative elites did not fail to utilize them to mobilize support for themselves and opposition to the government. Thus parties became, at one and the same time, important instruments for the elites' struggles for power, for their struggles for increased autonomy, for linking elites with the growing masses of voters, and also for public representation, since they structured alternatives which elections could resolve. They thus became, in Lipset's (1967, p. 48) words, "by far the most important representative structure in complex democratic society."

In Britain the names of groups that were later to become political parties: Tories and Whigs, had been current since the latter part of the seventeenth century (and similar groups were later formed in other Western parliaments as well). But for a long time groups of this kind had no life of their own except in parliament. They were but loose parliamentary factions or cliques rather than full–fledged parties. They were based mainly on the personal interests of their leaders, on those leaders' personalities and family ties, on regional and local economic interests, and only to a minor extent (or not at all) on common political programs. Their voters, still very restricted in numbers, represented the leaders' personal followers, their or their patrons' retainers, or those who sold their votes to them. Their full potential was not realized at the time, and only retrospectively could they be recognized as embryonic forms of a party system that developed much later (James, 1974).

As parties and their supporters were not clearly demarcated from each other, the government had to work continuously to ensure a majority for itself in Parliament. It did so by means of patronage, dispensed through the good offices of the patronage secretary:

> The patronage secretary had to supply the government with a majority as cheaply as possible. For a long time . . . he worked directly on the members and bought each of them individually. When, owing to the improvement in Parliamentary manners, these transactions perceptibly diminished or disappeared altogether, the patronage secretary, and his *vis-à-vis* on the other side, the Opposition Whip, bought constituencies, seats in parliament, for friends who were to vote as they were told. . . . The government Whip was in the best position for operations of this kind. He had secret service money at his disposal, George III contributed largely to it from his civil list." (Ostrogorski, 1902, Vol. 1, p. 139.)

Evidently, in this situation, since the government had no firm majority in parliament, it could not be said that it either won or lost an election. By the same token there was no clearly demarcated, not to say independent, opposition to the government. Up until the first Reform Bill there was also no real party system. The first government that clearly lost an election was that of 1830, and contested elections were rare until 1885.

It was not till after the Reform Act of 1832 that regular though embryonic party organizations arose in the country. Previously, parties had required little or no organization. As the electorates had been minute, and control over them had been so effective, it had not been necessary to set up large-scale organizations to elicit their support. But now, as the electorate grew, and as new regulations for the registration of voters came into effect, the organization of parties outside parliament was increasingly required to ascertain electoral support.

Initially, such party organizations outside parliament were established as a result of the defective provisions of the Reform Act for the preparation of electoral lists, which left registration for elections to private initiative. It thus gave rise to registration societies, whose task was to ensure that the supporters of their party were registered to vote. Thus registration became the means through which the parties, previously confined to Parliament, made their way into the constituencies.

The period immediately after the reform bill also marked the appearance of embryonic party organizations in London, at first in conjunction with political clubs. Such clubs had been in existence since the seventeenth century. During the second half of the eighteenth century, they had assumed a more political character, following the party division in parliament. But they had been meeting places of an open and casual character. Real clubs on the basis of formal membership did not appear until the nineteenth century and they soon began to supply the basis for the operation of politicians. In 1831 the first Tory club was created, and links with the constituencies were established. A committee of the club maintained relations with local agents in charge of electoral registration. The Liberals formed a similar institution in 1836. Both clubs were activated by the party whips, assisted by electoral agents, and thus formed the beginnings of the parties' central organizations outside Parliament.

Paradoxically, however, towards the middle of the century the party system was, if anything, weakened. Traditionally the Tories had been representing mainly the landed interests which opposed the new industrial classes (although they were eventually joined by some wealthy industrialists and merchants) while the Whigs—though also mainly aristocrats—were more open to the interests of the industrial and commercial classes. But towards the middle of the century the differences between the two parties grew less marked, whatever traditional party ties had previously existed slackened even further, and the system disintegrated into a variety of unstable factions with constantly changing allegiances. In this situation, too, no proper opposition to the government could develop. Personal loyalties and considerations still overrode political convictions, which counted for little or nothing, and voters who were not subject to deferential voting and were not bought, still had to be personally persuaded by the candidates or their patrons to vote for them.

It was after 1867, with the doubling of the electorate, that political parties began to organize much more thoroughly and on a much larger scale than before. Both the Conservative and Liberal party leaderships set up machineries for mass election campaigns and began to outbid each other in their competition for popular support, among other things, through programs of electoral reforms. "Believing that the triumph of Radicalism was inevitable, both Tories and Whigs rushed to meet it half-way, in a wild race in which each tried to outstrip the other" (Ostrogorski, 1902, Vol.1, p. 97). This was also the time in which elections became gradually freer from corruption, influence, and intimidation; parliament increasingly asserted its power to control ministers; and hence an independent parliamentary opposition became a formidable (though generally moderate) institution in its own right.

But even then, party organizations were still not fully developed, political programs were still less than binding, and there still was no party that could be seen as even remotely representing working class interests. Only at the turn of the century did parties become identified with more binding political programs, members and activists were widely solicited, and mass support was actively mobilized. It is at this time, too, that the Labour Party was created and eventually came to rotate with the Conservative party in opposition, and the party system in its present form thus emerged.

In France, the starting point for all political parties was the Revolution of 1789, for it brought about the pattern of conflict between conservatives and liberals that was to be perpetuated later on. Broadly, and with some exceptions, the conservatives represented the landed aristocracy, their chief electoral supporters were the peasants, and they supported the monarchy and the privileges of the nobility. By contrast, the liberals, drawn mostly from the bourgeoisie and the middle class, supported the ideas of the American and French revolutions: the idea of natural and equal rights for all men, and government by consent of the people as established through elections. But while the parties had their origin in the Revolution, during the first part of the nineteenth century the organization of parties working outside parliament was still little developed. The cadres of parties were formed before elections and broke up afterwards.

Also, both conservatives and liberals were subdivided into several brands of royalists and republicans, and neither formed a clearly separate and unified party. The socialist parties that were emerging at the time were also divided amongst themselves, and this party splintering in the nineteenth century has been regarded as one of the main causes for the present-day multiplicity of parties in France. But it did not prevent the development of a vigorous and eventually successful parliamentary opposition to the government—led by men of high calibre—in the latter part of the nineteenth century.

This opposition was made up of royalists, moderate constitutional liberals, republicans, socialists, and revolutionary communists, all with their own leaderships. The toughest opposition initially came from the liberals led by Adolphe Thiers and the republicans led by Leon Gambetta as well as by groups of eminent lawyers, journalists, and literary men. Gradually the opposition grew and gained strength: in the 1857 election only seven candidates hostile to the government were returned, and in the 1869 election ninety–three were returned. Later on, the toughest opposition was that of the socialists, who united into one party at the turn of the century. This opposition, too, grew over the years, and by 1914 there were as many as seventy–six socialists in the Chamber.

The process of the development of the opposition was not only one of numerical growth, however. As the government gradually lost the ability to manage and manipulate elections (see below), as the parties became better organized and more efficient in marshalling popular electoral support, and as the power of the opposition against the government thus rested increasingly on such support, its leadership became more independent from government control, more powerful, and hence successively more open and militant. As a consequence, freer parliamentary debates were eventually allowed, and ministers had to defend government policy in parliament, and became more accountable to it.

It can be seen, then, that before the development of party systems rulers and governments had no clearly demarcated opposition. In Britain the government could buy itself a majority in parliament and in France no opposition deputies were elected to parliament until after the middle of the nineteenth century. In other words, there was no independent elite that could clearly and continuously countervail the power of the governing elite. The process of the development of distinct, continuous, and powerful political parties—which was part and parcel of the development of democracy—was thus also one of the development of a coherent, independent, oppositional elite countervailing the elite of the government.

This was most clearly evident in Britain, which for most of its modern history (and despite some small third parties and independent M.P.s) basically had a two party system. For, in the words of Duverger (1964, p. 414), "the two-party system tends to make the opposition into a real institution." In a multi-party system, such as the French one, the demarcation between government and opposition has not become so clear-cut since, again, in the words of Duverger (1964, p. 415) "here no real organization assumes the function of opposition." Here, however, the "tradeoff," so to speak, has been that some of the opposition parties and leaders have tended to become more extremist, and thus have given evidence of their independence from the government through their more blatant divergence from it.

It could also be seen that the development of mass party organizations was intertwined with the recruitment of new elites, the elites of the ever increasing masses of voters. By fostering the recruitment of new elites from the masses, and by forging more direct links between these leaders and their supporters among the masses, the parties also rendered leaders, and particularly opposition party leaders, more independent of the machinery of the government and of the state. The development of party democracy was thus inextricably intertwined with the development of a new brand of more independent elites.

In sum, then, the struggle of new political elites for power and for incorporation into the existing structures of power involved the development of party systems and of successively new parties. This process of the development of parties, coming on top of the development of elections and the widening of the franchise, was also one whereby the new political elites gained increasing autonomy from the governing elite, and an increasing ability to countervail its power. Concomitantly, the same process manifested itself also as one which made it increasingly necessary for elites to rely for their power on the electoral support of the public, hence it forged closer links between elites and the public, and gave the public a clearer choice between elites. Thus, the process of the autonomization of political party elites manifested itself also as a process of the development of democracy.

The Autonomy of the Economic Elite and the Development of Democracy

The argument that the elites' struggles for power have resulted in their increased autonomy as well, and that this has been inextricably interlinked with the development of democracy, may also be illustrated from the domain of the economic elite. Towards the end of the eighteenth century and during the first part of the nineteenth century this elite, which spearheaded the development of capitalism, was also engaged in practically continuous struggles for independence from state (or governing elite) interference.

From the beginning of the seventeenth and up until the end of the eighteenth century, the prevailing economic policy in Europe had been that of mercantilism. "Basically, mercantilism can be understood as the economic complement of political absolutism involving, as it did, the subordination or, better, the subsumption of the economy under the polity" (Dowse and Hughes, 1986, p.99). State intervention, the extent of which differed from country to country, was not aimed at impeding the development of capitalism. Rather, it was the policy through which the absolutist state meant to set the conditions under which capitalism and the capitalist elites were to flourish. But it did so by interfering in the most minute details of economic life, including the fixing of prices, the regulation of imports and exports, the fixing of wages, and the like. Thus, the economic-capitalist elite was comprehensively dominated by the state, although this was the case in Prussia and in Russia more than in France and especially in Britain, where (relatively speaking) the capitalists had managed to retain a greater degree of structural independence from state intervention.

In any case, the then evolving capitalist elite did not welcome the state as regulator, and its intervention was thought to defeat its own purpose. Many of the capitalists therefore exerted pressure for, and eventually attained, a relatively large degree of autonomy for their economic activities. The essence of the transition to this new period of relative autonomy for capitalists is best brought out by an anecdote concerning Colbert, the finance minister to Louis XIV in France. "How may we help you?" wrote Colbert to a prominent merchant. The reply was *'Nous laissez faire'* which, translated into modern parlance would mean: "Just let us do our own thing." This expression subsequently became the slogan of the new nineteenth century economic regime, which came to be known as the period of laissez–faire capitalism (Heilbroner, 1962, p. 71).

Similar ideas and demands were also voiced by British economic elites. From the turn of the nineteenth century onwards many British landowners and their representatives in parliament, no less than urban capitalists, believed that wages ought not to be regulated by the state and ought to be allowed to find their own level. In 1820 London merchants presented to parliament a petition which embodied the following principle: "That freedom from restraint is calculated to give the utmost extension to foreign trade, and the best direction to the capital and industry of the country" (Thomson, 1966, p. 162).

Subsequently, in Britain, the struggle for economic freedom, or the autonomy of the economic elite, was also expressed as a struggle against the protectionist Corn Laws, and was led by the Anti-Corn Law League. The leaders of this league were obliged to lean, materially and morally, especially on the support of the middle class which had a direct interest in commercial freedom, and it relied mainly on persuasion rather than on mass agitation. Its leaders travelled continuously all over the country to carry on the free trade propaganda. The protectionists tried to counter the league by the same methods; landlords, whose representatives had a majority in Parliament, continued to resist it "but the mind of the country was made up, thanks to the League, and only a shock was needed to make the fruit drop from the tree. The bad harvest which supervened in Ireland supplied this" (Ostrogorski, 1902, Vol. 1, p. 132). A famine followed, and in 1846 the Corn Laws were repealed.

The desire to be left alone, to be able to engage in economic activities (including trade) exempt from state intervention, which on the practical level was expressed by the capitalists, was expressed on the theoretical level by Adam Smith and his fellow classical economists. These theoreticians taught that maximum freedom for the play of economic forces would, as though led by an "invisible hand" further the economic interests of all. The classical economists were thus the ideologues of the economic elite's struggle for autonomy, as they furnished the ideological legitimation for the laissez–faire economic system.

Their teachings were also intertwined with those of the (previously mentioned) philosophers of liberalism. These sought to restrict the powers of the state, which they saw as useless or even dangerous, except where it was designed to protect the rights of individuals; those individuals ought to be free to pursue their own preferences in all private, including economic affairs. Liberalism thus advocated a state whose functions were to be limited, while private property and the competitive market economy were to be the central mechanisms for coordinating individuals' interests. The development of laissez–faire as an economic doctrine, thus went hand in hand with the development of liberalism as a political doctrine, as both "separated out the realms of politics and economics" (Dowse and Hughes, 1968, p. 98), a separation which was then partly implemented in the economic structures and policies in the nineteenth century.

These structures, which culminated towards the middle of the nineteenth century in Western Europe and the United States, were indeed characterized by a relative freedom of play of economic forces, and thereby they also spelled freedom for the elites who activated those forces. This does not mean that government concern with the economy was absent. But many traditional restrictions on economic enterprise —production and trade— were removed: restriction of movement was abolished, duties were reduced, shipping restrictions were eliminated, and other free trade measures were introduced. Some European countries with strong feudal traditions, especially Germany, did not leave economic activity to free initiative to the same extent as did Britain and United States, but the thrust towards greater autonomy in the economic sphere (and thus for the economic elite) was a widespread Western phenomenon. Many of the laws and regulations which did exist, moreover, were geared primarily to *prevent* the intervention of noneconomic forces in the economic sphere (Knowles, 1932).

Contrary to what Adam Smith and like–minded thinkers had claimed, however, this relatively free play of economic forces did not serve the interests of all. Not only did the system have dehumanizing effects on the newly created industrial working class, but it was also beset by recurring economic crises. Or, as J.M. Keynes was to put it later on, "the invisible hand had become arthritic and had dropped its bundle." This became evident in the wake of the many economic crises that beset Western capitalism, which culminated in the stock market crash of 1929 and the depression that followed it. At that time the trend of autonomy for economic activity was reversed, and government intervention in Western economies became more pronounced.

Government guidance of the economy came to be especially pronounced in France, with its five–year plans somewhat reminiscent of those in socialist countries. But state intervention has penetrated all Western economies and is still growing. So the autonomy of the economic elite from the governing political elite has reached its peak around the middle of the nineteenth century, and to some extent has declined since then. But, importantly, the extent of the governing elite's intervention in the economic elite's affairs has never reverted to its extent in the pre-laissez-faire, mercantilist era.

Furthermore, the increasing government intervention in the economy was balanced by an unprecedented growth and concentration of economic enterprises and by the consequent monopolization or oligopolization of economic markets. This, in turn, has led to ever more powerful economic corporations (and the elites that own and manage them), having control over chunks of Western economies. Thus, the new balance between the political governing elite and the economic elite that has been established in the post–laissez–faire era has increased government intervention in the economy; but this has been counterbalanced by the economic elite's increased power. Hence, while the autonomy of the economic elite does not equal its extent in the laissez–faire era, and while its power still does not rival that of the state elites, the new balance has nonetheless left the economic elite with a considerable degree of autonomy and power.

Moreover, it has now become accepted as part of the mainstream of democratic theory in the West, and is also being argued here, that the principle of freedom of organization entails, inter alia, non-state (though not necessarily capitalist) economic enterprises, or an economy that has a partial (though not necessarily a total) immunity from state intervention, and that such an economy is therefore a sine qua non of Western democracy (see next chapter). In light of this theory, which (in some respects) is a descendant of nineteenth–century liberalism, it may be said that the degree of autonomy which the economic elite has been able to tease out from the governing political elite, and the balance of power and autonomy thus created, although it creates many inequities, and although it poses a severe dilemma for democracy—as argued below—nonetheless also forms one of the pillars of Western democracy. Its development, and partial preservation later on, may thus be seen as part and parcel of the development of that democracy.

The Autonomy of the Bureaucratic Elite and the Development of Democracy [2]

This chapter's argument can be illustrated also with respect to the autonomization of the bureaucratic elite and its inextricable interrelationship with the development of democracy. Even today bureaucratic elites in Western democracies are not totally disconnected from governing political elites. This is so because bureaucracy cannot be totally divorced from politics, or even from party politics. For the very formulation of policy—in which the bureaucracy is necessarily involved—has political, and frequently, party-political connotations.

Nonetheless, there was clearly a process of autonomization, or relative autonomization, of the bureaucratic elite, which occurred first, through the very development of bureaucracy as a separate structure, and subsequently through the gradual (albeit incomplete) dissociation of bureaucracy from party politics. This, in turn, was part of a process of differentiation within the political structures of Western societies throughout their modernization (Huntington, 1968) and it had important implications for the development of democracy. As will now be illustrated, it happened to a different extent and at a different pace in different democratic countries. And only where and when the bureaucratic elite succeeded in gaining a significant degree of autonomy from the political elite could electoral corruption be subdued and proper democratic procedures be put into place.

In feudal society each small entity was responsible for its own legislation (if any), judicial tasks, and administration, and these various activities were fused with each other and took place on an haphazard basis. The king's or prince's administration was part of the royal household. It subsequently became more elaborate, in an attempt to cope with administrative tasks with which the simple household organization was not capable of coping. But it remained partly fused with the household until the beginning of modernity.

The sixteenth century marked a watershed between feudal and modern administration. During this century administration was still based on personal relations; but with increasingly complex administrative problems, a differentiation between personal ties and administrative tasks became more noticeable. As well, functional differentiation between the judiciary and the administration became more emphasized.

Throughout the entire era of absolutism, however, although government administration became centralized, it was still rudimentary, unsystematic, and not clearly differentiated from other social structures. In the seventeenth- and eighteenth-century French administration, the personal and the impersonal, the private and the public, were still largely interlinked. During the reign of Louis XIII, for instance, it was Richelieu's firm policy to procure appointments for as many members of his family as he could, and afterwards, too, favoritism and nepotism continued to prevail. So, too, did the purchase of government posts.

At that time, in France as well as in Britain, the aristocratic society, with its peculiar codes of ethics, inevitably undermined all general laws and regulations, because privileges consisted of personal exceptions, and the personal always prevailed over the general. To this must be added regional variations, all of which produced a confusing array of governmental agencies, many almost useless. Also, at that time, government administration was still wholly or partly intermingled with politics. With the appearance of political parties, this took on the form of the interpenetration of administration and party politics.

In eighteenth–century Britain, for one, administrative departments were regarded as the private establishments of ministers. Consequently, appointment was by personal and political patronage, there was no clear-cut distinction between bureaucratic and political activities, and for many public servants they blended into each other. Even low-ranking public servants frequently had political tasks to perform, such as canvassing for parliamentary elections. And even administrative activities were subordinated to political considerations. Evidently, no clearly demarcated, let alone independent, bureaucratic elite could exist at that time.

Only in the nineteenth century did a government bureaucracy in the modern sense emerge. Napoleon built up such an administration as an instrument for his centralized state. Officials now became public servants and were paid regular salaries. Administrative capabilities became an important element in their selection. Administration was regularized, and this included the submission of exact accounts by each administrative unit and the establishment of a systematic tax collection system. But at this time, and throughout the nineteenth century, the government still had a great deal of political control over the administration and used it for its own electoral advantage.

The nineteenth–century British administration gradually followed its own path of reforms towards greater coherence and independence. The previously existing multiplicity of boards disappeared, a more logical articulation of functions took place, and administrative departments—to carry out each of these functions—were created. Administrative reforms proceeded on a considerable scale, and by 1832 the trend of divorcing the bureaucracy from partisan considerations was well under way. The leaders of the party in office still allocated jobs in the bureaucracy to their supporters, but the most evident subordination of administrative utility to party-political considerations had diminished. Moreover, by that time, the supply of patronage in the civil service fell far short of demand, and many politicians thus came to consider it as a burden.

The initial demands for reform had come from without, as part of the general call to abolish the inefficiency, patronage and corruption of aristocratic government. But they were soon internalized and taken over by pioneering reformers amongst the leading civil servants, including, for instance, Sir Henry Taylor, and several others. These civil servants were themselves products of the patronage system. "Yet they used patronage to dig its own grave" (Perkin, 1969, p. 337). Following their efforts, the next twenty years represented the key period for the reform of the home civil service, for it was during that time that the principles and procedures for a more professional and independent bureaucracy were worked out.

These developments set the stage for the subsequent reforms that were based on the Northcote-Trevelyan Report (submitted in 1854). Their essence was the separation between temporarily elected politicians and permanent, appointed, nonpolitical public servants. Recruitment to the public service was to be solely by merit. It was to be based on open, competitive examinations, conducted by a central board, and to be carried out without the intrusion of political considerations.

The implementation of these prescriptions was a protracted process, as some heirs of the previous patronage system—with vested interests in that system—attempted to preserve it. For a time, the civil service commission (appointed in 1855), had to be content with procedures entailing limited competition only. It was not until the 1870s that open, competitive examinations were established as the regular method of entry for most of the large administrative departments.

Even then, civil service patronage was still tenacious, and some posts were still used for this purpose. But both parliament and public opinion increasingly turned against the practice. Also, once independent public servants had been appointed, they played a leading role in the struggle for legislation furthering their own independent power. Hence, civil service political patronage declined steadily and with the close of the century was practically eliminated.

The new system, based on nonpolitical appointments and partisan neutrality of the public service, has been perpetuated largely into the present. According to Richards (1963), there are no such clear-cut barriers to patronage with respect to ministerial or administrative boards, public corporations, and the like. But as far as the civil service proper is concerned the possibilities for political patronage have been rather limited, and the British government bureaucracy has thus been relatively disconnected from party politics. Some recent commentators have seen in the Thatcher civil service appointments and promotions evidence of politicization (e.g., Wass, 1985). Although such appointments have been confined to the top, high level appointees can covertly influence less senior appointments to suit their political preferences. Even so, the British bureaucracy is less party-politicized than are its counterparts in most other Western democracies.

In France, the separation of the bureaucracy from party politics has not been as clear-cut as in Britain. It has been a long standing tradition for ministers to be supported by small staffs of politically loyal advisers—the ministerial cabinets. And even the dissociation of the regular and formally neutral bureaucracy from politicians and their intervention has not been as clear as in Britain; but it has nevertheless made some advances.

In the Third Republic, the governments followed the tradition of previous regimes in removing political opponents from the bureaucracy and substituting them with their own supporters. In the 1930s officials' positions became more secure and the most governments could do was to transfer their most formidable opponents to less influential posts. Under Petain, however, tenure was abolished and this increased the government's leverage over the bureaucracy: thousands of officials were purged.

After the Second World War, under the Fourth Republic, a reform came into effect whereby civil servants were recruited by general, competitive, entry examinations with uniform standards, which were kept above suspicion of political influence. Thus political appointments diminished, but high level appointments were still given to the governing politicians' political supporters, and administrative departments were still colonized by, or at least loosely connected to, the major political parties.

This situation continued also during the Fifth Republic, as ministerial and presidential staff scrutinized all senior appointments. By the late 1960s the Gaullist party, the *Union de Democrats pour la Republique,* had become France's dominant party, and it gained a strong hold over the bureaucracy. With the decline of this party in the 1970s, colonization of the civil service continued, but not with the same degree of forcefulness. Most recently, in 1988, President Mitterand has been accusing his principal political opponent, then Prime Minister Jacques Chirac, the leader of the neo-Gaullist RPR Party, of using or planning to use his political power to place his party's friends and supporters in key posts in the public and private sector. However, it is difficult to estimate the actual extent of such politicization. In the words of Searls (1981, p. 171), "It is easy to exaggerate the links and hard to estimate the impact which they had."

The gradual divorce of the bureaucracy from party politics, and the gaining of independence of the bureaucratic elite from the political governing elite, which happened to a relatively greater extent in Britain, and to a relatively more modest degree in France, has had important implications for the development of democracy. As long as the bureaucracy and its elite were party-politically dominated, electoral corruption flourished. In Britain this took the form of the bribing of voters in a variety of overt and covert ways. This was partly supported by government-administrative patronage, for instance by using government funds to buy constituencies for members of parliament who then supported the government (see above), and by providing administrative and other jobs for government supporters. In France, after the restoration and under Napoleon III, the administration itself played an active and formidable part in managing elections, and ensuring the election of government candidates and the defeat of their opponents.

In Britain, the decline of political influence over the bureaucracy was eventually followed by a decline of electoral corruption, which was practically eliminated around the turn of the century. In France, during the Third Republic, the bureaucracy still largely controlled the rural vote, but gradually the control of the bureaucracy over elections declined. During the Third Republic, and thereafter, it continued to be the custom for deputies of the government to boost their chances for reelection by making requests for favors on behalf of their constituents from the bureaucracy, and for the bureaucracy to be favorably disposed towards such requests. Even during the Fifth

Republic the deputies of the government parties, particularly the UDR, have still had direct access to the administration which was more responsive to their wishes than to those of the opposition parties' deputies.

Although senior administrators have increasingly come to resent this practice, they nonetheless have been forced to give priority to the wishes of government politicians, and this has given the latter an electoral advantage over their adversaries (Suleiman, 1974, pp. 292–363). In part, this situation was found to persist more recently as well. In a study conducted in 1977 Schonfeld (1981) found that Gaullist politicians still had significantly more contact with civil servants than their socialist counterparts although, again, the electoral impact of this advantage is hard to estimate.

It can be seen, then, that in both Britain and France there was a certain process of autonomization of the bureaucratic elite from the political elite, through the gradual and at least partial extrication of the bureaucracy from party politics, and that this has had important consequences for democracy. In Britain, where this autonomization was more pronounced, electoral corruption declined to a greater extent; in France, where this autonomization was more limited, bureaucratic control of elections in favor of the government declined, but some electoral malpractices persisted.

Conclusion

The last two chapters have illustrated that, historically, democracy has evolved out of the struggles not of classes as such, but of elites (some of which also represented the interests of certain classes, groups, or movements, and some of which represented no one in particular but themselves) in the modernizing and newly modernized Western societies. This was illustrated with respect to the struggles between the political elites: that of the aristocracy, whose power was challenged first by the political elites of the rising bourgeoisie and the middle class, whose power, in turn, was then challenged by the elite of the working class, and finally by that of women. It was also illustrated with respect to the economic elite, the elite of trade unions and workers' associations, and the elite of the bureaucracy. Processes such as these, here illustrated only with respect to Britain and France, occurred (mutatis mutandis) in other Western countries as well and included —besides the previously mentioned elites—also developments along similar lines for the judiciary, the elites of the security forces, and those of the media of mass communication.

These struggles among elites, which were basically power contests, or contests over the control of resources, manifested themselves also as struggles over the institutionalization of the principles of democracy. With respect to the elites, they resulted in a dual process: the incorporation of successive elites into the existing power structures (or into the political establishment) on the one hand, and the granting of greater autonomy in the control of resources to successive elites on the other hand. Concomitantly, they also resulted in (albeit belated and hesitant) socioeconomic reforms, and in the (albeit belated and hesitant) granting of successively greater democratic rights to the public, and the institutionalization of the principles of democracy. The dual historical process of the incorporation and autonomization of elites was thus at the core, if not the essence of, the development of Western democracy; its end result was the relative (though incomplete) autonomy of elites, which is at the core of Western democracy as we know it today.

Notes

1. It is often claimed, with a large degree of justification, that in Western democracies certain (formal or informal) limitations on freedom of association have continued to prevail even afterwards, with limitations upon communism during the McCarthy era in the United States being a prominent example. But this and similar cases elsewhere may be seen as aberrations of the general principle of freedom of association which, while it cannot be taken for granted, and while it has to be continuously reasserted, still prevails in Western democracies to a greater extent than it does in other regimes.
2. This part of the chapter is based in particular on Birch (1975); Bridges (1971); Gladden (1972); Jacoby (1973); Langrod (1967); Meynaud (1964); Parris (1969); Ridley and Blondel (1964); Williams (1954, 1964), and my own previous work (1979, 1985a).

5

Elite Power and the Contradiction of Democracy

"Yes We Have No Dilemmas"
(Title of an unpublished article by Marion Levy, Jr.)

Introduction

It will now be argued that the relative autonomy of elites as it developed over the last two centuries—which today is one of the most distinctive features of democracy—also creates an inherent contradiction for it: it is consistent with one democratic principle, yet inconsistent with another. The relative autonomy and countervailing power of elites thus is basic to the essence of democracy, yet also contravenes that very essence. It is further argued that this contradiction creates unclear, ambiguous and contentious "rules of the game" for democracy. Later on it will be shown that this contradiction, and the unclear rules it creates, have important implications for the manner in which the governing, political elite exerts, consolidates, and attempts to perpetuate its power and for the manner in which these attempts are countered in Western democracies.

Contradictions in Western Societies

The idea that societies, particularly Western, capitalist societies, are beriddled by contradictions has been central to several major theories in the social sciences. For instance, Marx and Marxist theories have long been harping on what they see as the major contradictions of capitalism: its tendency to lead to massive production, while depriving the proletariat of the means to consume the massive products thrown onto the market, thus creating crises of overproduction. Marxist theories have also been dwelling on the contradiction whereby capitalism maintains private ownership and control over production while it concomitantly creates a socialized mode of production in massive enterprises, a combination that generates a suppressed proletariat that is increasingly acquiring the organizational and political tools necessary for the system's destruction.

Recently some neo-Marxist scholars, including O'Connor (1973), Habermas (1975), and Offe (1984), have also highlighted what they see as the contradiction of the capitalist state: it must maintain the conditions of profitable accumulation for capitalism, yet also satisfy the popular expectations for democracy and social welfare, and maintain its image of an impartial arbiter of class interests, thus ensuring the legitimation of its own power. According to the above writers, the incompatibility of these requirements has the potential of leading to a crisis, including a fiscal crisis, of the capitalist state.

In contrast to the contradiction illuminated in Marxist theory, the contradiction here explored is not simply an incongruence or an incompatibility between two aspects of a social formation (e.g., production and consumption) which leads to a crisis and carries within it the seeds of the system's destruction. Rather, it is a compatibility, or even a necessity, coupled with an incompatibility for democracy. Contradictions of this genre have also been highlighted by various scholars.

Thus, Lindblom (1977) writes about the compatibility/incompatibility between capitalism and democracy: he argues that Western democracies resulted from struggles to win rights, which included, amongst others, the right to free enterprise. Further, "[t]he Liberal notion of freedom was freedom from government's many interventions, and for that kind of freedom markets are indeed indispensable" (p. 164). At the same time, a free enterprise, market economy generates large corporations and the power of capitalists who head such corporations, and who become greatly influential in shaping government policy. This power evidently is not congenial to democracy. Or as Lindblom (p. 356) put it: "The large private corporation fits oddly into democratic theory and vision. Indeed it does not fit."

On a similar line Dahl has recently argued (1982, 1985) that independent organizations are highly desirable in a democracy, and in all democratic countries such autonomous organizations do, in fact, exist. But such independence may be used by the organizations to do harm, to promote the interests of their own members over others, or even to destroy democracy. Besides, the "liberty to accumulate unlimited economic resources and to organize economic activity into hierarchically governed enterprises" (1982, p. 50) creates "inequalities in social and economic resources so great as to bring about severe violations of political equality and hence of the democratic process" (1982, p. 60). So, liberties inherent in the democratic process create inequalities which are inimical to the same process.

In my previous work (1985a) I have pointed to a parallel compatibility/incompatibility between bureaucracy and democracy: a powerful, politically independent bureaucracy is essential for the safeguarding of proper democratic procedures, yet the independent power of such a bureaucracy as against that of elected politicians also forms a threat for democracy. There is thus a symbiotic, though contradictory, relationship between bureaucracy and democracy.

Alford and Friedland (1985), for their part, have recently highlighted what they perceive as a contradiction or a compatibility/incompatibility among all three of the above: capitalism, bureaucracy (or the bureaucratic state), and democracy. As the authors perceive it, these elements are each dependent on the others, yet also incompatible with them. Thus, for instance, capitalism is dependent on a state which protects the conditions of accumulation, or profitability, yet also requires autonomy from the state whose excessive intervention might undermine it. It is supported by democratic institutions which make the power of capitalists less visible and thus legitimate capitalism. Yet it also limits the impact of democratic channels of participation.

The state is dependent on capitalist accumulation because the welfare of the population has come to be equated with a capitalist economy. At the same time, the state is faced with a combination of demands deriving from three components: rationalization (the bureaucratic aspect), participation (the democratic aspect), and accumulation (the capitalist aspect). The state must simultaneously appear to form policy rationally, to be responsive to popular participation, and to foster capitalist production, yet these three demands are contradictory, and the state is continuously torn between them.

Democracy, for its part, creates channels of political participation which legitimize the state and capitalism, yet these channels hamper the effective functioning of a rational state and a profitable capitalist economy, and hence are limited by the requirements of bureaucratic and capitalist institutions. Capitalism, bureaucracy and democracy, are thus symbiotic yet contradictory and mutually limiting aspects of modern, capitalist society.

Some recent thought in the social sciences has thus been moving in the direction of highlighting contradictions in the form of paradoxical mutual compatibilities cum incompatibilities, as they find expression in the arena of the modern, capitalist, democratic state. And, indeed, the contradiction here explored is partly overlapping with those previously identified contradictions. But the focus of the present analysis differs somewhat from the previous ones: it is both more narrow and broader than they are.

For here the emphasis is on compatibility coupled with incompatibility in the logic of the democratic political system as such, in the essence of its most basic principles, and therefore in the democratic role of, and relations among, the elites that have emerged in democratic regimes and are safeguarded and legitimized by those principles. The present analysis, thus is more narrow than the previous ones, in that it concerns not institutions or organizations — including capitalism and bureaucracy as such—but the elites of organizations which are here considered at the crux of how democracies function and malfunction.

But the present analysis is also broader than the previous ones, for besides taking account of the paradoxical status of capitalist and bureaucratic elites in a democracy, it takes account of the similar status of several other elites. Indeed, its focus is on all major (though not generally elected) elites in a democracy, arguing as it does that the relative autonomy of all those elites creates the same contradiction or dilemma for democracy as does the relative autonomy of capitalist and bureaucratic elites. In short, here the focus of the analysis shifts from organizations or institutions, such as those of capitalism and bureaucracy, to the elites of such organizations and institutions, and it further shifts to encompass the elites of other major organizations and institutions as well, and thus comes to cover all major elites in democratic societies. The analysis further encompasses elites of social movements, as explained below.

The analysis of the contradiction of elites in a democracy now leads us back to the definition of democracy as presented before. For it is my argument that the basic principles of democracy, as spelled out in this definition, and as actually (though imperfectly) realized in democratic regimes, are both consistent and inconsistent, both interrelated and necessary for each other, and also incongruous with each other, and it is this, which creates the contradiction of the countervailing power of elites in a democracy.

Consistencies and Inconsistencies in the Principles of Democracy

In some respects the principles, included in the previously presented definition of democracy, are internally consistent: all elements of this definition are not only interrelated but, indeed, serve as prerequisites for each other. Without freedom from harassment, freedom of speech, organization, etc., free elections would not be possible. And without free elections, the threat of elite replacement they involve, and the curbing of elite power they generate, the other political freedoms could not be safeguarded. Similarly, the general rules governing these freedoms and elections, and the general rules pertaining to the procedures of gaining and exercising power—also known as the "rules of the game" of democracy— are a sine qua non for those procedures and freedoms and vice versa.

In Western societies the rules that govern democratic freedoms and procedures and the exercise of elite power have taken the shape of constitutions (whether written or unwritten), supplemented by laws, regulations, conventions, and the norms of the participants. They have been the product of previous political contests and struggles—over the control of resources, or the exercise of power, between elites— which have continued for several centuries. But once settled upon, and at least partly stabilized, they have become constraints and restraints on further contests for, and exercises of, power. As such, they have also become safeguards (though not necessarily impermeable safeguards) of political freedoms.

As scholars (e.g., Sartori, 1987) have emphasized (and as has also been illustrated before), historically the constitutions designed to protect citizens from despotic rule and political harassment by the rulers originated from separate interests and philosophical-ideological strands, developed independently from, and indeed, preceded the development of democratic rules, institutions and practices. But they still developed in the same (i.e., Western) societies, in the same general historical era, and this is certainly not a coincidence. It can be explained by the fact that they are contextually interrelated.

Thus, as Sartori (1987) has pointed out, the security provided by legal limits on the exercise of power also permits alternation in power on the basis of elections. Or, as Adlai Stevenson is reported to have said, democracy is the regime "where it is safe to be unpopular." In the absence of such security power would be fought over ferociously and never relinquished voluntarily.

The constitutions, laws, and other rules governing democratic procedures have also set limits on what could otherwise become democratic despotism—e.g., the persecution of minorities by majorities, or the abolition of political freedoms by majority decree. The constitutions, rules, or laws of democracy thus safeguard democracy from destroying itself through its own institutions and procedures, while also safeguarding its basic freedoms. Hence democratic laws or rules on the one hand, and democratic liberties on the other hand, are inextricably interlinked or, as Rousseau, in his *Letters from the Mountain* (cited in Sartori, 1987, p. 310) expressed the idea: "Liberty shares the fate of laws; it reigns and perishes with them."

While constitutions and other rules that spell out citizens' liberties also protect the institutions of democracy from self-destruction, such laws and rules would not have much value without these self-same institutions to protect them. Constitutions, rules, norms, may serve to protect citizens' liberties by limiting the power of rulers or governing elites in principle or de jure. But it is only when elections create an institutionalized, recurrent threat of replacement, and when freedom of organization creates countervailing elites, that the power of governing elites can be limited de facto, and the freedoms of the individual can be protected in practice. Thus, the various principles of democracy are inherently interlinked and to the extent that they have been (though imperfectly) implemented in actual practice, they have acted to sustain each other.

At the same time there are also some major contradictions created by the principles of democracy, strangely enough, in particular between the principle of freedom of organization and the principle of free elections. On the one hand, of course, freedom of organization is a prerequisite for free elections, for without it competing groups, parties and candidates could not present their cases to the electorate. Also, as previously noted, freedom of organization is crucial for the limitation of governing elite power. For by making it possible for actual, free organizations to develop and persist, it safeguards the generation and stabilization of organizational elites. To the extent that such elites are powerful and at least partly independent from the governing elite, they countervail and thus limit its power. As such, freedom of organization, and the elites whose autonomy is sustained and protected by it, are part of the very essence of democracy.

On the other hand, the two principles also contradict each other: the power of the countervailing elites also contravenes the electoral principle and as such poses a threat to democracy. For, while the incumbent political elite is democratically elected by the entire population, the elites that may countervail its power are not. Indeed, being generated by individual, independent organizations, these elites cannot be elected by the entire population. In practice they usually acquire their power in a non–or a-democratic manner (e.g., by appointment, self-appointment, or inheritance), or are elected by only the members of their own organizations.

Hence, if these elites accumulate power beyond their own organizations, this contravenes the electoral principle, whereby power is gained on the basis of general elections by the whole population. And if their power is not controlled by the elected, governing elite, they may be accountable to no one but themselves, or to only part of the public. In addition, they frequently have nondemocratic (e.g., hierarchical) structures and tend to apply nondemocratic modes of action (e.g., by issuing decrees and regulations).

In other words, elites that countervail the power of the governing elite, are essential to democracy, yet also obviate its essence. This is but another way of saying that democracy, if drawn to its full, logical conclusion, would self-destruct and must therefore be curbed by non- or a-democratic elites, atop of non- or a-democratic institutions. Thus democracy must be curbed by nondemocratic mechanisms which, however, if drawn to their full conclusion would destroy democracy.

This inherent contradiction is manifested in several areas of sociopolitical life. For instance, one such manifestation stems from the power of economic corporations and their elites in Western-style democracies.

The Economic Elite and the Contradiction of Democracy

As was seen before, historically the association between Western-style democracy and a private enterprise-market economy has not been a coincidence: the economic elites' struggles for independence from government intervention over the control of economic resources, or for freedom of organization, have also constituted struggles for a free enterprise-market economy.

However, a free enterprise economy spells economic organizations in the form of capitalist corporations, with greatly powerful elites. It has frequently been asked how such power of capitalist elites squares with democracy. The plain answer, of course, is that it does not, as Marxists and others, including neo-pluralists such as Lindblom (1977), and Dahl (1982, 1985) have so convincingly pointed out. This economic elite can and does enter into collusions with the elected political elite. But it also has the power to obviate policies that run counter to its interests, even when those policies have been devised by a democratically elected government. As Lindblom (p. 189) further stresses, as a result we now have, besides the elected political leadership, another group of nonelected power-holders that is not accountable to the electorate.

On the other hand, again, the only way to abolish the power of capitalists would be to abolish private enterprise. Contrary to Lindblom's previously cited view, I do not argue that markets are necessary for freedom. But as many observers (e.g., Weber, 1968; Mosca, 1939; Moss, 1975; Djilas, 1981, among others) have convincingly indicated, the most likely alternative to free-market private enterprise capitalism, a state-controlled economy or state-socialism (sometimes called state-capitalism), creates more concerted, more powerful ruling elites.

Even under contemporary Western capitalism, the state controls a large proportion of economic resources directly, and also has some indirect controls over the rest of the economy. But where the state (or the ruling elite) has complete control over the economy, controls all means of production, is the sole employer of all, and controls all the means of consumption as well, only the most daring would object to its policies. In the words of Sartori (1987, p. 360) "when many capitalists are resolved into one, and, in addition, economic power joins forces with political power. . . . As the state becomes the sole employer and the controller of all the means of production, a truly formidable and indeed crushing disparity of power is created between rulers and ruled."

Some scholars have made the point that even in state-socialist societies the ruling elites are not necessarily unitary, that they frequently consist of different interest groups and factions that are in ongoing conflict with each other. Thus, in principle, opposition to prevailing policies would not be totally impossible. But independent opposition, opposition that does not have the blessing of any of the ruling elites or their factions—which also control the economy—would be obviated or greatly encumbered by the system and would be unlikely to arise. A totally state-controlled economy thus certainly is not congenial to democracy.

The other alternative to private enterprise capitalism is that of worker-owned enterprises (or cooperatives). Such a system is not incongenial to democracy. Indeed, it might well mitigate not only economic inequalities but power inequalities as well, and create internally democratic economic organizations. It would thus create economic democracy to complement political democracy, and as such it would be of considerable value in its own right.

But it cannot be disregarded that such a system would be apt to give rise to organizations which (as has been argued before) must necessarily generate their own elites. In fact, wherever cooperatives have been formed, and however successful they have been, this has occurred already (see e.g., French and French, 1975; Roy, 1976). The elites of cooperatives, though elected by their members, are not elected by the entire population. Yet they would countervail the power of the generally, democratically, elected political elite. Thereby they would pose the same dilemma for democracy that capitalist elites do today: they would be both a necessity and a threat to democracy. Democracy is thus beset by the contradiction of depending for its existence on non-state economic enterprise, the elites of which also jeopardize its existence.

The Trade Unions' Elite and the Contradiction of Democracy

A similar contradiction for democracy is also created by the trade unions' elite. While Lindblom (1977) sees only the elite of capitalist organizations as incongruous with democracy, here it is argued that the same is the case with trade union (and other) elites as well. Trade union elites have frequently been co-opted into the establishment, recently in particular through tripartite agreements with governments and employer organizations—as highlighted by the scholars of corporatism. But at times they have also clashed with governments. And although they have not necessarily emerged victorious from such clashes, they have frequently had considerable power in influencing government policy through their sheer potential of calling forth such clashes.

Lindblom (1977, p. 175–6) has argued that labor leaders do not equal capitalist elites in their power. For, while governments must make concessions to business that has a choice of either investing or not investing in the economy, they are not obliged to make similar concessions to labor, because workers have no choice but to work, whatever the circumstances. Hence general strikes are impossible, except for a few days, and the leverage labor leaders have over government is limited. However, while general strikes are indeed rare and brief, trade union leaders can achieve equivalent effects through large numbers of small strikes and other forms of industrial action which have a cumulative effect in disrupting the economy.

Thus, it is not unusual for the governing elite to make concessions to trade union leaders, and even when such leaders are co-opted through tripartite agreements, they frequently still succeed in wringing at least some concessions for themselves and their supporters. However, trade union leaders, though sometimes elected by the members of their own associations, are not elected by the public at large, hence their power in gaining such concessions obviates the spirit, if not the letter, of democracy.

Yet, as was seen, historically, the development of free trade unions, workers' and employees' associations has been one of the milestones in the development of democracy, as their elites have countervailed and continue to countervail (especially conservative) political elites, and thus form an important element in the limitation of governing elite power. And the elimination of such associations, or their subjugation by the state, has been one of the hallmarks of totalitarian and authoritarian regimes. Thus, independent, powerful trade unions form an important element of democracy. Here, too, then, democracy is faced with the internal contradiction of being supported by the very same organizations, and elite, that also threaten its proper procedures.

The Bureaucratic Elite and the Contradiction of Democracy

The same dilemma is also exemplified by the role of government bureaucracy and its elite in a democratic regime. Bureaucracy has been widely (and justly) accused of jeopardizing democracy because its nonelected elite frequently amasses great independent power as against that of elected politicians. Such accusations have been made not only by Weber, but also by adherents to the "technocratic" school of thought (see, for instance, Ellul, 1965; Meynaud, 1964; Peters, 1978), by several Marxist scholars (see, e.g., Mandel, 1975; O'Connor, 1978; Poulantzas, 1978), and others (e.g., Page, 1985. See also Thompson, 1983).

However, as Mosca (1939) and Schumpeter (1962)—but few others—have correctly perceived, a powerful, independent bureaucracy is also necessary for the safeguarding of proper democratic procedures. For the top of such a bureaucracy is another elite which countervails and thus curbs the power of the ruling political elite.

From my previous studies (1979, and 1985a) and from the foregoing analysis it could be seen that wherever the bureaucratic elite has been relatively deficient in such independent power, has depended on the governing political elite for its own rewards, and has buckled down to that elite, it has been used by it as an instrument of political manipulation and corruption. And this manipulation and corruption at times has greatly biased or obviated the democratic process. And only where the bureaucratic elite has gained greater control of its own resources and rewards, and thus has gained more independent power as against that of politicians, has this electoral manipulation and corruption been eliminated and proper democratic procedures have come into force. Hence, the thesis that bureaucracy, too, poses a practically insoluble dilemma for democracy. A powerful, independent, bureaucratic elite poses a threat to democracy and yet is also a necessity for its proper functioning.

The Media Elite and the Contradiction of Democracy

A similar contradiction recurs in the case of the media elite. Freedom of the media from government control is not only a basic principle of democracy but is also essential for exposure of the governing elite's abuses of power. In the absence of such freedom, the media elite can even be used by the government as an instrument of manipulation in its own right, designed to aid it in keeping itself in power indefinitely. On the other hand, freedom from government control does not imply citizens' free and equal access to the media. The modern mass media are large-scale organizations and as such—like other organizations—give birth to their own elites. And these act as gatekeepers who control, and practically monopolize, access to the media.

But although crucial in the political process,[1] the media elite is not elected by the public—and not accountable to it. Hence, it is also against the principles of democracy for this elite to exercise power exempt from the control of those who have been elected. Thus, for the media elite to hold independent power that countervails the power of the elected political elite is both a necessity and a threat to democracy.

Social Movements' Elites and the Contradiction of Democracy

One of the distinctive features of democracy, following from the principle of freedom of organization, is its tendency periodically to generate new social movements and their uninstitutionalized elites, and subsequently to absorb their modes of action and demands without this leading to a basic disruption of the system or to basic transformations to a new one. Some theorists (e.g., Eisenstadt, 1966) have long seen this as a hallmark of modern society's openness and flexibility. Others, in particular neo-Marxists such as Marcuse (1964), have viewed the self-same characteristics as evidence of capitalism's "repressive tolerance."

Seen from the present perspective this is yet another manifestation of the contradiction of democracy. The constant generation and regeneration of new movements— which could be seen to have occurred in the nineteenth century, and has certainly continued in the twentieth—has formed a crucial avenue of public participation in politics. It also has enabled minorities not adequately catered for by the majority principle embodied in elections to raise their voice and stand up for their rights. As such, it is of the very essence of democracy. Also, the elites to which such movements have given rise, have formed yet another type of elite which may countervail and curb the power of the governing elite—and thus they too are crucial to democracy.

But these elites frequently represent relatively small groups amongst the public, and the noise they make frequently is disproportionate to the numbers of their supporters. They thus tend to drown out the less audible but more widely based voice of the "silent majority," and in this sense, they also obviate one of the most basic principles of democracy. As was seen before with respect to the nineteenth century, and will be seen below with respect to the present, the leaders of such movements tend to become absorbed into existing structures and institutionalized elites. But before they do, or when they do not, they present yet another example of the aforementioned contradiction: they are both a necessity and a threat to democracy.

Moreover, in order to become politically audible, protest groups must be organized. The more organized they are, the better the chances that their demands will have an impact on government policies and on actual political developments. But the more organized they are, the more clearly are they themselves dominated by elites. And this in itself is still another contradiction which protest movements "contribute," so to speak, to democracy.

A Problem That Has No Solution

The contradiction of democracy and its various manifestations as analyzed above can also be seen as a dilemma, or as a problem that by its very logic has no solution. It can be somewhat alleviated by extending the electoral principle to some of the countervailing elites and the organizations they head. Thus, as noted, cooperatives headed by elected managers are internally more democratic than capitalist organizations; trade unions whose leaders periodically face free elections form internally more democratic organizations than do unions whose leaders hold life-long positions or whose elections are largely manipulated, and so forth. But in some cases the organization's effectiveness hinges on its top positions being filled by criteria of professionalism and competence rather than by criteria of popularity. This is arguably the case in the bureaucracy and the judiciary, in professional organizations—including media organizations—and even in economic organizations.

More importantly, even when the electoral principle is applied to organizations such as trade unions, cooperatives, and the like, it refers to internal elections only. From the viewpoint of the political system as a whole, the power such leaders acquire beyond the boundaries of their own organizations is still necessarily undemocratic as per the above definition of democracy. If, however, there were to be a law that the elites of such organizations must be elected by the public at large, this would contravene the principle of freedom of organization. Elites so elected would not be able to represent the interests of their own organizations, they would become merely another branch of the state elites, and their ability to curb those elites' power would be curtailed or obviated.

The Contradiction of Democracy: Some Implications

Thus it would seem that in one way or another, democracy must live with its inherent contradiction and with that contradiction's implications and consequences. One of these implications has to do with the "rules of the game" of democracy.

At their most basic level, the democratic "rules of the game," or the guidelines for action, which govern the relations and struggles amongst elites, and those between elites and the public in Western countries, are part of the above definition of democracy and are of primary significance for it. As indicated before, they are the result of protracted elite struggles. But once developed, they have been designed to set certain restraints on elite struggles and on elite power; and these restraints are of the very essence of democracy. It has been correctly observed that they are "the restraints that set us free."

It has been taken for granted by scholars of a variety of schools of thought that the actual, more detailed "rules of the game" as they developed in Western democracies, are in fact reasonably well equipped to bear this heavy burden. Since de Tocqueville, it has been assumed by such scholars that while democracy is based on controversy and conflict, it is based on an *institutionalization* of such conflict, which in turn presupposes not only clear, unambiguous rules but also widespread consensus over the rules whereby the conflict is waged. Further, it has been widely argued that such consensus over the rules of democracy is well entrenched, particularly amongst elites. Occassionally, empirical research has shown that this is not inevitably the case, that while consensus over rules is more widespread amongst elites than it is amongst the public, there are several areas where such consensus is absent even among elites (Dahl, 1969; McClosky, 1969; Pedersen, 1985). Nonetheless, the idea that consensus over the rules of democracy prevails, especially amongst elites, has continued to prevail and still is one of the stocks-in-trade of a variety of sociopolitical analyses (see e.g., Dye, & Zeigler, 1987, Ch. 1; Sartori, 1987, pp. 90–1).

But if, as has been argued before, democracy is faced with a basic, inherent, contradiction and dilemma, then this must necessarily find expression in some contradictions, and controversies with respect to the rules of democracy. If the role of elites in a democracy is beset by inherent ambiguities and dilemmas, then the rules governing their behavior, especially the rules governing the relations between various elites, must have a degree of ambivalence as well.

While there may be consensus on some general, abstract rules of democracy (e.g., the electoral principle) such consensus may be expected to diminish or be absent where concrete rules governing the actual interaction between elites are concerned.

And, indeed, my comparative study of bureaucracy in democratic countries (1985a) has shown that, while there are important differences between Western countries in this respect, there is usually some ambivalence in the role expectations pertaining to bureaucratic elites. By democratic "rules of the game" bureaucratic elites are in a double bind: they are expected to be under the control of elected politicians and yet exempt from such control, politically responsive and politically independent, at one and the same time. My recent study of national broadcasting corporations in Western-style democracies (1987)—as an example of both bureaucratic-style and media organizations with their own elites—has led to similar results: in fact there has been no consensus on how much independence from the governing political elite the broadcasting elite ought to have. The ambivalent rules governing relations between elites are further illustrated in Chapter 8.

Conclusion

To summarize then: the central, non-ruling elites have a relative (though incomplete) autonomy from the state, or ruling elites, and the nonelected state elites have a relative (though incomplete) autonomy from the elected, governing elite. This creates a contradiction for democracy, which may also be seen as a dilemma, or as a problem that has no solution. The contradiction of elite autonomy in a democracy frequently results in ambivalent and contentious rules governing the relations between these elites.

The combination of all these factors has essential implications for the manner in which the power of elites is exerted and countered in a democracy. Their main result is to create some restraints on governing elite power, but also to render these restraints at times inadequate, and at all times exceedingly fragile. Since democracy is itself dependent on these restraints, the overall effect of the contradiction, and the unclear rules that emanate from it, is to render democracy itself a rather precarious institutional structure. These points will be further explicated and illustrated in the next chapters.

Notes

1. On the basis of research carried out in the 1950s and 1960s, social scientists had long argued that the effect of the media on public opinion was rather limited and served mainly to reinforce existing attitudes. More recently, however, research has shown that the media (and hence their elites) do have a more substantial effect on public opinion than was previously believed, especially in making the public aware of, and focusing its interest on certain issues which, for their part, may work in favor of, or against certain parties, politicians or the government of the day.

6

Elite Power, Manipulation, and Corruption

Introduction

The relative (but incomplete) autonomy of the central non-ruling elites from the state, or ruling elites, and the nonelected elites from the elected, governing elite, is now further explained. And it is argued that it has important consequences: it makes it both possible and necessary for the governing elite to exert and attempt to consolidate its power through various strategies of control that are based on the utilization of non-coercive state resources. And, especially when the rules that circumscribe this relative autonomy are unclear, it encourages the governing elite to do so through certain abuses of its power, in less than fully overt and legitimate ways, that is, through manipulation and corruption. It also encourages the other elites to curb and counter such attempts, though not always with the determination and success that would be required for their prevention or elimination. Indeed, the ability of the non-governing elites to counter not only the governing elite's power in general but also its manipulation and corruption—albeit only in part—is one of the most distinctive features of Western democracy. This argument is now developed with the aid of a three–dimensional model of governing elite power, manipulation, and corruption.

Frequently, power is viewed by social scientists as the central component of political structures while manipulation and corruption are viewed merely as aberrations. Often, therefore, they are not included in the mainstream of the analysis of power and are dealt with as separate (and secondary) issues. Consequently, the literature on political power (referred to in the previous analysis), that on political manipulation (e.g., Edelman, 1971; Mueller, 1973; Qualter, 1985; Riker, 1986), and that on political corruption (e.g., Peters and Welch, 1978; Johnston, 1982; Nas et al, 1968) have developed largely as disconnected entities.

Here, by contrast, political manipulation and a major form of political corruption are seen as an integral part of the pattern of the exercise of power in Western democracies. They are also regarded as fairly prevalent in such democracies on the assumption that there is often more to manipulation and corruption than meets the eye. Hence these phenomena are here analyzed in conjunction with the analysis of legitimate power, in the framework of a general model of the exercise and countering of power in a democracy.

The Relative Autonomy of Elites and the Utilization of State Resources

In a democracy, the governing elite (which, for the sake of variety will also be referred to as the elite that holds office, or the incumbent political elite) attains power by the consent of the majority of the public—as expressed, albeit imperfectly, through elections—and this endows it with a certain legitimacy. Nevertheless, that elite cannot rely on electoral legitimation alone in order to exert and sustain its power: widespread dissatisfaction with its rule amongst other elites and amongst the public might well cause noncompliance and civil unrest, and even force it out of office prematurely. Hence, once elected, that elite must devise ways and means to exert and consolidate its power in practice and preferably, from its viewpoint, to perpetuate it into the future. For this purpose it requires the compliance, support or acquiescence of the other elites, as well as the continuing consent or acquiescence of the majority of the public.

Ostensibly, the governing elite should be able to attain at least compliance and acquiescence through its ultimate control of those state institutions which have charge of the instruments or resources of coercion. But actual use of these means of coercion is severely restricted by democratic rules, which in this particular area are quite clear and restrictive. Also, the direct control of these instruments has come to be in the hands of specialized and themselves relatively autonomous elites: those of the military, the security services, and the police. Their utilization by the incumbent political elite presupposes the support of the elites in charge of the instruments of coercion—a support that cannot be taken for granted, unless the relevant rules are observed. In practice this signifies that the elite that holds office in a democracy, beyond certain narrowly defined limits, cannot rely on coercive means to secure acquiescence of the other elites and of the public to its rule.

This, therefore, is an additional factor (besides the protection granted by the rules of democracy themselves—as previously noted) that explains why the governing elite does not have total control of the other elites, and why it cannot rely on automatic compliance from them and from the public. *Thus, since it cannot coerce it must devise other strategies of control* in order to gain the support or acquiescence of the other elites and of the public.

At the same time, the fact that—apart from the instruments of coercion—the governing elite has charge of other state resources on which the non-governing elites and parts of the public may at times be dependent (for their elite positions, or for a variety of supplementary benefits) enables the former to utilize those resources for such strategies of control. It does so by using them as negative sanctions (curbs), thus withdrawing them as a penalty for nonsupport or opposition, or—more prominently—by applying them as positive sanctions (inducements), thus handing them out in return for support or acquiescence.

In other words, if the governing elite had total control of the means of coercion and through them of the other elites (and the public) it would not be necessary for other state resources to be used as curbs or inducements in order to gain compliance, support, or acquiescence. If the other elites (and the public) had total independence from the governing elite and if that elite thus had no leverage over them at all, it would not be possible for it to do so. The intermediary situation of the relative autonomy of elites, thus both enables and requires the elected, governing elite to use state resources as sanctions, as part of its strategies of exercising and consolidating its power.

The Relative Autonomy of Elites, Manipulation, and Corruption

This situation has an additional effect: given that the governing elite does not have total control of the other elites, and given that the rules that govern this imperfect control are frequently contradictory and ambivalent, this encourages the incumbent elite to resort to certain abuses of power: it encourages it to utilize the state resources for the exertion and consolidation of its power in non-overt and non-legitimate ways, that is, through manipulation and corruption.

For in this situation of imperfect control, or relative independence, the other elites are jealous in safeguarding whatever independence they do have. Hence, the elite that holds office must use the state's resources in its strategies to secure support or acquiescence of those elites to its rule but, to a large extent, it must do so without being seen to be doing so, and thus without antagonizing those elites. The independence of another elite (e.g., the bureaucracy) may also have the support of still other elites (e.g., the media and the opposition) and of large parts of the public. The governing elite must therefore attempt to exercise and consolidate its power over that other elite without incurring the wrath of those third elites, the ones that support the other elite's independence, and might make unfavorable publicity for the governing elite amongst the public.

In addition, some of the relatively autonomous elites (in particular, again, the opposition and the media) are likely to demystify and counter the government's attempts to produce consent by making favorable publicity for itself amongst the public, that is, through what is commonly known as propaganda. And the more blatant the government's propaganda, the greater the success of the other elites in countering it is likely to be. In this situation, the governing elite's attempts to manufacture consent for itself, too, are likely to be most effective when carried out in subtle and devious ways. In other words, because the other elites have relative autonomy, the governing political elite is under pressure to exert and stabilize its power in non-overt ways, that is, through manipulation.

Also, when the autonomy of the other elites from the governing political elite is precariously balanced, and when the perpetuation of its own power is thus frequently at stake, this encourages the political elite to do whatever it can to ensure the maintenance of power, even through less than fully legitimate means. And when the rules pertaining to this autonomy are hazy, they may be more easily interpreted to suit one's own interests. Moreover, hazy rules leave greater leeway for activities that are neither clearly within, nor clearly outside their boundaries and which, according to our definition (see below) may still be conceived of as corruption. Finally, where rules are ambivalent and contentious, they may be more easily circumvented without incurring official sanctions. In other words, contradictory, ambivalent and hazy rules encourage corruption.

The reader may have noticed that there is a certain similarity between what here is termed manipulation and what in Marxist parlance (following Gramsci) has been labelled as hegemony. But there are two basic differences. First, here, the manipulation referred to is that by the governing political elite rather than that by what Marxists call the ruling class. Thus, this analysis does not share the Marxist assumption that the governing elite is invariably in league with what is here termed the economic elite, when it either exerts its power, or manufactures consent for itself, in devious ways. Second, while, as was seen before, several Marxists share the implicit assumption that hegemony is fairly pervasive and almost invariably successful in befuddling the gullible masses, here the view taken is that manipulation may be resisted and countered, with varying degrees of success, as will be further clarified below.

State Resources and Their Use: A Classification

This argument is now explicated with the aid of the following classificatory scheme. In Chapter 2 it has been noted that (in addition to its control of the resources of coercion) the state has control of a variety of symbolic, power, and material resources. Thus, the state-controlled resources, and the strategies whereby the elite that holds office attempts to use them for the exertion and consolidation of its own power (jointly referred to as devices), may be classified as follows:

Symbolic Devices. The incumbent elite has certain symbolic resources at its disposal. These derive from the legitimacy and the charisma of office, at times intermingled with personal charisma (in Weberian terms). The symbolic resources that accrue to the governing elite are further enhanced by certain channels of mass communication (the media) that are generally keen to report on the deeds and pronouncements of the governing elite, even when they are critical of it. The governing elite's symbolic resources also derive from its control of various symbolic benefits that form part of the state apparatus.

Thus, the governing elite's attempts to ensure compliance, support, or acquiescence for itself through symbolic resources may assume a variety of forms. They may take the form of attempts to produce political support through the use of symbols: spoken or written words, visual symbols, music, or symbolic actions, in order to predefine the situation for others in such a way that political support may be expected to ensue. That is to say, such attempts by the governing elite to create support spell the creation and dissemination of propaganda in its own favor (see Edelman, 1971; Mueller, 1973).

The use of symbols as part of the exertion and perpetuation of power may also occur through the bestowing of approval, prestige, or honors in return for compliance or support, or the withdrawal of such rewards and the imposition of disapproval, scorn and low prestige as a penalty for nonsupport or opposition.

Power Devices. The incumbent political elite also commands resources of "pure" political power, as it were, or imperative control (in Weberian terms) based on its control of certain of the state's regulatory structures which, themselves, are also sources and resources of power. It may thus offer power or the semblance of power as an inducement for compliance or support (a device also known as co-optation). Conversely, it may use withdrawal of power and power-related privileges as a sanction for nonsupport or opposition.

Material Devices. Additionally, the elite that holds office has control of a wide array of material resources derived from taxation, control of public economic enterprises and, more broadly, from certain controls over the economy, as specified before. It thus can use all or some of these resources as inducements through the awarding of material benefits in return for compliance or political support, or through the withdrawal of benefits or the imposition of material penalties in return for nonsupport or opposition.[1]

These devices, of course, frequently do not appear in actual reality in their "pure" form, but rather are used in various complex combinations. But they may be classified as symbolic, power, or material devices according to the element which is most prominent in them. When a strategy is used in which inducements of two or more types are about equally prominent, they may be referred to as mixed devices.

Each strategy may be employed with various degrees of determination and success. In each case, there may be an actual application of the device, or there may be a (sometimes equally effective) promise or threat of such application. The resources may be deployed in return for active or passive support or acquiescence at present, or in the hope that —out of gratitude or a sense of obligation—support or compliance will be forthcoming in the future. Or else, the resources may be deployed precisely where one fears non-compliance or opposition, in the hope that this will help dispell grievances and create at least quiescence, if not actual support. Also, the resources may be handed out in return for other resources which can then be deployed to amass political support. All this should become clearer from the examples cited below.

The Utilization of State Resources: Manipulation and Corruption

A crosscutting way of classifying the governing political elite's utilization of the state's resources in the exercise and perpetuation of its power, is by the degree of overtness vs. covertness or deviousness with which it is employed. Thus, one may distinguish the entirely overt application of such devices, which the elite publicizes and for which it is willing to take full credit or responsibility—as the case may be. There is then the semi-overt application of these devices, which is generally well known, but not officially admitted and not publicized by the elite—or, if engaged in publicly, is practiced in devious ways, and not admitted by the elite to be part of its attempts to exert and remain in power. There is, third, the covert application of these devices, which the governing elite makes deliberate efforts to conceal. The latter two forms may be labelled as manipulation.

Yet another crosscutting classification of such devices is by the degree of their legitimacy by the norms and values commonly held by the participants. Following Nas et al (1986) and others (with some variations), the non–legitimate utilization of the control of state or public resources for the benefit of the utilizers is here labelled as political corruption. However, this analysis is not equally concerned with all varieties of such corruption. Its chief concern is not with what is usually known as favoritism (such as that by the politician who never did any special favors except for his own friends), or with what is usually known as nepotism (such as that by the minister who appointed his brother-in-law to conduct a study of nepotism in his department), even though it may be assumed that the politicians themselves eventually benefit from the favors they hand out. Nor is its chief concern with what is usually known simply as bribery, that is, with corruption the proceeds of which go into politicians' or officials' own, private pockets (in connection with which one-time Israeli Prime Minister, the late Levy Eshkol, once invoked the commandment "Thou shalt not muzzle the ox when he treads out the corn" Deuteronomy 25:4).

Rather, my concern here is chiefly with that type of political corruption (or non–legitimate use of state resources) which is engaged in by the governing political elite as part of its exercise of power, or in its attempts at consolidating and perpetuating its power. In other words, I am concerned with the incumbent elite's non–legitimate distribution of state resources in return for political support or acquiescence to its own rule, or in return for resources which are then utilized to amass such support. It is possible to distinguish legitimate, semi-legitimate and illegitimate applications of this device. On the basis of the above definition, both semi-legitimate and illegitimate applications of this device are here labelled as corruption.[2]

There is a widespread custom in the social sciences to dichotomize behavior as either legitimate or illegitimate. This, however, leaves out a distinctive type of social actions which fall into the no-man's land, the grey zone, or the "twilight zone," in between behavior that is fully condoned and that which is flatly condemned in a given society or group of societies. It is this category of behavior that may be termed semi-legitimate. It is frequently behavior that is widely considered as being in line with some deeply rooted, widely accepted norms, but contrary to other deeply rooted norms. Alternatively it is behavior that is considered as contrary to some important norms, but at the same time serves to promote some powerful interests.

Semi-legitimate behavior may be recognized by the ambivalence with which it is regarded. Such ambivalence may find expression, for instance, in the fact that the behavior is officially condemned but unofficially condoned. Or, it may find expression in the fact that the behavior is condemned by some, but condoned by others in the same society. Or else, it may be widely condemned, for instance in the media, in the state comptrollers' and official inquiries' reports; yet, even when it is in transgression of the law, and even when publicly revealed, it rarely meets with effective sanctions. This is distinct from illegitimate behavior, which, when exposed, does meet with sanctions such as dismissal from office and/or indictment, conviction, imprisonment. Although many who engage in such illegitimate behavior may get away with it, those who transgress the eleventh commandment ("thou shalt not be found out")— besides creating a "furor" or a "scandal"— usually meet with retribution.

The combination of all these dimensions and categories creates a three-dimensional, three-category classificatory model which graphically may be presented in the form of a cube as shown in figure 6.1.

A basic advantage of this model over other, more prevalent analyses of power, is that it covers all principal attempts by a governing political elite to consolidate and perpetuate its power—whether overt or covert, legitimate or illegitimate. It thus incorporates straightforward and legitimate exertions and attempts to perpetuate power together with attempts at manipulation and

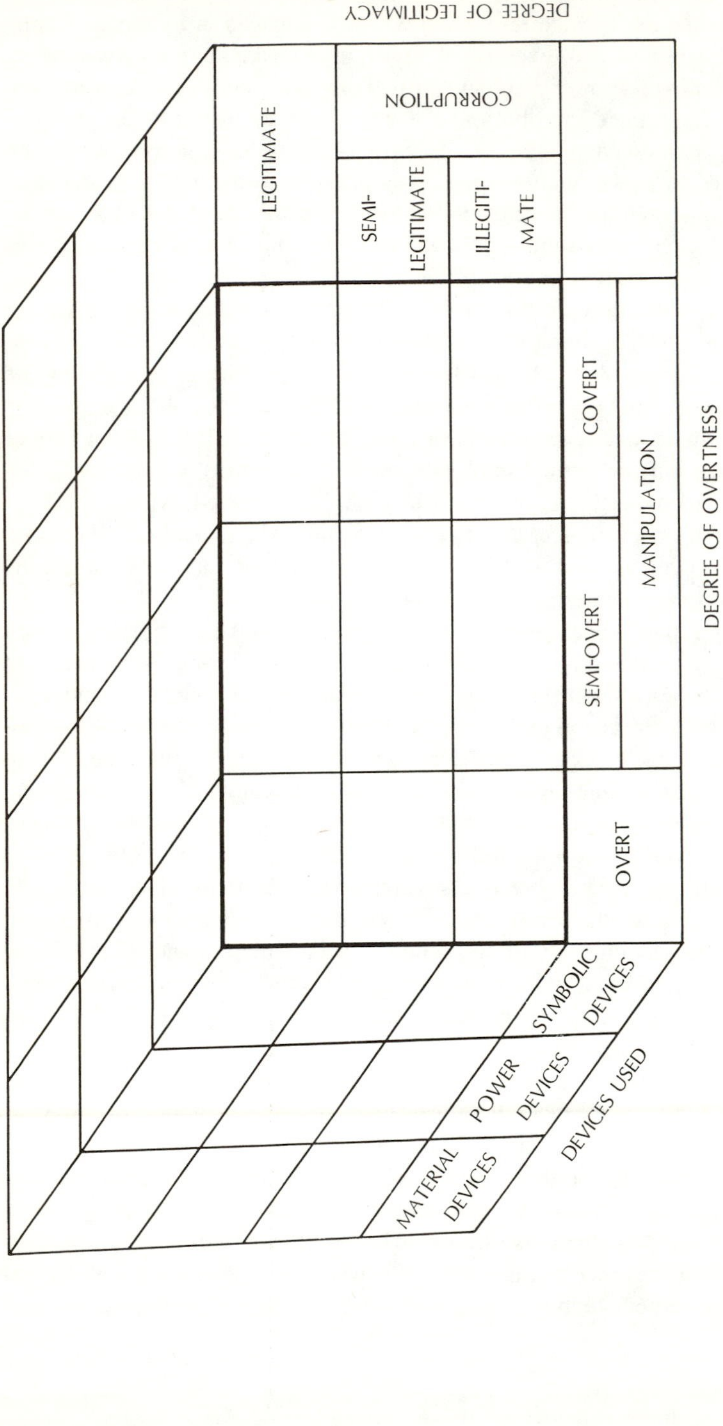

Figure 6.1. Model of Governing Elite Exertion of Power, Manipulation, and Corruption.

corruption— all in one model. It thereby brings out the affinities as well as the differences between them.

It stands to reason that there is a positive relationship between the latter two dimensions of the model, manipulation and corruption, in the sense that corruption usually implies manipulation. This is but another way of stating the obvious, namely, that when a governing elite engages in corruption it is in no rush to publicize this fact, and the less legitimate the practice, the more likely is it that attempts will be made to conceal it or to employ it in devious, obfuscatory ways. This does not mean, of course, that the elite's attempts to conceal corruption are necessarily successful. But even when the elite's corruption is publicly exposed, it must still be classified as manipulation, if the intent was to practice it in a less than fully overt manner. Thus, several instances of the governing elite's attempts to amass support for itself fall on the diagonal lines of the model, as illustrated above.

While corruption generally implies manipulation, the opposite is not necessarily the case: there are instances of manipulation which—by commonly accepted standards—would not be considered as corrupt. Thus, some rubrics that are not situated on the diagonal lines of the model, are not necessarily left empty, as also exemplified above.

On the basis of this model it is now possible to assemble the various pieces of the argument: the relative (but incomplete) autonomy of the other elites from the incumbent political elite, and the relative ambivalence and contentiousness of the rules pertaining to the relations between them, make it both necessary (or at least expedient) and possible for the governing elite to utilize state-controlled (symbolic, power, and material) resources in order to exert, consolidate, and perpetuate its power, and encourages it to do so in less than overt and legitimate ways, that is, through manipulation and corruption. This argument may be clarified through the following examples.

For the purpose of the graphic presentation of these examples, the above model is being divided into "slices" so that symbolic, power, and material devices for the exertion and stabilization of power can be presented separately.

Symbolic Devices: Some Examples

A prominent symbolic device for the exertion and perpetuation of power is that of propaganda, for which the elite that holds office utilizes state resources, such as the legitimacy and the charisma of office. Propaganda is never fully covert, in the sense that its very essence lies in its publicity. But it is possible to distinguish overt or straightforward, and semi-overt or devious propaganda. The former includes, for instance, election campaign speeches and slogans mapping out past and projected policies and calling on the public to vote the incumbent party, elite, or politician, back into office. The latter may entail, for instance, the use of emotive language so as to predefine the situation for the public in a manner that favors the government (see Edelman, 1971). It also includes the use of other emotive symbols, such as the flag, the national anthem, or even religious symbols to promote support for the government elite. In the framework of our model, this type of propaganda may be classified as symbolic manipulation.

When propaganda, for instance in an election campaign, is carried out in a wholly straightforward manner, it is obviously considered legitimate, indeed, part of the proper procedures of democracy. But even where propaganda is practiced in less than fully candid ways, in the form of symbolic manipulation, for instance through the use of emotive symbols, this is (within certain limits), still a commonly accepted practice. In fact, it is what the public has come to expect as routine behavior from politicians, and hence may be considered as legitimate.

Where propaganda, including election campaigns, presents knowingly false promises or misleading statements, this is usually considered less than legitimate in democratic countries. Given, however, that it is a common practice amongst politicians to make such statements, yet those who make them are not commonly tried and punished, and frequently are even elected or reelected in the wake of such statements, they would have to be classified as a semi-legitimate type of manipulation.

The rather widespread practice of politicians uttering false promises and misleading statements, classified before as semi-legitimate, ought to be distinguished from straightforward, factual lies, which politicians occasionally utter in order to keep themselves in power. While other elites and the public commonly denigrate, yet are usually willing to tolerate the former, they apparently are less willing to tolerate the latter (unless legitimized by other, e.g., patriotic symbols). This is evidenced by the rare but celebrated cases in which politicians, having been caught lying, have been forced to resign their posts. Outstanding examples would be the Profumo affair in Britain and the Watergate affair in the United States. Lies of this type may thus be classified as illegitimate. They may also be seen as semi-overt in the sense that the statements themselves are made in public, but the fact that they do not correspond to the truth is concealed.

Another symbolic device for the mobilization of political support is the awarding of honors, or honorific positions, in return for political support for the governing elite, or in return for campaign funds or other financial contributions to the governing elite or its party. A prominent example would be the awarding of peerages and other honorific titles so as to favor supporters of, or financial contributors to, the political establishment in Britain and other Commonwealth countries. This device may be considered as semi-legitimate: the public usually believes that honors ought to be awarded to express appreciation for objective achievements. But when they are awarded in return for political or financial-political support, the only adverse reaction is usually contained in cynical remarks in the press or in informal conversations.

Yet another symbolic device takes the form of discreditation and delegitimation of radical movements, or conversely, of supportive statements and other symbolic actions to signal recognition for less radical but still potentially divisive groups or movements and their elites, in the hope that these will help placate such groups and elites, and thus will help elicit at least their acquiescence, if not their support of the governing elite. Such symbolic acts are usually deemed legitimate, and where tokens of recognition for disadvantaged groups are concerned they may even be considered morally desirable. But although the symbolic acts are publicly employed (and, here, too, their very essence lies in their publicity), their purpose of placating the potentially divisive groups and elites usually remains latent or, at least, is not publicly admitted. Hence they may be seen as semi-overt. Concrete examples of this device will be presented in the following chapter. Together with the other examples cited before, this device may be graphically presented in the framework of our model, as in figure 6.2.

Power Devices: Some Examples

One of the most salient examples of the governing elite's utilization of the state's power structures for the consolidation of its own power is that of coalition agreements with other political elites and their parties. At times, a political elite, which obtains a plurality (but not a majority) of the popular votes in an election, enters into such an agreement in order to be able to assume power. At other times, an elite which obtains a (possibly narrow) majority of the electoral votes could hold office on its own, but for whatever reasons considers it prudent to share power with another party or parties. Having done so, it accords that party or parties a chunk, and frequently a disproportionate chunk, of power. In return, it can then rely on its or their support in parliament, and thus consolidate its own power by democratic rules. Italy, France, Israel, and Australia are prominent examples of countries that are always or frequently ruled by coalition governments. The religious parties in Israel are prominent examples of parties that have been perennial coalition partners of practically all governments thus far, have thereby secured a share of power —particularly in devising religious policies— while helping sustain the governments in office.

Since coalition agreements of this sort frequently are necessary to obtain and retain power by democratic majority rules, and since, in any case, they always follow the letter (if not necessarily the spirit) of those rules, they are entered into overtly and are considered legitimate. Even if, at times, rumblings are heard concerning small parties' inordinate power accorded to

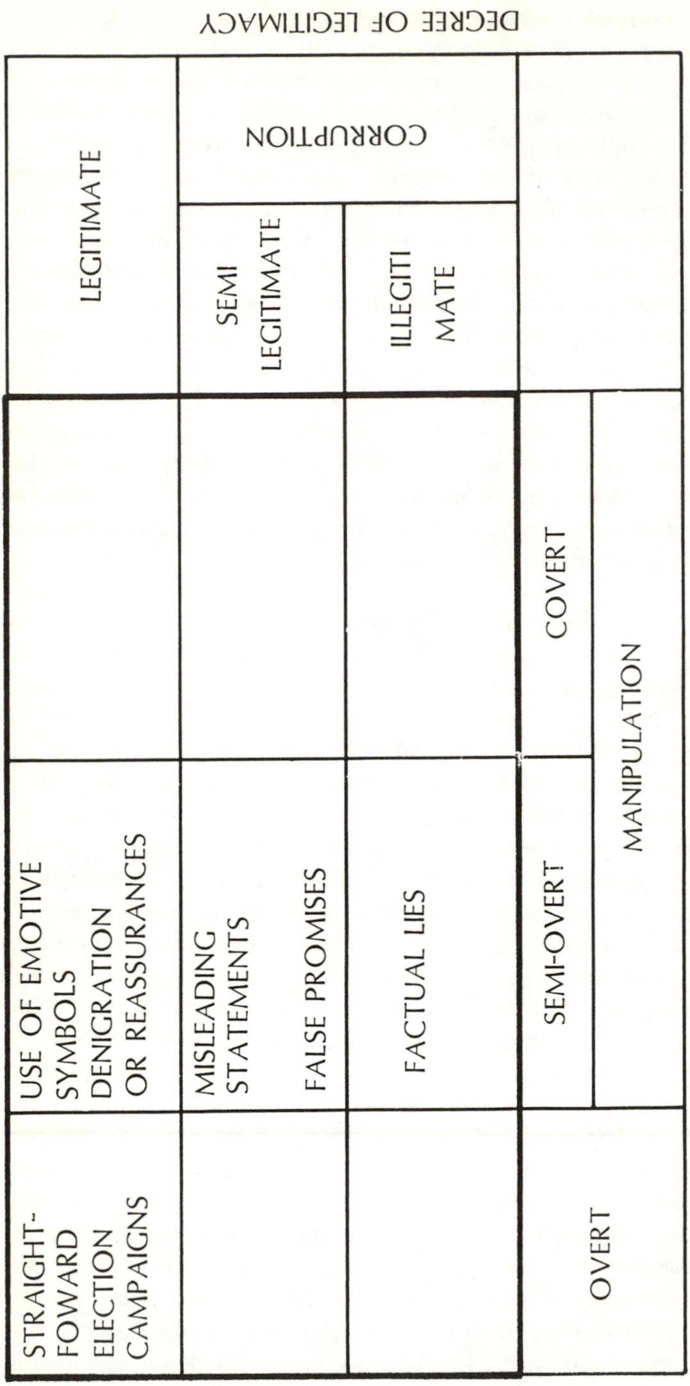

Figure 6.2. Model of Governing Elite Exertion of Power, Manipulation, and Corruption: Examples of Symbolic Devices.

them by coalition agreements, it is still normally considered that governments have the right to make such arrangements within the democratic framework.

Also legitimate, though less overt, are various forms of co-optation of other elites by the governing elite. Co-opted elites are commonly those that have the potential of counteracting, undermining or destabilizing the power of the governing elite. But in return for being given a share of power, they may be counted upon to curb their own destabilizing potential, or even to support the governing elite, and thus help it exert and consolidate its power.

A greatly pervasive example of this practice is the co-optation of business and union leaders by the government through tripartite agreements, especially on economic policies. Through such agreements, business and union elites' power is legitimized by the state, and they are accorded some influence in the shaping of economic policies to suit their own interests. In return, the governing elite may expect not only to stave off confrontation with them, but also to gain their support for, and complicity in, the policies in the design of which they have themselves participated. In Australia, for instance, such an agreement has been engineered by the Hawke Labor government in the form of a "Statement of Accord by the Australian Labor Party and the Australian Council of Trade Unions Regarding Economic Policy" (February, 1983), also known as the Prices and Incomes Accord. Subsequently, the government orchestrated a National Economic Summit Conference (April 1983) in which business leaders participated as well and accepted the basic spirit of the accord.

Agreements such as these are not only publicly known, but indeed, are deliberately publicized by the government. But usually they are declared to be aimed at ensuring economic stability, industrial harmony, a just "social contract," and the like. Their equally important aim of helping the government maintain power is not generally publicized. Hence, such forms of co-optation may be considered as semi-overt. These arrangements, too, frequently give rise to rumblings in the media and the community. The government making them may be taken to task for leaving other interest groups out in the cold, or for bypassing parliamentary, democratic procedures. But, ultimately, the government is still considered to be within its rights in hammering out such agreements —hence they may be considered as legitimate.

Another example of co-optation would be the incorporation into the establishment of leaders of potentially divisive ethnic, minority or protest groups, in the hope that giving them a share, or a semblance, of power will placate not only themselves but also the groups they lead. The appointment of an aborigine to head the Department of Aboriginal Affairs in Australia is one of many cases in point. Other cases will be presented in the next chapter. Power devices for the mobilization of support are presented within the framework of our model in figure 6.3.

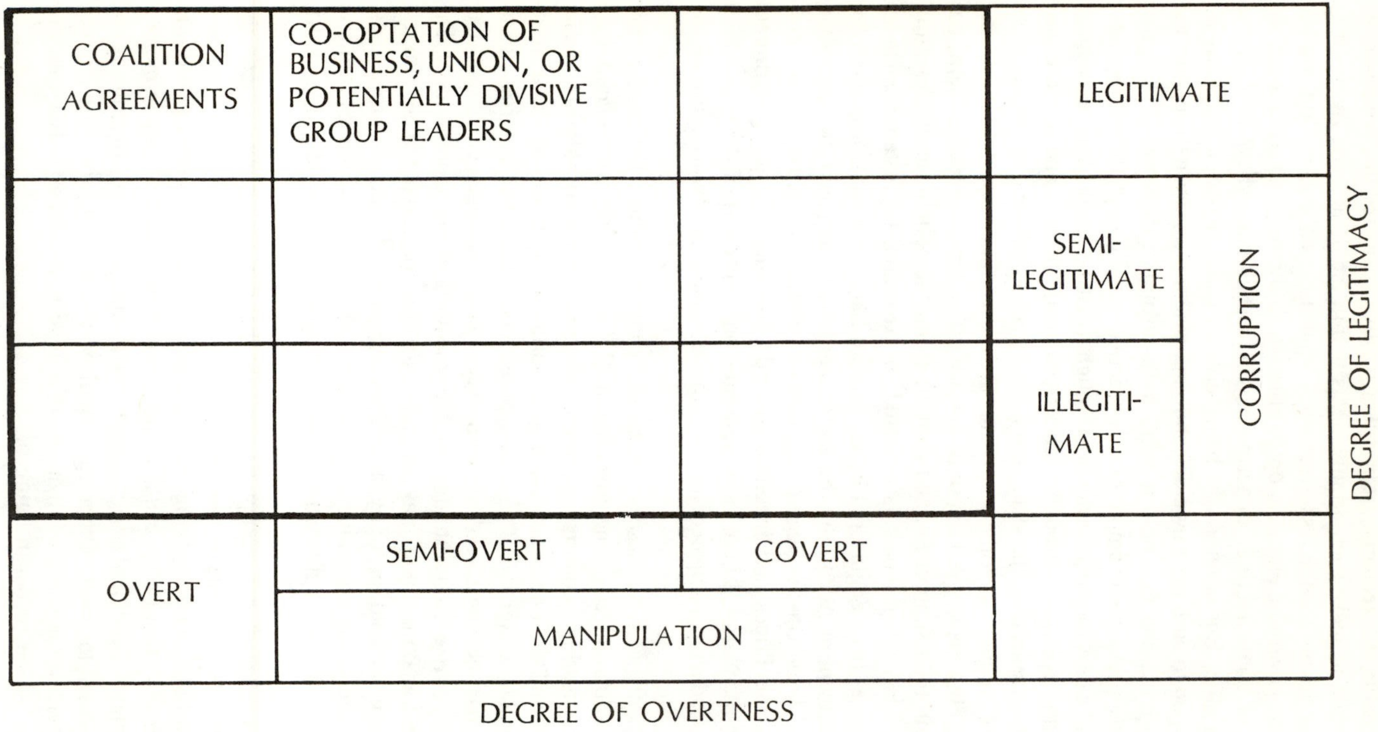

COALITION AGREEMENTS
CO-OPTATION OF BUSINESS, UNION, OR POTENTIALLY DIVISIVE GROUP LEADERS
LEGITIMATE
SEMI-LEGITIMATE
ILLEGITI-MATE
CORRUPTION
DEGREE OF LEGITIMACY
OVERT
SEMI-OVERT
COVERT
MANIPULATION
DEGREE OF OVERTNESS

Figure 6.3. Model of Governing Elite Exertion of Power and Manipulation: Examples of Power Devices.

Material Devices: Some Examples

The devices whereby the governing elite uses its control of state or public material resources in order to consolidate its power by increasing support or acquiescence for itself may take place on various levels. On the macro level, it consists of shaping economic policies (which are basically general guidelines for the allocation of material resources) to suit the perceived preferences of the electorate. A case in point would be the introduction of lenient tax policies before an election.

On the intermediary level the device may consist of shaping policies so as to penalize certain interest groups for non-support, or so as to favor other interest groups whose support or acquiescence is then expected to follow. Examples of the latter would be tariff protection for business and export subsidies for farmers. On this level, too, would be the shaping of economic policies in favor of potentially divisive or dissenting groups, further illustrated in the following chapter.

On the micro (or particularist) level, the device consists of providing state resources (such as public funds or government contracts) to individual institutions, companies or persons, in return for political support or acquiescence, or in return for resources (such as campaign fund contributions) which may aid the recipients in gaining political support.

On the macro level this practice is engaged in overtly and (unless it entails obvious damage to the economy) is considered not only as legitimate, but indeed as a basic component of democracy, indicating —as it does— government responsiveness to the wishes of the public. On the intermediary level, the device is commonly applied with public knowledge, although its aim of ensuring compliance and support for the government, and thus perpetuating governing elite power, normally is not publicly stated. Thus it may be seen as semi-overt. On this, the intermediary level, this widely used device, although manipulative, is generally seen as inevitable, and hence is considered as being within the boundaries of what is acceptable in Western democracies.

However, the practice is considered as increasingly illegitimate as one moves down to the level of the individual institution, company, or person. It is at this level that the practice runs counter to democratic procedures (as per the definition of democracy presented before) for it helps a governing elite to exercise and perpetuate its power not on the basis of its advocated policies, but on the basis of the largesse it can distribute to its supporters. It is at this level, therefore, that the practice runs counter to generally accepted rules and norms, or falls into the twilight zone of what the norms neither fully condone nor fully condemn.

On the micro level, the practice is thus semi-legitimate or illegitimate, depending upon the directness of the exchange. When an immediate exchange takes place, this is generally labeled as bribery; it usually contravenes the law, is engaged in covertly and is considered illegitimate. A case in point would be the direct bribery of voters at an election. This is known to have occurred on a fairly large scale, for instance in nineteenth century England and Australia. While it is not widespread today, it has not been totally eradicated. Thus, a few years ago, an Israeli personality was convicted in court for bribing his way into parliament by distributing monies to the tune of hundreds of thousands of dollars to voters.

More common, however, and, indeed fairly widespread, are the cases where the exchange is indirect, in the nature of "cast your bread upon the waters," and no express tit for tat may be shown to exist. These practices are generally employed in semi-overt ways, in the sense that they are not engaged in publicly, but are nonetheless reported in the media and are well known to the public. They may be seen as semi-legitimate in that they commonly raise widespread criticism in the media, occasionally give rise to commissions of inquiry or even police investigations, but normally do not lead to culprits being tried, convicted, and punished. Cases in point would be a large part of what has been known as machine politics in the United States, and similar practices in, for instance, Italy, Belgium, and Israel. More concrete examples would be some aspects of the recent New York City scandals, and the allocation of funds to educational institutions by political criteria in Israel. These examples are presented in figure 6.4, and some of them are reviewed at greater length and analyzed in Chapter 8.

Combined Devices: Some Examples

Some of the measures employed by a governing elite to consolidate its power are clearly combinations of symbolic, power, and/or material devices, where all components are about equally weighted. A most prominent example would be the awarding of posts in a government bureaucracy, or in a government-related authority, to the supporters of the party (or the elite) in office. In the United States, for instance, a few thousand appointments at the top of the federal civil service are routinely made on this basis. In West Germany, Italy, Belgium, and Israel, for instance, such party-politicization penetrates the middle rungs of the bureaucracy as well. Such bureaucratic appointments, in turn, endow their holders not only with power, but also with relatively high material rewards and with prestige.

Where, as in the United States, such practices are in accordance with formal civil service rules and regulations, they are engaged in overtly and may be considered legitimate. Where, as in Israel, civil service regulations call for appointment by objective criteria of merit, political appointments are made in semi-overt ways: they are not publicized but are generally known to occur. When pressed, politicians tend to admit to these practices, but justify them on

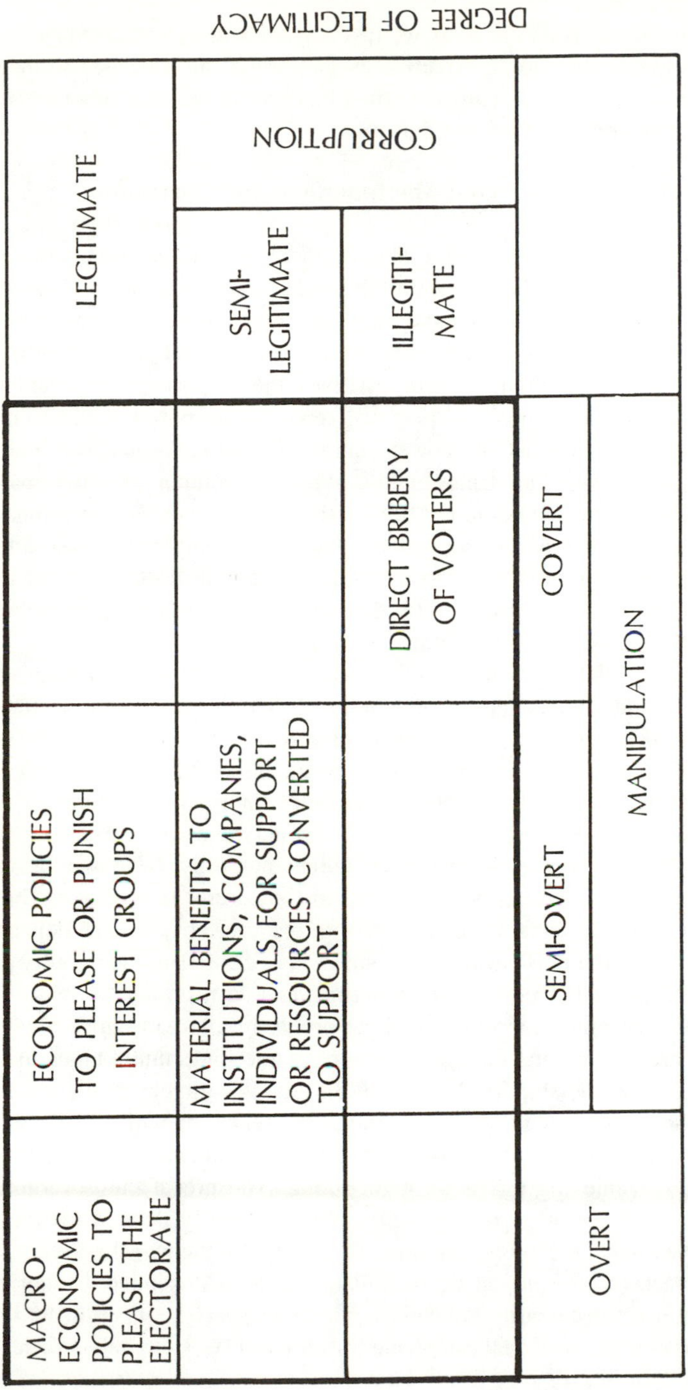

DEGREE OF LEGITIMACY
LEGITIMATE
CORRUPTION
SEMI-LEGITIMATE
ILLEGITI-MATE
MACRO-ECONOMIC POLICIES TO PLEASE THE ELECTORATE
ECONOMIC POLICIES TO PLEASE OR PUNISH INTEREST GROUPS
MATERIAL BENEFITS TO INSTITUTIONS, COMPANIES, INDIVIDUALS, FOR SUPPORT OR RESOURCES CONVERTED TO SUPPORT
DIRECT BRIBERY OF VOTERS
OVERT
SEMI-OVERT
COVERT
MANIPULATION
DEGREE OF OVERTNESS

Figure 6.4. Model of Governing Elite Exertion of Power, Manipulation, and Corruption: Examples of Material Devices

the ground that their rivals do so as well. They are widely criticized in the press, but these critiques are as effective as they would have been, had they been critiques of the weather. Thus they may be classified as semi-legitimate. Graphically, they are presented in figure 6.5.

The Countering of Power, Manipulation, and Corruption

Each of the devices covered by the above model, as well as combinations thereof, may be resisted and countered with various degrees of determination and success. The countering of these devices entails the rejection of the inducements and/or the willingness to bear the penalties derived therefrom, separately or in combination. It also involves the imposition of counter penalties, and such countering, too, may utilize symbolic, power, material, or combined resources. Material and power counter penalties, for instance, may involve work stoppages and strikes, while symbolic counter penalties may involve exposure of the devices to public scrutiny and their public condemnation, or the dissemination of counter-propaganda. Combined power and symbolic penalties may involve protest rallies and demonstrations. A threefold combination of counter penalties (with respect to corruption) may involve indictment, trial, conviction, fining and imprisonment.

The countering of the governing elite's devices for the consolidation of power, its manipulation and corruption is led by other elites.[3] But these elites can do so only if they have at least some autonomy in the control of resources on which their elite positions depend. And the likelihood of their doing so is increased if they can thereby preserve or enhance their own resources. It is here, in particular, that we may speak of the distinctiveness of Western style democracies. For in such regimes other elites not only have a relative autonomy from the governing political elite in the control of resources, but frequently can, in fact, enhance their control of resources by, or even depend for their resources (and thus for their very survival as elites) on, their ability to curb the governing elite's power, manipulation, and corruption.

Thus, economic elites can enhance their profits by blocking government policies that are incongenial to their members, while trade union elites may depend for their leadership positions on displaying suitable militancy in blocking policies incongenial to their members. The opposition can gain power only by decreasing public support for the government, and frequently its best hope of achieving this is through public exposure of the governing elite's abuses. The members of the media elite frequently depend for their standing in the eyes of the public and thus, indirectly, for their livelihood, on a critical approach to government deeds and misdeeds. Consequently, such a critical (though not necessarily radically critical) approach to government by the media has come to be a well established tradition in Western democracies.

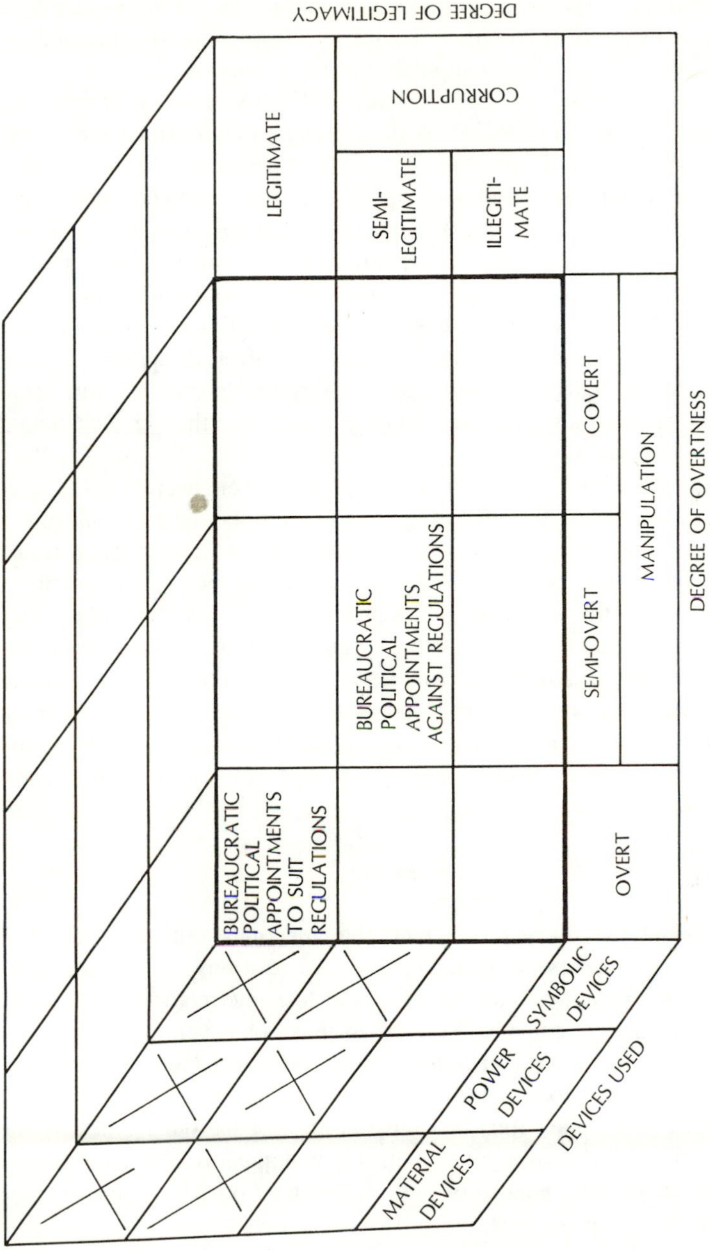

Figure 6.5. Model of Governing Elite Exertion of Power, Manipulation, and Corruption: Examples of Combined Devices

In particular, investigative journalists frequently build their careers and reputations on the exposure of political corruption. And some members of Western academic elites (particularly social scientists) similarly specialize in the demystification of power, manipulation, and corruption.

Finally, there are in Western democracies, factions within bureaucratic and judicial elites, whose raison d'être is the exposure of governing (and other state) elites' corruption. These special factions of elites include inspectors, commisions of inquiry, state and municipal comptrollers, ombudsmen. These factions of elites are usually brought into being by the governing political elite itself in order to follow formally proper procedures, in order to be seen to be doing something to prevent corruption, or in order to gain a moratorium, some breathing space, when corruption has been revealed. But once these bodies have come into being the governing elite (like the sorcerer's apprentice) may find that they are difficult to control; in some cases it may be in their interest to become more zealous in the exposure of corruption, than their creators would have wished them to be.

Yet, as was noted, even in Western democracies all nongoverning elites are, at times, vulnerable to the governing elite's power because of that elite's control of state resources on which—in the form of various allocations, subsidies, exemptions, contracts, congenial policies, laws and regulations, information, appointments, salaries and promotions—these other elites may at times be dependent, and whose authority and power over themselves is not always clearly defined. All this encourages attempts by other elites to counter the power, manipulation, and corruption of the governing elite, but without overly antagonizing that elite. This means that, at times, these elites are less than fully forthright and steadfast in combating governing elite manipulation and corruption.

Conclusion

In conclusion, the manner in which the governing elite exercises and attempts to perpetuate its power depends on its relationship with the other major elites. Or, to put it differently, there is a close interrelationship between the balance of elite dependence, and the exercise of governing elite power through strategies of control including curbs and (even more prominently) inducements, manipulation, and corruption—although the relationship is not a simple, or a linear one. Total, coercive control of the other elites by the governing elite would make such controls, manipulation, and corruption superfluous. Total independence of the other elites from the governing elite would make them impossible.

Given that in Western democracies there is never such total control, nor such total independence, but rather a relative (but incomplete) autonomy of the other central elites from the governing elite, this makes it both necessary and possible for that elite to exert and perpetuate its power through strategies derived from its control of state—symbolic, power, and material —resources. And this, together with the frequently unclear and contentious "rules of the game," encourages it to do so through certain abuses, that is, through manipulation and corruption.The relative autonomy of elites also encourages the other elites to resist and counter such attempts. Although the degree of the other elites' independence, and their consequent ability for confrontation, is not always sufficient to render them a truly effective bulwark against manipulation and corruption, they still have a curbing, or limiting effect on these abuses which is peculiar to Western democracies.

This conclusion gives rise to two propositions. First, because of the relative autonomy of elites and the frequently ambiguous and contentious rules in Western democracies, governing elite exertions of power through strategies of control as illustrated before, even in devious, hidden and/or corrupt ways, are likely to be widespread. Second, under the circumstances prevailing in Western democracies, the greater the dependence of the other elites on the governing elite, and the more ambiguous and unclear the rules, the less the ability of those other elites to counter the governing elite's control strategies, including those involving manipulation and corruption, and vice versa. Relatively less independent elites, and relatively more ambiguous rules, thus, provide the conditions under which manipulation and corruption are likely to flourish; relatively more independent elites, and clearer and more consensual rules, provide the conditions under which manipulation and corruption may be curbed.

Illustrative support for the first proposition is brought in the next chapter, which reviews the manipulative strategies employed by governing elites in Western democracies in dealing with the elites of social protest movements. Illustrative support for the second proposition is brought in the chapter after next, which reviews some cases of corruption and shows how these were encouraged by relatively dependent elites and discouraged or curbed by relatively independent ones.

Notes

1. For a similar scheme (albeit for the exertion of power within organizations) see Etzioni (1961).
2. Sometimes, the term *corruption* is being used by scholars to signify illegitimate material transactions only. Here, the term is used more broadly, to include all less than fully legitimate transactions (including such symbolic transactions as well).
3. These elites may, of course, exert power and engage in manipulation and corruption of their own, but this is beyond the scope of the present analysis.

7

Elite Power and Manipulation: The Absorption of Protest

Introduction

Some people say that the acid test of democracy is not to be sought in free elections or the countervailing power of elites, nor yet in freedom of speech and organization. Rather, it is to be sought in the responsiveness of the governing elite to the demands of the rank and file public. Some have added that it is precisely in this that Western-style democracy is deficient. With respect to Israel, for instance, satirist Ephrajim Kishon observed that while there is clearly freedom of speech, or a law that anybody can say whatever he wants to, there is no law that says that anybody has to listen. Some would say that this observation holds true with respect to Western-style democracies in general. But is this in fact the case? This chapter analyzes the response of Western governing elites to social-protest movements and, thereby, is designed to provide at least some preliminary and partial answers to this question.

It has been noted before that social-protest movements (like other social groups, organizations or endeavors) generate their own elites. These are more fluid, and initially noninstitutionalized, or not as institutionalized as other elites. But they still are elites by our definition, for they control resources on which the movements' supporters are dependent—even if these are only resources of time, energy, and personal charisma—which serve to rally supporters, to set the movements into gear, and to consolidate them into going concerns (in the literature these people are also referred to as leaders of social-protest movements or counter-elites). The reaction of the governing elite to such movements is therefore both a response to public political participation, and a response to countervailing elites. As such it may also be conceptualized as part of the previously presented scheme on the governing elite's attempts at exerting and perpetuating its power.

The Contradiction of Democracy and the Elites of Social-Protest Movements

Because of the relative autonomy of elites, the contradiction this creates, and the frequently contentious rules to which all this gives rise in democratic regimes, we have said, the governing elite displays a widespread tendency to exert power through non-coercive strategies of control, and particularly through inducements, even in hidden and corrupt ways. And it does so, *inter alia*, through manipulation and corruption. This conception gains illustrative support in this chapter with respect to the elites of social-protest movements.

For it can be seen, firstly, that the counter-elites of such movements do in fact have a relative autonomy from the governing elites in Western democracies. On the one hand, these counter-elites usually have sources of livelihood that are not dependent on, or controlled by, the state. Also, their elite positions are accorded to them by their supporters; so for these, too, they are not dependent on the state or the governing elite. Then, too, they have gained the democratic right to protest and (unless violent) their activities cannot be suppressed by the governing elite without incurring the wrath of the other elites and of the public.

Hence, although at times these movements' activities have resulted in clashes with the authorities, and although some of their activists have been harassed (Bottomore, 1979), mostly they have been allowed to express their grievances. As long as they have remained nonviolent, they have come to be largely tolerated. And the fact that social-protest movements have been able to exist and function relatively free of shackles all over the Western world, is itself evidence of the fact that they have gained a measure of independence from the governing elites.

On the other hand, again, in order to maintain their elite positions, the elites of social movements must be able to "deliver" at least some achievements to their supporters. And for such achievements they are frequently dependent on the governing elite. In addition, while they may have independent sources of livelihood, their personal rewards may be greatly enhanced if they are co-opted by the governing elite and made part of the establishment. Thus their independence from the governing elite is always relative, never complete.

It can also be seen that this relative autonomy, or countervailing power, of the elites of social movements from the governing elite poses a basic contradiction or dilemma: it is both a necessity and a threat to democracy. For, on the one hand, the very existence and proliferation of such movements, giving rise to ever new, fluid, relatively independent elites that are in close contact with groups of rank-and-file citizens and serve as a mouthpiece to their concerns attests to the openness of Western democracy to public participation in politics. The acceptance and implementation of their demands attests to the responsiveness of the governing elite to voices from the public, which is of the very essence of democracy.

Yet there are frequently large numbers of people who have diametrically opposed views to those promulgated by the movements and their leaders. Thus, the voice of the protesters frequently overrides the voice of their opponents, who may well be in the majority. These opponents may be no less concerned about the same issues. But since (for whatever reason) they prefer not to organize, to generate their own leaders, and to engage in protest, they may be practically disenfranchised.

It may be argued that they, too, have the democratic right to organize and make themselves heard through protest movements. But, by the same token, they also have the equally democratic right not to organize, and to have their preferences mediated through the institutionalized, electoral, democratic process. Yet protest movements may well detract from this right or obviate it. One of the most democratic forms of public participation is thus also one of the most nondemocratic forms of participation. The responsiveness of the governing elite to the leaders of such movements, their supporters, and sympathizers, also spells its non-responsiveness to other—and possibly larger—sections of the community.

Further, this chapter gives illustrative support for the thesis that because of this contradiction the rules that govern the relations between elites in a democracy are frequently ambiguous and contentious: perhaps in part because of the above mentioned contradiction, Western democracies and their governing elites have not devised clear guidelines for dealing with social movements and their elites. Because of the principle of freedom of speech and of organization their activities cannot be forbidden. In fact, they have come to be not only an accepted but an expected component of political life in the West. But in dealing with their demands the governing elite cannot follow clear-cut democratic rules: if it rejects those demands—it is accused of undemocratic rigidity, of lack of responsiveness to citizens' concerns. If it accepts those demands and gives in to them, it is accused of spinelessness, of surrendering to the blackmail of rowdy minorities, of undemocratic disregard of the wishes of the majority.

Finally, this chapter gives illustrative support to the argument that because of this relative independence of elites, the contradiction and the unclear rules, it is a common practice for the governing elite to cope with other elites through strategies for the consolidation of power derived from its control of state resources, including those that involve manipulation and corruption. It will be shown that this conception well fits the response of Western governing elites to social-protest movements, much of which can be subsumed under the heading of manipulation (though not necessarily under the heading of corruption).

In a way, the governing elite is practically forced into responding to the counter-elites and the social movements they represent through manipulation. For social-protest movements confront the governing elite with an additional dilemma. The rejection of such movements, their elites, and their demands, may well lead to even more widespread dissent, hostility and even rebellion, and thus jeopardize the governing elite's own power. Their acceptance and incorporation into the governing elite's own structure, platforms, and policies may well lead to the movements' elites taking over. It, too, may thus jeopardize the governing elite's power.

Hence the widespread pattern of the governing elite responding to social-protest elites and movements through manipulative strategies which are hereby referred to as "the absorption of protest." They consist basically of attempts to curb the movements through negative sanctions (such as restrictive legislation) or of attempts to placate the movements and thus elicit their support for the governing elite, or at least their acquiescence, through positive inducements. I would argue (although I cannot provide quantitative proof for this) that the strategies of governing elites with respect to the recent social–protest movements have been most prominently those that employ positive sanctions or inducements, rather than negative sanctions or curbs. These involve granting the movements' leaders, their supporters, or both, some benefits derived from the state resources. This may involve some changes in policies in response to the movements' demands. Such changes are introduced, however, without allowing the movements and their elites to cause major upheavals in existing benefit and reward structures, upheavals which might have threatened the governing elite's own established bases of power.

These devices can be regarded as manipulation even though they are usually applied quite openly (indeed, sometimes their very essence lies in the openness with which they are applied). This is so because the purpose of these devices, that of dissipating the movements' threat to the governing elite's power is—as a rule—not publicly admitted. Indeed, it is a moot point whether all members of the governing elite themselves are fully aware of this purpose. Hence, these devices may be classified as semi-overt by the previously proposed classificatory scheme.

In what follows it will be illustrated that while the devices which form part of these (advertent or inadvertent) strategies for the absorption of protest take on a variety of forms, they generally fall into the interrelated categories of symbolic, power, and material devices (or various combinations thereof) and they may be classified in the framework of the previously presented model as seen in figure 7.1. But first a few words must be said about the background of social-protest movements in Western democracies.

Background: Recent Social-Protest Movements in Western Societies

Following Bottomore (1979, p.41), a social-protest movement is here defined as a relatively unorganized collective endeavor to promote (or resist) social change, engaging in relatively uninstitutionalized or "direct" modes of

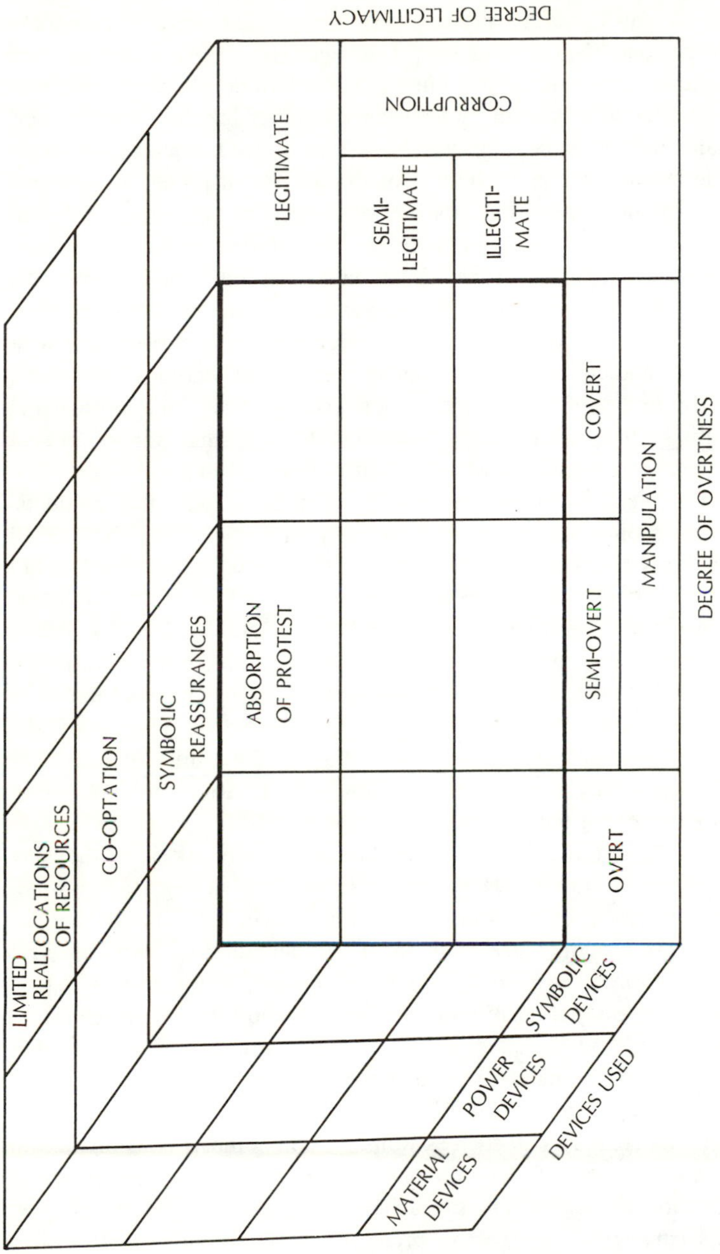

Figure 7.1. Example of Manipulation: The Absorption of Protest

action. This as distinct from other political endeavors—such as pressure groups—which may also aim at promoting or preventing change, but are more fully structured, and engage in more institutionalized modes of action.

Social-protest movements are not unique to Western democracies. Previous and other societies have known millenarian and other religious movements, slave, peasant, and other popular rebellions and, indeed, social movement-initiated revolutions. But in Western democracies social-protest movements have become far more pervasive: they have undergone unprecedented proliferation both in their own numbers and in the numbers of their members, supporters and sympathizers. Such movements have multiplied all over the Western world, especially from the 1960s onwards. In the previous decade it was widely believed that the West was experiencing growing contentment with rising prosperity and consequently a stage of the "end of ideology" (see e.g., Bell, 1961). But in the 1960s not only political establishments but political and social scientists, too, were caught unawares by a rising tide of protest activities, expressing massive discontent with the social order.

The leading element in this upheaval, of course, was the Students' Movement, interconnected with the New Left Movement, which rejected existing structures and demanded not only a restructuring of universities, but also, a (vaguely defined) restructuring of the entire social order. The Students' Movement was also interrelated with the Civil Rights and Black Power Movements, demanding an end to the discrimination against blacks in the United States, the Anti-Vietnam-War Movement, and the Women's Liberation Movement, demanding socioeconomic equality for women. Besides voicing their own demands these movements also voiced a common demand for participatory democracy, for increased citizens' participation in the decision-making processes of all public institutions (Desai, 1985).

The peak of these movements was reached in 1968, marked by the May Revolt of students in France. Thereafter, these movements began to subside. Their decline, however, was not followed by quiescence, but rather by an even greater proliferation of movements in the 1970s and 1980s. Thus, in West Germany alone, there have recently been an estimated 38,000 citizens' action groups, backed by two to three million members, supporters and sympathizers (Mushaben, 1985). And the situation is not much different in several other Western countries. Nedelman (1984) has noted the great variety of movements that have recently appeared on the Western scene. This variety refers first to the issues and demands raised, such as women's and homosexuals' liberation; a more equitable treatment for certain national, ethnic or racial groups; a halt to the production of nuclear energy; a halt to nuclear armaments or even unilateral disarmament; peace; active protection of the environment; greater citizens' participation or grass-roots democracy; demands for tax cuts; a stop to abortions, to consumer rip-offs, and a variety of other demands.

The variety also refers to the types of activities through which the demands are being voiced. Since the 1960s these activities have included marches, demonstrations, and rallies, sit-ins, teach-ins, camp-ins, and various "happenings" in public places, sometimes shading over into acts of civil disobedience, or even violence. In the 1970s and 1980s these types of activities have proliferated even further; at times they have been carried out in conjunction with more institutionalized types of action (such as signing of petitions and lobbying). But the movements' main thrust has remained in the great proliferation of their protest activities. "Moreover, these different types of movements very often act in parallel or co-operate temporarily" (Nedelman, 1984, p. 1033), so much so, that according to some jesters it is not unusual, these days, to come upon an all-purpose protest: bring your own food and cause.

The Absorption of Protest

Researchers agree that there are great difficulties in gauging the response of governing elites to protest movements and in measuring the movements' actual impact on social policies and social structures. For if actions or changes occur *following* the movements' pressures, it is difficult to demonstrate that they have occurred *because* of these pressures. With this reservation in mind it must be added that most researchers still conclude, on the basis of their studies, that there has in fact been some real influence of movements on policy outcomes, and that there have thus been some tangible responses by Western establishments to the movements and their leaders. For reasons explained before, these are here conceptualized as the absorption of protest, and are presented in the framework of our classificatory scheme as symbolic, power, material, or combined devices.

As is the case with other strategies, the devices of the absorption of protest, too, usually have various aspects to them, such that the awarding of symbolic resources, for instance, also entails the awarding of material and power benefits, and vice versa. In other words, the strategies, or devices, for the absorption of protest do not usually appear in actual reality in the form of one of the model's "pure" categories alone. They will still be classified as falling into one of those categories if they have an especially prominent symbolic, power, or material component. But when two, or all three, components are about equally prominent in them, they will be classified as "combined" devices for the absorption of protest.

1. Symbolic Devices

Recently, symbolic devices have come most prominently as symbolic reassurances to the movements and their leaders. Such reassurances may take the form of public statements made by political leaders in support of the movements' causes and demands, or in support of the groups the movements represent. A good example (out of a myriad of others) would be statements made by Australian political leaders in support of Australian Aborigines and their demands. This group of black Australians has long protested against its treatment by white Australians, but has stepped up its protest on the occasion of the bicentenary of white settlement in Australia, in 1988. Thus, Aborigines held a special day of protest on 26 January 1988, the 200th anniversary of the landing of the first fleet of white settlers. On this day some 20,000 Aborigines from all over Australia gathered and staged a protest march in Sydney. On the same day, the Australian Prime Minister, Bob Hawke, released an Australia-day message which included the following statement:

> On December 10, 1987, the Minister for Aboriginal Affairs, Gerry Hand, delivered in the parliament the policy statement entitled Foundations for the Future. I believe that was a landmark for the Australian Aboriginal people, a landmark for all the Australian people. It acknowledges the descendants of the Aboriginal people of Australia as the prior occupiers and original owners of this land. It acknowledges the dispossession of their land by subsequent European occupation.... It acknowledges the deep disadvantages and deprivations the Aborigines have thereby suffered—and continue to suffer. And it pledges the Australian Government and the Australian people to an earnest and continuing effort of rectification and reconciliation. (*The Australian*, 26 January 1988, p. 15).

It is not difficult to perceive that statements such as these are designed (amongst other things) not only to reassure the activists of a protest movement, but also to reassure those members of the public who might otherwise be inclined to join the protest.

Apart from soothing statements, symbolic reassurances frequently take the form of some actions in favor of the movements, which have prominently (though not necessarily only) symbolic value. For instance, they may take the form of public announcements or other symbolic indications to the effect that the issues and demands brought up by the movement are being studied and are under active consideration. This might find expression, for instance, through the establishment (and the publicity surrounding the establishment) of commissions of inquiry to investigate the movements' complaints and demands, and the subsequent publication of their reports.

Examples of this practice from the United States include the President's Commission on the Status of Women and its report *Women in America* (1963); the President's Task Force on Women's Rights and Responsibilities and its report *A Matter of Simple Justice* (1970); the U.S. Commission on Civil Rights and its periodic reports (e.g., 1970, 1973, 1975, 1978) and the Report of the President's Commission on Campus Unrest (1970). Further examples include the Royal Commission on Environmental Pollution in Britain, which submitted its tenth report in 1984, and the Equal Opportunities Commission in Britain which has been publishing periodic reports as well. Finally, examples of this kind include responding to the Women's Movement, the Civil Rights Movement, the Peace Movement, and the Environmental Movement through the establishment at universities of units for Women's Studies, Black Studies, Peace Studies, and Environmental Studies, respectively.

Symbolic devices for the absorption of protest may also take the form of public announcements or other signals to indicate that steps are being taken to resolve or alleviate the problems or to meet the protestors' demands. A case in point, would be the introduction, in legislatures, of bills on matters of concern to women. According to Costain and Costain (1985) most bills introduced in the U.S. Congress, for instance, constitute symbolic acts by legislators, designed to express sympathy for the causes promoted by particular groups of people, without those legislators committing themselves to spending the time and effort that would be necessary to get the bills passed. Consequently, only a small proportion of bills introduced actually become laws. The authors' analysis shows that members of Congress did, in fact, apply this measure to the Women's Movement: during the years in which the movement was most active, the number of bills on women's issues introduced into Congress soared.

2. Power Devices

The most prominent of these devices is also known as co-optation. It entails the movements' incorporation into existing power structures, while leaving those structures basically unchanged. As Philip Selznick in his now-classical study *TVA and the Grassroots* (1949) has clarified long ago, there are different grades of co-optation: some involve the granting of real power, others involve the granting of merely potential power, or even only a semblance of power to the co-opted. Moreover, there are various gradations of—and in between—the two, and they are not always easily distinguishable. Here, they are all subsumed under the heading of co-optation as long as they involve the incorporation of outsiders into existing power structures, without those outsiders being allowed to take over the structures. It is argued that this is, in fact, the manner in which the elites of protest movements frequently have been handled in Western democracies.

In the case of such elites and their movements in Western democracies co-optation may assume several concrete forms. It may take the form of the movements' leaders or potential leaders and supporters being incorporated into existing power structures. It may also take the form of the movements' demands being incorporated into the platforms, agendas and policies of existing power structures. This, too, gives the movements a certain share, or a potential share in power, for instance by making it possible for them to put their initiatives before the public at the ballot box. Yet this is generally done without making it possible for the movements and their leaders to take over, and mold the structures to suit their own preferences.

Either of these forms of co-optation can take place through incorporation into previously existing bodies. Alternatively, it can take place through allowing the movements to create new bodies which are then absorbed into the overall, existing establishments. These cross-cutting possibilites are summarized in table 7.1 below.

Table 7.1. Co-optation of Social-Protest Movements

	Incorporation of Personalities	Incorporation of Demands
Direct Incorporation into Existing Structures	1	2
Acceptance of New, Movement–Created Structures as Part of the Overall Political Establishment	3	4

Cases in point for 1 and 2 would be the incorporation of movements' leaders and potential supporters, or their demands, into governmental structures, possibly via the creation of special subunits to accommodate the movements' personalities and demands. Other cases in point would be the incorporation of movements' personalities into existing political parties and the incorporation of the movements' demands into those parties' platforms. Cases in point for 3 and 4 would be the movements creating their own political parties, or instigating the creation of new political parties. These parties, which incorporate the movements' leaders and adopt the movements' demands as major planks in their programs, are then accepted within the established electoral systems of Western democracies.

A comparative analysis of the fate and fortunes of different movements in different Western countries shows that (with some exceptions) there is something akin to a trade-off between different forms of co-optation: where the tendency has been to emphasize 1 and 2, there has also been a tendency to de-emphasize 3 and 4 and vice versa. In other words, where movements' leaders and demands have been successful in penetrating preexisting power structures, they have not tended to form their own political parties, or have not been greatly successful in these endeavors. By contrast, where existing power structures have been relatively closed to movements' activists and demands, the movements have been more successful in setting up their own separate parties or fielding separate, independent candidates, which have then participated in elections (see Harmel, 1985; Bürklin, 1985; Müller-Rommel, 1985b).[1]

A prominent example of co-optation type 1 and 2 is the establishment's reactions to the Civil Rights and Black Power movements in the United States. These movements led to acts and amendments abolishing measures that had previously hindered the voting registration of blacks in the South. Especially successful from this viewpoint was the Voting Rights Act of 1965. For instance, in Mississippi, beforehand, only 6.8 percent of voting age blacks were registered to vote. That proportion has subsequently grown to 70 percent and in 1980 almost 60 percent of them actually voted (Berns, 1984, ch. 17). Pursuant to the surge of blacks' rights' movements, and the growth of blacks' voting participation, blacks also began to be incorporated into the political elites of the existing parties. Thus, by 1966, 90 blacks had been elected to state legislatures and municipal offices—many in the South (Carter, 1973, p. 69). Since then, major Southern cities have had black mayors, and recently there have been almost 2,000 black elected officials in the six states of the deep South (Berns, 1984, p. 282).

Furthermore, the War on Poverty program initiated by the Johnson administration was (at least partly) a response to the demands of these movements. A new agency, the Office of Economic Opportunity, was created and put in charge of the program. Besides the goal of bettering the condition of the poor, the agency also adopted as one of its major aims the co-optation of the more active personalities amongst the poor and the blacks. This was to be achieved by eliciting their "maximum feasible participation" in the War on Poverty program, even though the eventual success of this endeavor was rather meagre.

With respect to the Women's Movement this type of co-optation was evident by a gradual, limited, but nonetheless perceptible growth in the proportion of women in politics. For instance, following the Feminist Movement's assertion that "A woman's place is in the House—and also in the Senate" there has, in fact, been a certain, though limited incorporation of women in the legislatures of several Western countries. For instance, in 1980–81, in the West German Bundestag 8.8 percent of representatives, and in the Austrian Nationalrat 9.8 percent of representatives were women (see, e.g., Etzioni-Halevy and Illy, 1986). Women have also been elected in greater numbers to various other public offices. For instance, in 1975 there were 566 women mayors in the United States; by 1982, the number had grown to 1,670 (U.S. Bureau of the Census, *Statistical Abstract of the United States*, 1986, p. 253).

Additionally, there has been a tendency for special agencies, dealing with women's issues, to be set up as part of existing governmental structures.

Examples include the Women's Bureau and the Office of the Status of Women as part of the public service in Australia. Women have also been appointed to various senior positions in government and other public bodies, in particular (but by no means only), to staff the agencies concerned with women's issues. Finally, equality of opportunities for women was adopted as part of the platforms of established parties in different Western countries. Concomitantly, no separate blacks' or women's parties have gained representation in Congress or in Western parliaments respectively.

The trade-off between different forms of co-optation is especially evident with respect to the recent environmental, anti-nuclear and peace movements. In France, for instance, the established parties have not been accessible to the demands of anti-nuclear and environmentalist movements, and these movements have also met with indifference or even hostility from the executive authorities. But, on the other hand, the ecological candidate in the presidential election of 1981 received almost 4 percent of the vote on the first ballot. And two ecological parties, participating in the 1984 European election, together won 6.7 percent of the vote (Kitschelt, 1985).

In the United States, the closest equivalent to an ecology party, the Citizens' Party, has not become very significant. At the same time, extensive provisions have been made for citizens' involvement in the enforcement and monitoring of environmental laws and programs (Desai, 1985). In 1970, the Environmental Protection Agency was set up, and at times environmental and anti-nuclear activists have also been able to strengthen their positions in the executive. Thus, during the Carter administration, anti-nuclear activists were appointed to high-ranking positions of this and other energy and environmental agencies.

No peace parties have gained representation in Congress. But, on the other hand, the leadership of the American Peace Movement has been interconnected with the leadership of the left wing of the Democratic Party. In addition, in the late 1970s, the Anti-nuclear Movement succeeded in placing anti-nuclear referenda on the ballot in a number of states. This action, and the favorable public response to it, sensitized legislators to the issue. Possibly as a response, more members of Congress, regardless of party affiliation, have adopted anti-nuclear positions (Kitschelt, 1985).

In Sweden, the Ecological Party failed to receive 2 percent of the vote in the *Rijkstag* election of 1982, and has remained well below the 4 percent threshold needed for representation in parliament. Possibly, however, this is because there have been two parties that were able to absorb environmentalist and anti-nuclear demands into their own platforms: the Communist Party and the Peasants' Party—later the Center-Party. Since the 1950s this latter party has been advocating anti-technological and environmental values, and in 1973 it became the first established party to adopt a formal decision against nuclear energy. But, significantly, once in government, this party was not able to maintain its strict opposition to nuclear energy and was obliged to make some compromises (Nedelman, 1984; Kitschelt, 1985). In Norway and Denmark too, left–wing liberal parties have taken over the issues of the environmentalist and peace movements (Müller-Rommel, 1985a and b).

In Britain there is an Ecology Party, and the Communist Party has adopted anti-nuclear and environmental issues. But neither the Ecology nor the Communist Parties have gained representation in parliament. Concomitantly—and no doubt partly as a response to various movements such as the Campaign for Nuclear Disarmament (CND), European Nuclear Disarmament (END), and the Greenham Common's Women—the Labour Party, at a recent conference, adopted a policy of unilateral nuclear disarmament that was also against the stationing of American nuclear missiles in Britain (even though its leadership later partly reneged on this decision). A recent annual conference of what was then the Liberal Party also voted in favor of unilateral nuclear disarmament, although this stance was not favored by the party's leadership and by its Social Democratic partners to what was then the Alliance. As a result, the recently formed Liberal and Social Democrats have adopted a rather unclear policy on nuclear disarmament.

In West Germany, various groups rejecting the ecological, social, and peace policies pursued by the government and the established parties, have been brought together in the Greens Movement, which came into being in the late 1970s. At first the established parties, including the Social Democratic Party (SDP), decided against absorbing the movement into its own ranks and policies. So the Greens Movement became institutionalized to some extent by transforming itself into a political party, and since 1979, it has been able to win more than 5 percent of the vote in most state elections. It also managed to gain representation in the *Bundestag*: in the 1983 federal election it obtained 5.6 percent of the vote and in the 1987 election, 8.3 percent of the vote. In recent years, however, the SDP had changed its strategy, adopting some of the movement's demands as part of its own platform.

All in all, then, the recent social movements have had some visible political achievements. But these achievements have also been visibly limited and have not led to any real takeovers of existing power structures: although their numbers in politics increased, neither women as a group, nor blacks, have become major political power holders. Although some of the peace and environmental movements' leaders were absorbed into existing political establishments, nowhere did they actually become a major component of those establishments.

3. Material Devices

Material Devices entail some limited changes in the allocation of material resources in response to the movements' demands, while the basic patterns of resource allocation persist as before, or else continue to change in the direction in which they were heading before the movements came upon the scene. There is, of course, no generally accepted yardstick to indicate where a limited change ends and a fundamental change begins. But two criteria have been used here: first, wherever changes in the allocation of resources have occurred they have not measured up to the movements' demands. Second, where disadvantaged groups have been involved, the changes in the allocation of resources have not abolished those disadvantages, and have not put the disadvantaged on an equal footing with the rest of society.

Thus, the Civil Rights and Black Power movements in the United States helped bring about a number of federal measures designed to better housing, education and job opportunities for blacks. They also helped to increase enrollments in welfare programs. Yet, when we look at the distribution of resources between blacks and whites in the United States, we see that no basic changes in it, or in its trends, have occurred since the respective movements presented their demands.

While the proportion of people living in poverty[2] in the United States declined in the 1960s, this was because of overall growing prosperity at the time and not because of the deliberate programs to fight poverty, which turned out to be no more than "a drop in the Ghetto." This is evidenced by the fact that after the economic downturn of the 1970s, the proportion of people living in poverty grew once again. Moreover, while the proportion of blacks living in poverty has declined from 56 percent in 1959 to about 34 percent in 1984, it was, and has continued to be, disproportionately high: since 1959, it has continued to be about three times that of whites. And the differential in earnings between blacks and whites has remained more or less constant as well: the median income of black families as a percentage of white families was about 54 percent in 1950, and about 58 percent in 1984 (U.S. Bureau of the Census, *Statistical Abstract of the United States*, 1986, Tables no. 751,752,767).

Some tangible achievements in resource allocation have also been evident for the Women's Movement. For example, according to Costain and Costain (1985), who conducted a detailed study of legislation on women's issues in the United States, such achievements were clearly evident there. In the periods in which social movements were mobilized in support of women's rights, Congress reacted not only through the symbolic gestures of the introduction of bills—referred to before. It also reacted through the passage of actual laws aimed at improving the socioeconomic position of women such as the Equal Pay Act of 1963, and the Intergovernmental Employment Act of 1970. Further achievements of the Women's Movement include the Affirmative Action Regulations of 1965 and 1972.

In Australia, to cite another example, there is an elaborate quasi-judicial system of wage fixing, the decisions of which had long set women's pay at a lower rate than men's pay. But pressures from the Feminist Movement and the unions in the 1960s helped pave the way for two equal-pay decisions in 1969 and 1972. These decisions, together with parallel decisions in the States, have effectively eliminated direct wage discrimination against women (Jones, 1983, 1984).

Despite all this, men have maintained significant advantages over women in the distribution of material resources. While greater proportions of women have entered the labor market, and while legislative and policy measures have led to a certain narrowing of earning differentials between men and women, men still enjoy substantially higher incomes than women in practically all Western countries. For instance, in the United States earning differentials between men and women have changed, but not substantially, since the 1930s. In 1939 the median income of women was 60.8 percent of that of men; in 1970 the figure stood at 59.2 and by 1985 it had risen to 68. (England and McCloughlin, 1979; U.S. Bureau of the Census, *Statistical Abstract of the United States*, 1987, p. 402, Table 680).

In part, earning differentials are due to differences in education, skills and long-term attachment to work. Conceivably, therefore, the lack of more substantial changes in earning differentials between men and women in the United States might be due to greater numbers of unskilled, less work-committed women having entered the labor market. But a nationwide study by Corcoran and Duncan (1979) found that the earning advantages enjoyed by men over women in the United States could not be explained primarily by men's superior qualifications and greater long-term attachment to work. And Cook (1975) reported that even when adjustments were made for various factors, such as schooling and age, the gap between men and women's earnings in America was still a substantial 12–37 percent. And this situation has not changed substantially since then: an 1987 report of the Bureau of the Census shows that 35 to 40 percent of the earnings gap between men and women could not be explained by "tangible" factors, such as education, work experience, and work interruptions.

In Britain, the overall earning differentials between men and women did not decrease between 1935 and 1960. Although the differentials decreased for women in the professions, in management, and in skilled work, they increased in semi-skilled and unskilled work. All in all, women's median income from wages and salaries as a percentage of that of men was 56 in 1935 and 54 in 1960 (Meehan, 1985, p. 7). Some, but no great changes were evident from 1970 onwards: the median gross weekly earnings of women in manual occupations as a percentage of that of men in similar occupations was 57 in 1970 and 61.8 in 1984. The median gross weekly earnings of women in non-manual occupations was 51.8 percent of that of their male counterparts in 1970; in 1984, the figure stood at 60.1 percent (Great Britain Central Statistical Office, *Social Trends* 1986, p.78).

Australia, for one, is a country in which a substantial decrease in the earning gap between men and women has taken place in recent years, as can be seen from table 7.2. However, a persistently high degree of occupational segregation between men and women, with women tending to gravitate towards the lower paying occupations, and lower paying jobs in similar professions, makes it questionable whether equal pay decisions can lead to any further increase in the lifetime incomes that women earn compared with men (Jones, op.cit.).

Generally, the situation is not much different in other Western countries. Thus, according to a cross-national survey (OECD, 1980) cited by Scott (1984, p. 26), there is a persistent and basically similar segregation in the job market between men and women in the twenty–four most industrialized Western countries. And according to Scott (p. 29), the average women's pay for full–time, year-round work, is 77 percent of men's pay in the Netherlands, 74 percent in Austria, 73 percent in France, and 66 percent in Canada.

TABLE 7.2. Full-Year, Full-Time Workers: Female/Male Mean Income Ratios (by occupation)

	1968–69	1978–79	1981–82
Occupation			
Professional and administrative, etc.	0.48	0.69	0.75
Clerical	0.59	0.71	0.72
Sales	0.51	0.60	0.66
Tradesmen, production-process workers, etc.	0.52	0.70	0.71
Service, sport, and recreation	0.57	0.67	0.69

Source: *Social Indicators—Australia*, 1984, p. 184.

The environmental movements also have had some tangible achievements in the form of legislation and regulations for environmental control. Thus, in Britain, from 1969 to 1981 twenty–five acts of parliament, regulations, and orders have been brought down, including the Control of Pollution Act of 1974, which established new mechanisms for monitoring and controlling pollution (Dix, 1981). In the United States, too, a whole network of federal laws (such as the Clean Water Act of 1972), supported by volumes of regulations for environmental protection have eventuated, and similar laws and regulations have been brought into effect in most other Western countries (Elseworth, 1984). These laws and regulations have had a certain effect on the manner in which funds (material resources) are distributed: many billions of dollars have been allocated for the control of pollution. In the United States, alone, for instance, since the Clean Water Act of 1972, governments and business have spent some $300 billion to combat pollution (Holgate, 1979, Ch.8; *The New York Times*, 26 August 1987, p. A 22). Other countries, though more limited in their capabilities, have been following suit.

But here, too, only limited changes in preexisting trends have so far been evident; indeed, pollution of the environment has continued to make considerable progress. Although some actions have been taken in various countries to scale down or limit pollution, and although billions of dollars have been poured into these activities, so far they have not been greatly effective. This is evident from the fact that widespread atmospheric pollution (also known as acid rain) has recently become a major threat to the environment in many Western countries. As the director of the United Nations Environmental Program (cited by Elseworth, 1984, p.12) stated: "In North Europe, Canada and the North-Eastern United States, the rain is turning rivers, lakes and ponds acidic, killing fish and decimating other wild life . . . it may even threaten human health, mainly by contaminating drinking water."

And the situation does not seem to have greatly improved since then. With respect to the United States, for instance, *The New York Times* in a leading article (see above) writes on the one hand that industrial pollution has been considerably reduced and, moreover, without the Clean Water Act, pollution would have been far worse. Yet it adds that despite all this, in 1987, the Eastern Seaboard of the United States was approaching a pollution-induced ecological crisis. And the same was evident in 1988 as well.

Various Western countries now seem to be taking more drastic (though belated) action with respect to pollution. But so far the results have not been greatly visible. And even if they do become manifest they can no longer be seen as a reaction to environmental movements: opinion polls all over the Western world now consistently show that the population at large has become greatly concerned with the aggravating threat of the contamination of the environment.

Anti-nuclear movements in Western countries seem to have fared somewhat better: some of them have been rewarded by scaled down nuclear programs. For instance, of the four countries studied by Kitschelt (1985), Sweden and the United States were the most tolerant to the anti-nuclear movements, and also had a steady or declining number of nuclear plants during the preceding decade. West Germany's nuclear program was also, if only temporarily, restrained and only France's program has continued to grow rapidly in recent years.

Despite differences between various movements and various Western countries, overall it may be said that the recent social movements do seem to have led to some changes in the allocation of material resources in their respective areas of activity. But the changes, where they occurred, seem to have been of a limited nature, by the criteria set out before; they certainly have not satisfied the movements' demands, or resulted in equality between previously advantaged and disadvantaged groups in society.

Mostly, to be sure, the social protest movements of recent years have not been aimed at abolishing inequities and inequalities to begin with. Thus, as various observers have noted, the most recent movements have been concentrating in particular on "post-materialist" issues, and they have been lukewarm at best with respect to the socialist parties' and labor unions' more traditional concerns, such as income distribution, welfare policies, and working conditions. But this is not true for all movements. The Civil Rights Movement in the United States, for one, has been concerned with the disadvantages (including the material disadvantages) suffered by blacks; the Women's Movement has been concerned with the disadvantages (including the material disadvantages) of women. Yet blacks have not come to equal whites in America, and women have not come to equal men in the material resources that accrue to them from their work, in practically all Western societies.

4. Combined Devices

Apart from responses that may be categorized as primarily symbolic, power, or material devices, social-protest movements have also met with combined responses, that have followed basically the same logic. For instance, the peace movements have elicited responses which have had combined (though limited) material and power implications. Those concern (besides physical human existence) material well-being (connected with the level of expenditure on armaments) and military might. The Anti-Vietnam War movement in the United States has had some important effects: according to a study by Small (1984), most observers agree that it contributed substantially to the pressures that eventually produced the U.S. withdrawal from Vietnam. The response to the more recent peace movements is more difficult to assess. Up until recently they have not fared well: the nuclear arms race—to which they object—has still been forging ahead at full speed. This is exemplified by the fact that in 1970 the United States had 7,502 deliverable nuclear warheads (as against the Soviet Union's 5,662); in 1986 the United States had 12,846 such warheads (the Soviet Union had 10,176) (International Institute for Strategic Studies, *The Military Balance* 1970–71, p. 89; 1986–87, p. 222–23).[3] Recently, of course, an accord between the United States and the Soviet Union on the elimination of intermediate ballistic missiles in Europe has come into force. But it is difficult to gauge how much influence the peace movements may have had on this event.

The Counter-Reactions of the Movements' Elites

In the face of the governing elite's strategies of the absorption of protest, the counter-elites of social movements face a problem: just as they themselves (and the movements they head) pose a dilemma for the governing elite, so the reaction of the governing elite poses a dilemma for them. This dilemma is the same as that faced by the elites of the social movements of the nineteenth and early twentieth century (as analyzed before): if the elites of social movements let themselves be co-opted, they usually gain personal rewards, and can usually show evidence of some achievements to their supporters. But at the same time they are forced to compromise, to settle for much less than they initially demanded. If they refuse to be co-opted, and maintain their ideological purity and their organizational separateness, they not only miss out on personal rewards, but their tangible achievements are usually just as limited, or even smaller.

Consequently, some recent counter-elites have preferred (or have been forced to) maintain their uninstitutionalized character, for instance the Greenham Common women in Britain. More frequent, however, have been the cases where elites or potential elites of protest movements have preferred (or succeeded) in entering the establishment, for instance by accepting governmental positions, or through the electoral process, as illustrated before. Some protest groups' activists have endeavored, and succeeded, in gaining the best of both worlds: they have maintained their rage, as it were, or have remained anti-establishment, even as part of the establishment.

Thus, the Greens in West Germany—now a legitimate parliamentary party— have recently given evidence of their anti-establishment tendencies by joining forces with 200 local protest groups in a boycott campaign against Germany's first census in seventeen years. They have argued that the census is a form of state control of citizens and violates privacy laws. Hence they have urged people to refuse to heed the government's call to sit down and be counted.

Whether they remain outsiders to the establishment or become insiders, or succeed in being insiders and outsiders (that is outside-insiders, or inside-outsiders) at one and the same time, may make some difference at a specific time, at a specific place. But overall the results are still similar; some, but mostly limited achievements for the movements they lead.

Conclusion

This chapter has illustrated how the relative autonomy of elites, the contradiction and the unclear rules thus created, lead the governing elites in Western democracies to cope with other elites through various strategies of control, including, most prominently, inducements applied in less than fully overt and straightforward ways, that is, through manipulation. The strategies here illustrated, employed in relation to protest movements and their elites, have also been referred to as the absorption of protest. They include first and foremost symbolic reassurances, the co-optation of the movements or their leaders into existing power structures, and limited acceptance of some of the movements' demands for the reallocation of material resources. Yet no basic restructuring of power has occurred, and where the movements' demands have involved the reallocation of resources in favor of disadvantaged groups, this reallocation has not gone as far as to put those groups on a par with the more advantaged groups in society.

This is not to say that the overall balance of forces and resources created by this interchange has been deliberately masterminded by anyone in particular, or by the governing elite in general. It is more likely the result of a wide variety of factors, including (besides unclear rules) the pressures applied to the governing elite by protest movements and their elites, the counter pressures of other interest groups and their elites, the interests of the governing elite itself, and a variety of other factors over which neither the governing elites nor the protest movements and their elites have had control.

But, whatever the constellation of factors that have shaped them, it is still noteworthy that the manipulative devices employed by the governing elite at the same time have also spelled certain achievements for the social-protest movements and their elites. While these achievements, where they occurred, have been of a limited nature, this is not to say that they have not been valuable, or that no real and substantial changes may result from them. For, in the first place, it is possible that without the movements' intervention the situation against which they have protested might have deteriorated even further. In the second place, even small achievements may be incremental and add up to more significant achievements in the long run. Indeed, as will be argued below, the processes whereby noninstitutionalized elites are able to gain (even limited) achievements in favor of their supporters—before or in the process of themselves being co-opted into the establishment—are major, processes through which democracies change, and through which they may become more democratic and equitable democracies in the future.

Notes

1. However, electoral laws also are important for the success or otherwise of new parties (see Harmel, 1985).
2. As defined in U.S. official statistics.
3. This statement, of course, is intended neither as a comparison of the nuclear strength of the two superpowers, nor as an evaluation of each side's "contribution" to the continuing arms race. It is merely intended as a shorthand documentation of the escalation of nuclear armaments.

8

Elite Power and Corruption: Some Case Studies

Introduction

Elites of social-protest movements differ from other elites in Western democracies not only in that (unless co-opted) they are not institutionalized, but also in that they therefore have fewer connections with the institutionalized, or established elites. When the established elites alone are looked at, it is clear that there are multiple connections within and between them. Such connections are created by the relatively small numbers of their members, those members' frequently similar social backgrounds, the informal social relations that often develop among them, the fact that they interact in their official capacities within the system, and the fact that they all share a common inside knowledge of the machinations of this system. This may well be conducive to political manipulation and corruption, as expressed in the popular saying "You've got to know the ropes to pull the strings." But it is not the foremost factor in creating or sustaining those practices.

More important, from this viewpoint, are the resources which prop up the elites' power. It is here that the precarious balance of power, or the relative autonomy of elites in a democracy comes in: relative autonomy is not complete autonomy, and even in a democracy elites may be partly dependent on each other. So, not only may it be the case that the other elites are dependent on some resources of which the governing political elite has control, and vice versa, but there also may be a partial, mutual dependence between various other elites and fractions of elites. In a democracy, I have argued, this is a major factor in hampering elites from countering (especially the governing elite's) manipulation and corruption. Hence it is also a major factor in helping sustain such manipulation and corruption as, once more, well expressed in the popular saying "You've got to go along to get along."

Since the relations between elites are so precariously balanced, the balance may be tipped either way: at times the relative autonomy of elites is wider, at times it is more limited. Because there is always a jockeying for position between elites, the outcomes vary from one democratic country to another, from one subsystem to another, and from one elite, or elite-faction, to another, in the same country. And so it is also with respect to the rules governing the relations between elites: because of the contradiction of democracy there always is some ambivalence and contentiousness in those rules, but their degree differs between and even within democratic countries.

Hence the argument that the actual degree of manipulation and corruption depends on the way in which the balance is tipped: relatively less independent elites, more ambiguous and contentious rules, are likely to encourage manipulation and corruption (of the type here canvassed); relatively more independent elites, and clearer and more consensual rules, are likely to limit it. This chapter provides illustrative support for this argument.

Ideally, it would have been desirable to substantiate this argument through a large number of illustrations from a great number of democratic countries. However, the illustrative substantiation is based on my own study, and the intensive (rather than extensive) research methods involved make this impracticable. Hence, it has been necessary to confine the analysis to two case studies of political manipulation and corruption. The cases selected for study are the recent corruption scandals in New York City, U.S.A., and the recent allocation of funds to educational institutions by political criteria in Israel.

The set of practices to be illustrated through those case studies is the handing out of material resources to individual institutions, enterprises or persons, in return for political support or in return for resources which may be used to amass political support. It will be recalled that these practices have been classified as a semi-overt or covert type of manipulation, and as a semi-legitimate or illegitimate type of corruption, depending on the directness of the exchange. In terms of our three-dimensional model this set of practices has been presented in figure 6.4. Although these practices may be subsumed under the headings of both manipulation and corruption, their most prominent feature is that they are corrupt by the norms of the elites in the societies in which they have occurred, as the analysis will show. Hence they are here regarded chiefly as case studies of political corruption.

It will be shown that with respect to these practices the relationship between the governing political elite on the one hand and the economic, bureaucratic, and judicial elites on the other hand is of strategic importance. It will further be shown that relations between different components of the same elites are relevant as well: apart from unclear rules, the interdependence between various parts of the political elite or the bureaucratic elite may also help fertilize the soil on which the exchange of benefits for political support is likely to flourish.

The phenomena under study—manipulation and corruption, the degree of elite dependence/independence on each other's resources, and the clarity vs. ambiguity of rules—are obviously not amenable to conventional research methods such as surveys via questionnaires or large scale interviewing and quantitative analysis of the data. In most cases it also is not possible to gather the information through participant observation. Hence, besides previous analyses, one must rely on documents (particularly on reports of commissions of inquiry, comptrollers' reports and the like) and/or on key informants who, on the basis of personal trust, may be convinced to divulge the sensitive information concerned. These were, in fact, the methods of study here employed.

The New York City Corruption Scandals

These scandals had two related components. First, they involved senior city officials giving favored treatment to some people and firms in return for bribes and kickbacks, and/or subjecting the representatives of such firms to extortion. Second, they involved senior, elected, city officials obtaining major campaign fund contributions from people and firms doing business with the city, and/or having matters pending before them. The first type of corruption is not our chief area of interest and, had it occurred on its own, it would not have been dealt with. But it is briefly mentioned because it was inextricably interlinked with the second type of corruption—which is our main concern—and some of the same personalities were entangled in both.

The first type of corruption was clearly deemed unacceptable, or illegitimate, as several of the principals involved were indicted and subsequently convicted for the offenses involved. The second type of practice, though widely condemned, was neither illegal nor totally unacceptable. The officials who received campaign contributions from people who had business pending before them, or before bodies with which they were connected, were not brought to trial and convicted, nor were they required to resign because of these practices. Accordingly, they may be classified as falling in the "twilight zone" between the legitimate and illegitimate, by the standards of the participants.

While the officials concerned attempted to conceal bribery and kickbacks, with respect to campaign contributions their attempt was not so much to conceal the practice as such, but rather the possible link (which could never be conclusively proved) between such contributions and favored treatment from the city government. Accordingly, these latter occurrences may be seen as semi-overt. They may be presented on our model of manipulation and corruption as shown in figure 8.1.

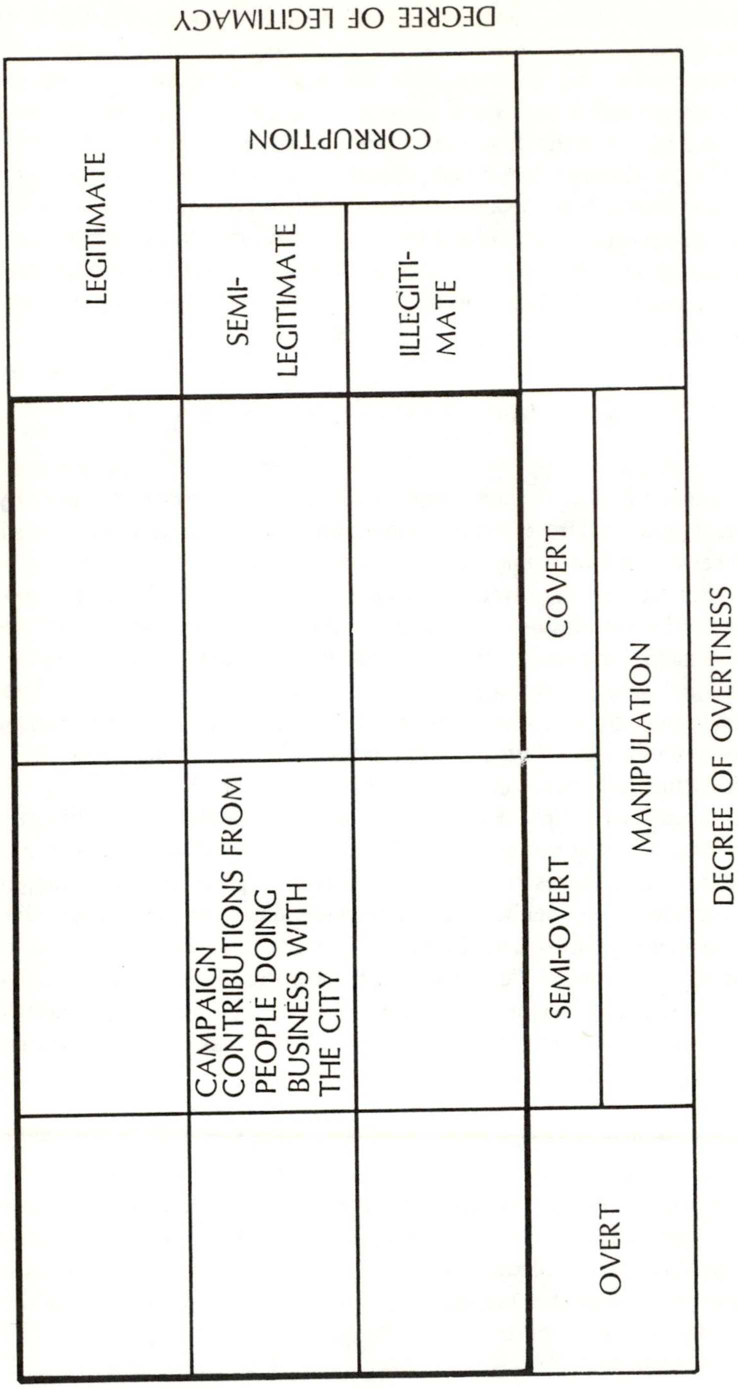

DEGREE OF LEGITIMACY
LEGITIMATE
CORRUPTION
SEMI-LEGITIMATE
ILLEGITI-MATE
CAMPAIGN CONTRIBUTIONS FROM PEOPLE DOING BUSINESS WITH THE CITY
COVERT
SEMI-OVERT
OVERT
MANIPULATION
DEGREE OF OVERTNESS

Figure 8.1. Example of Corruption Through Material Devices: The New York City Corruption Scandals

A Brief Account

The corruption scandals that were at the center of public attention in 1986–87 were preceded by recent, similar, though less widely publicized, occurrences. One example, reported by Gross and Kraus (1982), concerns New York City's Industrial and Commercial Incentives Board. The board, set up in 1976, was designed to provide subsidies when tax incentives were required to attract construction. Ten major contributors to the campaign fund of a senior official received more than $64 million from the board. Other corporations, financing senior officials' election campaigns, were benefiting from similar largesse.

In 1986 the corruption scandals have focused on five municipal agencies[1] and in particular on the city's transport agencies. The most extensive were two scandals at the city's Parking Violations Bureau (PVB). The first involved noncompetitive contracts entered into by the PVB with collection agencies, including Datacom, the Bureau's largest contractor for the collection of overdue parking fines. The Sovern Report (1986b) asserts that the percentage rate established to compensate Datacom for the collection of fines was excessive, and that, in addition, the collection agencies had pocketed fines. Some senior PVB officials had engaged in extortion and received large-scale bribes over several years in return for these parking violations fine contracts. They were subsequently indicted on extortion, racketeering and fraud charges. One of New York's boroughs' (Democratic) presidents, who in the meantime had committed suicide, was named as an additional conspirator. Reportedly, some collection agencies that had received favored treatment from the PVB had made substantial contributions to his election campaign fund.

The second scandal centered on PVB's $22.7 million contract with Citisource for the purchase of a hand-held computer to manage parking violation information, and for data processing on a sole-source basis. According to the Sovern Report (1986b), the system had been manipulated to push through the selection of Citisource. The chairman of one of New York's Democratic Party committees was a major shareholder and stock owner in Citisource. He (besides several officials) was subsequently convicted of federal corruption charges.

The third major scandal centered on the New York City Taxi and Limousine Commission (TLC). The Trager Report (1986) cited substantial evidence that an individual at TLC had schemed to exploit the mayor's directive calling for a new meter for taxis, for his and his friends' benefit. He had aided friends, who had formed a company for this purpose, to produce a taximeter mandated by the TLC. By discouraging competition, he had aimed to guarantee the major share of the market for this company. In addition, more than $2 million of the funds of a credit union were fraudulently misappropriated to finance this company's operations.

The investigation also found that a TLC-initiated program for testing diesel-powered taxicabs was exploited to funnel 123 taxi medallions to an owner of a New York City taxi fleet, and thereby to generate large-scale profits for him. The bogus nature of the diesel program was revealed by the fact that fewer than 25 percent of the taxicabs utilized in the program were actually tested, and by the fact that twenty-three more medallions than authorized by the TLC were actually issued, even after the expiration date of the program had passed and all testing had ceased.

In addition, the Trager Commission reported that two friends of a senior TLC official and an "undisclosed principal" had acquired 75 percent ownership of a car service corporation. The commission obtained evidence that the TLC official was actually that "undisclosed principal," a fact he had denied under oath. Finally, the commission found that the TLC had been subject to influence by certain groups within the taxi industry, such as the Metropolitan Taxi Board of Trade (the trade association of taxi fleet owners) which has often been represented legally by a Democratic political leader. As a consequence, these groups had received favored treatment as compared to all other cabs. Following these revelations, the TLC official resigned and was later indicted on federal fraud and bribery charges. Further instances of corruption were revealed later on, but are not at the focus of the present analysis.

The Corruption Scandals and Relations Among Elites

The Governing Political Elite and the Economic Elite

The relations between the governing political elite and the economic or capitalist elite are of great importance for corruption, for each of these elites has resources that, at times, the other may need to consolidate its own elite position, whether in legitimate, or in non-legitimate ways. But there are differences in these respects, as noted before. The New York City corruption scandals show that when the two elites become intermeshed, or when their need for each other's resources becomes overwhelming, this fertilizes the soil on which corruption is likely to flourish.

One of the major conclusions reached by the Sovern Report (1986a) was that the corruption scandals were rife with conflicts of interest, whereby political leaders, who were also major city officials, were simultaneously involved in private enterprise, particularly in firms doing business with the city. Thus, one politician was a principal in a firm doing business with the PVB; he also represented private clients who pursued contracts with the city, including (as noted) an association of taxi fleet owners having dealings with the TLC. Also, a TLC official was a principal in a transportation corporation having dealings with the TLC. The Sovern Commission (1986d, p. 23), also expressed concern at the currently "legal but disturbing practice" for legislators and members of their staffs to represent private clients before city government agencies. Couched in the terms of our analysis, these conflicts of interest involve the intermeshing, or overlap, of the political and the economic or capitalist elites because some people form part of both elites, or because of close, personal, financial ties between members of those two elites.

Related to this was the interdependence between the capitalist elite and the political elite created by the New York City contract system in conjunction with the American electoral system. The New York City government has charge of large scale resources, some of which it hands out to business people, in the form of contracts for various goods and services. The Sovern Commission (1986b) noted that in order to fulfill its many functions the New York City government awarded 100,000 contracts each year, and for the fiscal year of 1985, for instance, total city contract spending had amounted to no less than $5,177 billion. To become eligible for such contracts business people had to have their own resources to begin with and of those, of course, they were free to dispose as they saw fit. But many of them were nonetheless dependent on city contracts for profits, to keep themselves in business and thus maintain their resources, or to amass further resources.

There was also a certain dependence of the political elite on the economic, or capitalist elite, created by the fact that election campaigns required extraordinary amounts of money and these could frequently be acquired through contributions from business people, particularly from those obtaining, or hoping to obtain, contracts from the city. This opened the door for a fruitful, though non-legitimate, exchange between the two elites.

According to some observers (cf. Scanlon, 1986), the reforms of previous years had rid the system of strong party machines which had supposedly caused this sort of corruption. They were also supposed to have cleared up corruption. But they did not have this effect, for party organizations, by helping candidates fund their election campaigns, had given them a certain independence from capitalists. Hence their decline had had an unexpected side effect: candidates for elections now had to acquire and pay for everything they needed for their campaigns, including offices, equipment, and consultants. They thus became more dependent on private sponsors, particularly business people. Also, campaigns now took place chiefly through the media, and candidates had to fund their own exorbitant media time. Hence the funds candidates required and spent skyrocketed and, in the words of the Sovern Report (1986d, p. 5), had reached "obscene levels." Thus politicians came to be greatly beholden to their financiers.

This mutual dependence between business people and politicians was expressed in the manner in which city contracts were allocated. Noncompetitive contracts (the contracts chiefly involved in the corruption scandals) have to be ratified by the New York Board of Estimate (BOE). The board is composed of five borough presidents, the mayor, the city comptroller, and the president of the city council. According to the Sovern Report (1986b), members of the BOE were frequently recipients of massive campaign contributions from the very business people to whom they allotted contracts.

Similarly, a study by Democratic State Senator for Manhattan Franz Leichter (1986) found that most of the people making large-scale contributions (of millions of dollars) to the campaign funds of members of the BOE had business with the city. Of the 200 largest contributors 60 percent had business with the city. Of the 50 largest contributors 70 percent had business with the city. Of the five largest contributors 100 percent had business with the city. Significantly, the bribery scandals involved at least one board member, and the investigation of two others. Senator Leichter also claimed that one board member had obtained campaign contributions from companies involved in the PVB corruption scandals, although contributions tainted by the corruption scandals were later returned.

The Governing Political Elite and the Bureaucratic Elite

The relations between the governing political elite and the bureaucratic elite are also of prime importance for the manner in which the former can use public (state) resources to consolidate its power and particularly for its ability or otherwise to do so in corrupt ways. For while the utilization of public resources for the consolidation of power is designed to serve the interests of the political elite, frequently it must be executed by, with the active participation of, or with the connivance of, the bureaucratic elite: top or middle ranking civil servants at either the central government, the state, or the municipal level.

In Western democracies the bureaucratic elite is never completely dependent, nor completely independent from the political elite (and vice versa). But where the two elites are clearly distinct from each other, where, in addition, the appointment and advancement of bureaucrats takes place without political intervention, on the basis of relatively objective, nonpolitical-partisan criteria, the bureaucratic elite has relatively more independence from the political elite; hence its activities are not likely to be guided overwhelmingly by the party political criteria that concern politicians. In cases such as these, bureaucrats still allocate public, state resources, but they are not likely to have an interest in doing so in corrupt ways, to further the interests of politicians.

Where, however, the bureaucratic elite is more closely intermeshed with the political elite or dominated by it, where there is involvement of politicians in the appointment of bureaucrats, where the latter then owe their allegiance to their political appointers and depend on them for advancement, they are more likely to be willing to engage in activities that promote those appointers' interests, even if these activities are not aboveboard. They also are less likely to stick their necks out and oppose or expose such activities when politicians themselves engage in them.

It is, therefore, of importance that the corruption scandals also revealed close interconnections between the governing political elite and the bureaucratic elite within the New York City government. In the past, the entire American bureaucracy—on the federal, state, and municipal levels—was highly party-politicized. This has been explained by the fact that America was born with governmental institutions imported from sixteenth—and seventeenth—century Britain which, at the time, knew no clear separation between politics and administration. And while these institutions were being gradually changed in their home country, they took root, and some of their aspects were maintained to a marked degree, and much longer, in America (Huntington, 1968).

Even so, on the federal level, successive civil service reforms have led to a situation where today only a top layer of officials in the administration are party-political appointees (the president can make only some 4,000 appointments) and career bureaucrats have a certain, if only a partial, independence from straightforward political intervention (although this independence has decreased somewhat under the Reagan administration—see e.g. Goldenberg, 1984). But on the municipal level party-politicization of the bureaucracy has remained much more pervasive.

In New York City, in particular, the municipal bureaucracy has remained highly party-politicized. Thus, according to unpublished data supplied by the New York City Municipal Reference and Research Center, in 1983 the city of New York had 200,267 employees (not including those of independent agencies). Of these only approximately 80 percent were employed on the basis of objective merit criteria, as ascertained by competitive examinations. The rest were not so appointed, either because their positions were exempt from examinations (6 percent) or because they held provisional or temporary positions (14 percent).

By the testimony of an official of the Department of Investigation, such provisional appointments opened the door for political considerations to enter into the appointment process. Formally, provisional positions were not to be held in excess of nine months. But in fact, according to an audit carried out by Arthur Levitt, and cited in an article in *The Village Voice* (23 June 1980, supplied to me by an official of the Municipal Reference and Research Center from the center's own Archives) most of the provisionals held their positions for much longer periods. An informant also testified that after 1983 the center was no longer furnished with data on provisional and exempt appointments in the city administration, because the administration did not wish these figures to be known.

Further, according to the article cited, the city administration at the time had added many thousands of provisionals to the city payroll over and above those employed by its predecessor; a large number of these had connections with the Democratic Party, including also with Democratic politicians' campaign workers. This claim was corroborated and supplemented by an article in the *Daily News* (17 March 1986, also supplied by the official of the Municipal Reference and Research Center from the center's Archives). According to this article, the city administration had illegally increased the number of nonpermanent civil service workers on the city payroll by more than 13,000 since 1978. Of these, 1,400 had been referred to city agencies by mayoral aides in City Hall, and, in addition, the administration was in the process of exempting hundreds of permanent jobs from the civil service regulations.

The officer of the Department of Investigation also explained that the possibilities for political considerations entering into the appointment process were open, especially in the roughly ten to fifteen thousand managerial positions in the city bureaucracy. According to the above cited article from the *Daily News*, in 1984, a Manhattan Supreme Court Judge ruled that the city had illegally delayed the holding of tests for 3,000 civil service managerial jobs for no less than eight years.

On top of all this, even appointments made ostensively on the basis of objective examinations have been open to political fiddling. Thus, according to the above informant, at times city officials with party sympathies may notify certain political organizations or clubs of vacancies in their agencies, and influence the intake in this manner. Or else, job specifications may be drafted in such a way that they fit one's political cronies. At times, officials who have objected to this, for instance in the Parking Violations Bureau, have been fired.

Even the competitive examinations themselves are not foolproof in eliminating political considerations from the appointment process. Employers are free to select any one of the three highest scorers on an examination, which still leaves employers some discretion in the selection procedure. And, according to Rich (1982, p. 64), the personnel department could delay an appointment until an outside candidate lost interest, and an insider could then be appointed. The availability of this option thus supported the sponsorship system of appointments and promotions.

Our main concern is obviously with the positions at the top of the hierarchy, and it is these positions which have been most closely connected with the corruption scandals. Indeed, at that level some administrative and political functions have been intermeshed, and this has had clear implications for corruption.

Thus, at least four of New York's political leaders were involved in the city agencies' corruption scandals: at the time of writing three had been named in indictments and one had been put on trial. This has been due to the close bureaucratic-political connections, in particular to the overlap between the Board of Estimate and the Democratic Party committees. The previously mentioned study by Leichter (1986, p. 2) dwells on these interconnections. It states that some members of the board were also heads of Democratic organizations in their respective boroughs. Thus "persons with matters before the BOE can give either to the Board member or to the party organization he heads or is close to." In fact, people with matters pending before the board had made massive contributions to these organizations. And (one may add) who is to say where a "contribution" ends and a "bribe" begins?

In part, at least, the problem has stemmed from the fact that the Board of Estimate, which ratified contract allocations, was both an administrative and a political body at one and the same time. The Sovern Report (1986b) commented that this situation politicized the contracting process, which frequently involved political horse trading. This would not have been the case had politically independent, appointed officials been in charge of awarding contracts. The situation was further exacerbated by the fact that the Parking Violations Bureau, the site of the major corruption scandals, was also politicized. According to an official of the Justice Department (quoted in *The New York Times*, 25 January 1987, p.6), the PVB was the "preserve of the Democratic organization." It was thus dominated by the same political party, and the same political elite, which also dominated the BOE. Also, when the corruption scandals erupted, fifteen of the agency's twenty-three top jobs were held by provisional employees and six of these had close political ties to a former borough president.

The manner in which close relations between the governing political elite and the bureaucratic elite contributed to corruption was also evident at the Taxi and Limousine Commission. Prior to the creation of the TLC in 1971, rate and rule making for the taxi industry was the responsibility of the New York City Council and the mayor. But because of the unpopularity of fare increases, the council and the mayor had wished to distance themselves from the process. Consequently, the TLC was formed, ostensibly as an "independent" organization, and put in charge of rate making and regulation. However, the Trager Commission (1986, p.5) reported that "in fact, this salutary, if unrealistic result has not been achieved. Instead, the TLC, which in political reality is as accountable to the mayor as mayoral agencies, performs a masque of independence."

The lack of the TLC's political independence was also evident in its structure and the manner in which the senior appointments within it were made. The commission, established by the City Council, had a full-time, salaried chairman, and eight part-time unsalaried commissioners. Five commissioners were appointed by the council, while the chairman and three commissioners were designated by the mayor. Thus, all were political appointees, and since they were all appointed by closely related political bodies and personalities, it is not surprising that, as the Trager Report (1986, p.5) found, the TLC's eight part-time commissioners provided only "negligible oversight of its operations and habitually followed the Chairman's lead in casting their votes." Consequently, the TLC lacked "internal controls to guard against the corrupt or abusive exercise of authority by its chairman."

Relations within the Bureaucratic Elite

The corruption at the TLC, or at least its perpetuation, may also be partly explained by the lack of independence of a part of the bureaucratic elite, its inspectorate, from another part of the bureaucratic elite, the heads of the bodies it was supposed to inspect. The city's inspector general (IG) system was established in the 1970s, and further developed by Mayor Koch in 1978. Its purpose was to prevent and eliminate corruption in the city government. It consisted of twenty-eight inspectors general who oversaw the activities in city agencies and in several quasi-independent authorities. At the time of the corruption scandals and up to the end of 1986, inspectors general reported to both the commissioner of investigation and the chairman of the agency they oversaw, who controlled their budgets, salaries, and promotions.

An internal report of the city's Department of Investigation (Conboy and Hutchinson, 1986) placed the blame for failure to prevent or uncover the municipal corruption scandals in part on this deficient structure. In relation to this, the Department of Investigation conducted a review of the IG system. A randomly selected sample of 160 case files, in one–third of representative IG offices, was examined in depth by the department's senior attorneys. A significant number of poorly investigated or uninvestigated criminal complaints was discovered. Of the 160 investigations evaluated, 46 percent were rated as poor or very poor. In some cases no investigations were made at all. Many cases were allowed to languish and were not brought to a timely conclusion. There was also a failure to develop self-initiated criminal investigations. In conclusion, "the survey indicated the overall inadequacy of the criminal investigative effort" (Conboy and Hutchinson, 1986, p.20).

The report of the Department of Investigation explained this poor record by the inspector general dependency system: IGs who were supposed to detect and prevent corruption were under the control of, and dependent for their resources on, the very agencies they were supposed to monitor, and on the agency heads, who might have been implicated by their investigations. A number of IGs interviewed by the department stated their belief that they had been sidetracked by their respective agencies: their offices had been assigned service, support, and disciplinary functions, to prevent them from initiating investigative probes. Often IGs would accept or even seek such assignments as a means of providing contributions that would be appreciated by the agencies to which they were assigned, and thus increase the stature of their offices within those agencies. Under the system of dual reporting the commissioner of investigation lacked the authority to prevent the IG offices from fulfilling such functions.

This dependency pattern was eminently evident in agencies connected with the corruption scandals. An IG responsible for one of the agencies involved, when questioned by the Department of Investigation about his lack of aggressiveness in pursuing irregularities in it, explained this by the fact that "the Agency head, butters the bread" (Conboy and Hutchinson, 1986, p.3). The Trager Commission (1986) found that the effectiveness of the IG in another agency was diminished by his lack of independence, in particular by his desire to obtain a senior administrative position in that agency, and by the fact that not only his budget, staffing, and salary but his promotion prospects, too, had been controlled by it. When called upon to inquire into irregularities in one of this agency's programs, he subsequently reported to the Department of Investigation that there were none. His investigation, however, had consisted of an interview with a senior agency official. And not only did the IG fail to conduct a proper investigation, he also disregarded evidence of improprieties that were surfacing at the time. Later on he was promoted to a senior position in that agency. In more general terms the Trager report (1986, p.66) concluded that in the absence of "independence and the objectivity it engenders, inspectors general are at risk of being co-opted by those whose conduct they oversee."

Mayor Koch subsequently announced a major overhaul of the inspector general system, whereby the final control of inspectors general would now be held by the city commissioner of investigation and IGs would be barred from accepting promotions from agencies for which they had been responsible—heretofore a common practice. At the time of this study it was still too early to tell how effective the new system would prove to be in counteracting corruption.

The Governing Political Elite and the Judicial Elite

Also, albeit of somewhat lesser importance in this respect, are the relations between the governing political elite and the judicial elite. Judges are wielders of power: through their application, interpretation, and (to some extent) shaping of the law they have a substantial say in the allocation of resources.

When independent from the political elite they are better placed to exert their influence on the allocation of resources so as to countervail that elite's power, manipulation, and corruption. Of course, the autonomy or otherwise of the judicial elite from the political elite is always relative, or partial. In no Western-style democracy is the judicial elite completely integrated with, or dependent on the political elite, and nowhere does it enjoy total autonomy from it. But there are differences of degree in this respect among different democratic countries, and even within them.

By comparison to other democratic countries, in the United States political influence in the selection of judges and, consequently, the dependence of the judicial elite on the governing political elite has been uncommonly pervasive. The explanation given for this is similar to that provided for the long-time though only partly persisting party-political character of the American bureaucracy: initially, the judicial practices in America were the ones imported from sixteenth– and seventeenth–century Britain, before various state and governmental institutions had been clearly separated from party politics, and this fused pattern was then maintained in America (Huntington, 1968).

Thus, in the United States, federal judges have customarily been appointed, while on the state and municipal level a large proportion of judges have been elected. In both the appointment and election of judges political influence has been prominent. In the case of appointed judgeships politicians have at times been directly or indirectly involved in the appointment process. In the case of elected judgeships, the slates have been drawn up by party leaders whose decisions are frequently merely ratified by voters. All this has tended to entangle judges in political ties that have seriously undermined their independence. Most states have now introduced reforms to overcome some of these weaknesses. And it is certainly not the case that the American judiciary has been totally subjugated by politics. But, all in all, political ties of the judicial elite in the United States are still stronger than they are in most other Western democracies (see, e.g., Abraham, 1980).

Such relatively close relations between the political and the judicial elites have been clearly evident in New York, and the recent corruption scandals have also been influenced by them. The judiciary in the state of New York is mostly elective[2] and judicial elections are part of the party-political process. Judges are nominated in judicial nominating conventions, managed by political parties; voters usually do not know the candidates and tend to vote for their parties' nominees. Judges are then elected in partisan elections following campaigns which—like other election campaigns—are dependent on contributions. The Sovern Report (1986d) found that campaign contributions for judicial elections gave an appearance of impropriety, reinforced by the interdependence between the courts and the political parties.

An official of the Department of Investigation stated that the nomination process and, thus, to a large extent, the selection of (ostensibly elected) judges, was controlled by party-political leaders, namely the (presently Democratic) borough presidents, who handed out judgeships as a reward for support of the Democratic organization. According to the Sovern Report (1986d), this control was demonstrated in 1983, when a Democratic leader effectively ousted two highly regarded Supreme Court justices by declining to support their reelection and endorsing two other candidates. And since he resigned—following his conviction—his handpicked successor would now select New York's judges. More recently, the Sovern Commission reports, similar influence was wielded by the Republican chairman of a county. He refused to cross-endorse highly respected, non-Republican sitting judges, who then had to run on the Democratic line and lost.

According to the official of the Department of Investigation, where there are appointments of judges in New York City, these have not been clearly divorced from politics either. Appointments were made on the basis of recommendations from a merit selection committee chaired by a prominent legal personality. But whenever there was more than one recommended candidate to choose from, and one of them had the backing of a borough president, or of people influential in the city administration, that candidate would be given preference over the other candidates. Naturally, people influential in the city administration were also the ones whose judgment was trusted by the decision makers. Thus it was "sticky" to distinguish between objective and political considerations in cases such as these.

The Sovern Commission further points out that, consequent to the close interdependence between the judiciary and political parties, these parties could depend on jobs in the judicial system for their supporters. It was also revealed that people obtaining appointments from the courts had to pay kickbacks to party officials. Thus, a federal inquiry into guardianship appointments in Queens courts focused on assignments awarded to several lawyers, who all said they had given kickbacks to a Queens Democratic Party official.

Similarly, the official from the Department of Investigation informed me that a well-known personality had been appointed as executive of an estate because he had political connections with a former Queens borough politician with whom the judge—who awarded the position—was also related, through that politician having been influential in the awarding of judgeships in Queens. Also in the same vein, FBI officials inquiring into the corruption cases announced that they saw a link between payoffs at the PVB and corruption amongst Queens Judges and Queens Democratic Party officials. They further announced that the central figure connecting the cases was a Queens lawyer, who also had connections to a company that collected fines for the PVB. Also involved in payoff schemes was a justice of the State Supreme Court who had connections with a Queens politician.

And these are probably merely some of the many intricate judicial-political ties that have surfaced with the investigations into New York City's corruption scandals. Evidently not all of New York's judges are inextricably interlinked with politics, and not all judges with political links are inevitably corrupt. But the introduction of politics into the judiciary seems to be especially conducive to corruption.

Relatively Independent Elites

At the same time there have also been some relatively independent elites, or parts of elites, in New York City, and these have given evidence of their independence in the corruption scandals. Indeed, it is due to that independence that the corruption scandals came to light, were publicized, and at least some of the culprits of the more blatant types of corruption were brought to trial and convicted.

As the officer of the Department of Investigation explained, corruption cases had a good chance of coming to light in New York City because there were several agencies that competed with each other in uncovering corruption, and whose resources would be enhanced when they were instrumental in doing so. Thus, besides the Department of Investigation, there were five local prosecutors, two federal prosecutors, a special state prosecutor, as well as the attorney general's office; they all competed with each other in revealing and developing corruption cases, and were all in a race with each other to bring the cases to court, and profit from the publicity attached to such achievements.

The local prosecutors were elected in the boroughs and some of them had close political connections with party organizations and leaders. But others were divorced from politics. The Brooklyn prosecutor, for instance, had succeeded in beating the machine candidate at the election, and had gained her political independence in this way. Moreover, even prosecutors with political ties had a motivation to uncover corruption, as their professional reputations, and hence their ability to attract the best attorneys to their offices, and thus further enhance their reputations and careers, depended on their successes in this domain.

The same goes for the attorney general. Thus, in August 1987, the United States attorney in Manhattan, W. Giuliani, was planning to become a candidate for the United States Senate. On this occasion, Mayor Koch told reporters at City Hall, that the attorney would be an awesome contender. "He has a first rate reputation . . . And his success to date in rooting out corruption has made him a household name" (*The New York Times*, 27 August 1987).

No less aggressive in the race to reveal and publicize corruption were investigative journalists who "generated" many of these cases and led to their subsequent investigation. They did so because corruption scandals created a good press and increased sales. In particular *The Village Voice* had built up a reputation of aggressiveness in the discovery and unveiling of political corruption in New York City.

Commissions of inquiry, too, have been drawn from relatively independent elites, particularly from academia. For instance, the Sovern Commission has been headed by the head of Columbia University Law School. These commissions of inquiry have given evidence of their independence by naming and castigating culprits, and some judges have shown independence by bringing down convictions of those actually involved in the more blatant forms of corruption, who have been brought to trial before them. But, overall, they did not have it in their power to eliminate corruption, which was also exacerbated by unclear rules pertaining to the relations between elites.

Unclear Rules

Such unclear rules were evident for instance in the area of conflict of interest, or the overlap and intermeshing of the governmental and the economic elites, as well as in the more general area of the relations between them. Thus, the Sovern Commission (1986a) found that although the city laws on conflict of interest were adequate, laws of the state of New York did not draw a clear line between acceptable and unacceptable conduct, and that they therefore were both unclear and unenforceable. The Sovern Commission (1986b) reached similar conclusions with respect to the laws and regulations relating to city procurement and contracts. The commission noted that the laws pertaining to such contracts were complex and difficult to access and the range of their applicability was not clear.

For instance, noted the commission, the city Charter provided that the principal method of contracting should be by competitive, sealed bidding. But such bidding was considered inappropriate for health and human services and for a variety of professional services, because the award would be affected by important considerations other than price, such as the bidders' qualifications and experience. Accordingly, noncompetitive contracts had amounted to 38 percent of total contract expenditure. Most recent contract-related corruption involved such noncompetitive contracts.

In addition, the Sovern Commission concluded, the obscurity and confused state of the more specific rules of doing business with the city contributed to the ability of the principals of the corruption scandals to manipulate them for their own ends. The commission (1986d, p.3) summarized its conclusions on this topic in the following words: "Corruption and abuses of trust . . . thrive in the confusion and opacity of procurement laws . . . that lack clarity, consistency and uniformity." Similarly, the Department of Investigation, in its review (Conboy and Hutchinson, 1986, p.1), concluded that dishonest politicians and officials had "profited from a contracting process that lacked uniformity [and] clarity in standards."

The Allocation of Funds to Educational Institutions in Israel

One type of corruption that has become pervasive in Israel in recent years concerns the allocation of funds to educational institutions by criteria of affiliation to political parties—the aim being that of increasing political support for those parties. Such allocations have been taken to task by the High Court of Justice, by the attorney general and (repeatedly) by the state comptroller—as being contrary to fair and proper governmental practices. Yet they have been made at the instigation and with the blessing of Israel's most senior politicians. Hence they have continued despite the strictures, and their perpetrators have not been prosecuted, convicted, or punished. They are accepted informally, even if they violate formal rules (Sharkansky, 1986). Thus they may be classified as falling into the "twilight zone" between the legitimate and the illegitimate, or as semi-legitimate.

The allocations were made on the basis of coalition agreements between the various parties and thus the fact that they occurred could not be concealed from the public. But the details of the arrangements, the identities of those who benefited from them, the fact that there were no proper criteria for the allocations and no proper controls on how the monies were spent, were initially concealed, and only some of the information came to light in the State Comptroller's reports. Accordingly, they may be classified as semi-overt, and placed into our classificatory scheme of manipulation and corruption as shown in figure 8.2.

A Brief Account

Israel has a long tradition of politicization in education. This tradition dates back to the pre-state era, in which education was divided into three major political "streams": the Labor Stream (affiliated with the Labor Movement), the General Stream (affiliated with various center-right wing political groups) and the religious stream (affiliated with religious parties). With the establishment of the State, in 1948, Prime Minister David Ben Gurion endeavored to abolish these streams, but he unified only the "Labor" and the "General" Streams, while the Religious Stream remained a separate entity. Religious education, in turn, was subdivided into "State-Religious Education" —

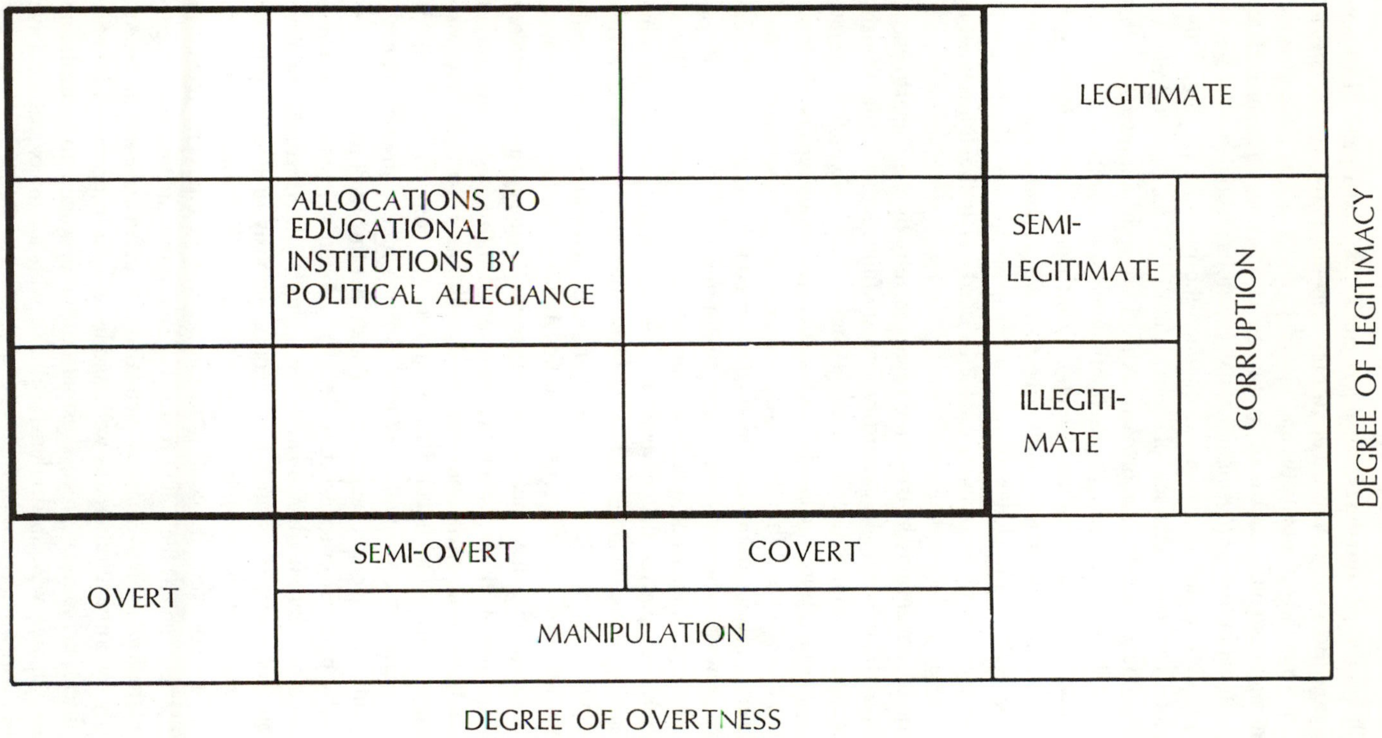

LEGITIMATE
SEMI-LEGITIMATE
ILLEGITI-MATE
CORRUPTION
DEGREE OF LEGITIMACY
ALLOCATIONS TO EDUCATIONAL INSTITUTIONS BY POLITICAL ALLEGIANCE
OVERT
SEMI-OVERT
COVERT
MANIPULATION
DEGREE OF OVERTNESS

Figure 8.2. Example of Corruption through Material Devices: Allocation of Funds to Educational Institutions in Israel

informally connected with the National Religious Party (NRP) and "Independent Religious Education" affiliated with the orthodox party *Agudat Israel*.[3]

In recent years the division between "General" and "Labor" education has crept in again through the back door, as it were. This has occurred through the fact that schools in the *Kibbutzim* and some vocational schools have been (at least informally) related to Labor. Also, when the majority of parents in a given school demand it, that school's curriculum is shaped so as to reflect a Labor ideological bent; the Labor parties then have a special interest in that school's well–being and prosperity. Schools in the settlements in the territories (the West Bank and the Golan Heights), for their part, have an ideological affinity with the religious parties and/or the right wing *Likud*,[4] which also has at least one college affiliated with it. A certain proportion of educational institutions are thus in one way or another, directly or indirectly, related to political parties.

Educational institutions in Israel are funded chiefly by the Department of Education. Religious educational institutions are funded also by the Department of Religious Affairs. In addition to the regular funding which is given to all educational institutions, some institutions receive allocations on the basis of coalition agreements. While Israel's difficult economic situation has forced it into severe cutbacks in the regular funding of education, political allocations have grown, particularly since 1981, and in recent years many millions of dollars have been distributed in this manner (see, e.g., Sharkansky, 1986).

Ostensibly, the parties that have been profiting most from this funding process have been the religious parties. For educational institutions receiving special funding on the basis of coalition agreements have been mostly institutions affiliated with the religious parties *Agudat Israel* and the National Religious Party, and they include kindergartens, primary and secondary schools, Institutes of Higher Religious Education (*Yeshivot*) and institutions of adult education. But institutions affiliated with other parties have also received their share: the Israel State Comptroller's Reports (1984, 1985) named a college connected with the *Likud* as being funded in this manner.

Also, some regular allocations to educational institutions have been influenced by political criteria. Thus, by the account of inside informants, educational institutions in the *Kibbutzim*, indirectly affiliated with Labor, have been favored in covert ways: they have been generously funded, despite the small numbers of their students. On top of this, allocations of funds to institutions not connected to education, but directly or indirectly related to political parties, such as the health funds (the largest of which is connected to Labor) and the *Kibbutz* movement as such (also connected to Labor) have been made partly by political criteria as well, and have been incorporated into the same political bargaining process as allocation of funds to educational institutions. In this way, institutions affiliated with all major parties have benefited in one way or another.

The state comptroller, in his previously mentioned reports (1984, 1985), documented the fact that despite a previous High Court of Justice verdict, and despite the attorney general's instructions to the government (of 1 December 1985) demanding the establishment of objective criteria for fund allocations (see below), both the Department of Education and the Department of Religious Affairs continued to make allocations to educational institutions by unclear criteria. Further, the state comptroller found that the departments did not follow orderly administrative procedures in making the allocations, had no proper inspection systems of institutions obtaining the special funds, and did not themselves vet, or insist on, proper financial reports from the institutions on how the monies were spent. When reports were submitted, their claims were not checked or verified by the departments.

The state comptroller's report (1984) further stated that even institutions belonging to the same political party did not obtain equal treatment: some secondary schools connected with the same party received no special funding; others did, depending on the factions within the party with which they were connected. Some institutions received special allocations from both the Department of Education and the Department of Religious Affairs, and there were no procedures to monitor such double-dipping. At times, grants made to institutions exceeded their requirements and the institutions invested the surplus funds on the stock exchange; at times the monies were given to general associations with which the individual institutions were affiliated, and in at least one case the association did not transfer the entire sums to the institutions for which they were designed.

In his subsequent report (1985), the state comptroller further stated that there were incongruencies between the numbers of students some institutions claimed to have enrolled and their actual student numbers; some students were listed simultaneously by different institutions; students who had transferred continued to be listed in their previous institutions. Yet, the Departments of Education and of Religious Affairs did not make effective examinations of the numbers of students actually attending, so that allocations for nonexisting, or nonattending students could be deleted. Inspections by the departments were rare, and in some cases 60 percent of the students for whom the institutions had claimed allocations were absent at the time of inspection. Nonetheless, no steps were taken to penalize such institutions. Especially large sums were given to two institutions which, in fact, were under one, single management; it was never clarified how these sums were spent.

Despite allocations based on coalition agreements being made in particular to religious institutions, the secretary general of the National Religious Party claimed that the educational institutions connected with his own party were shortchanged in comparison with other educational institutions. This was so, he argued, despite the fact that the educational institutions connected with the NRP had 22 percent of all student enrollments. It occurred because they no longer had a strong political backing: the NRP's bargaining power in the coalition had recently decreased, following its decline to about 5 percent of the popular vote in the then most recent elections.

Funding of Education and the Relations Among Elites

Relations Within the Governing Political Elite

As previously noted, in Western-style democracies the opposition is usually one of the major elites that countervail the power of the governing political elite and help to stem its attempts at manipulation and corruption. However, during the years in which allocation of funds to educational institutions by political criteria skyrocketed, Israel was governed by a broadly-based coalition government—in which all major political parties participated—and an opposition was effectively lacking. This broad coalition created a situation in which the leaderships of the major parties, while maintaining their organizational separateness, could all share in the bounty of the state-controlled material resources.

It is this collusion among disparate fractions of the political elite which bred the mutual generosity enshrined in the coalition agreements at the expense of the taxpayer. Had Israel been governed by a one-party or a narrow coalition government, the ruling party or parties' leaders could still have distributed benefits to the institutions connected with their parties. But since fewer parties would have been involved, the dimensions of the practice would necessarily have been more limited. Also, a strong opposition could have raised a furor which might have forced the governing parties to limit the practice.

Thus, the allocations had to be ratified by the Parliament's Finance Committee, in which all major parties are normally represented. Had there been an effective opposition, it could at least have attempted to block such payments when they came up before the committee, and generally put more obstacles in its way. As it is, the broad coalition and the collusion amongst party leaders forged thereby, ensured that they all obtained a share of the booty, were thereby placated, and opposition to the arrangements was effectively lacking.

According to key informants, in the Finance Committee the allocations were agreed on through inter-party horse-trading. Representatives of the various parties on the committee made it eminently clear to the representatives of the other political parties that unless grants to institutions connected with their own parties were made, grants to institutions (and not merely educational institutions) connected with those other parties would not be forthcoming either, or would be restricted. Since all parties had something to gain from the allocations, they were all ratified.

The Governing Political Elite and the Bureaucratic Elite

Although the grants for educational institutions are decided on by politicians, the actual allocations are made by civil servants, or bureaucrats. Hence it is of relevance that the Israeli bureaucracy has long been party-politicized (See, e.g., Etzioni-Halevy, 1985a). This has been explained by the fact that the formative period of Israel's governmental structure was mainly in the pre-state, or *Yishuv* era. But while, during this formative period, the country had been under British Mandatory rule, the Israeli government bureaucracy has not grown out of the British Mandatory government's administration. Rather, it is the outgrowth, and successor of the internally autonomous governmental authorities, built up by the Jewish community under British rule. These authorities have been party-politicized to their very roots.

This, in turn, has been explained by the fact that the political culture from which the *Yishuv's* founding fathers originated was the Russian-East European one, where politicization of the bureaucracy was accepted as normal, and in which no clear separation between politics and administration was known. And it is on this political culture that the founding fathers drew in devising the nation's budding governmental structure, which has therefore remained party-politicized (see, e.g., Etzioni-Halevy with Shapira, 1977).

In Israel, as in some other democratic countries, recently there have been attempts at bureaucratic reforms. But as Werner (1983) has correctly noted, nonetheless "internally, structures and behavior remained informal." And in recent years the bureaucracy has still been beset by political partisanship, and particularly by partisan appointments. Recently, for instance, the (*Likud*) Minister of Labor and Social Security has been taken to task in the press for making pervasive political appointments in his department (see, e.g., Ehrlich, 1987). Subsequently, Labor activists have compiled a list of 100 such appointments. The minister did not deny making them, but claimed there was nothing unusual in this, and that the same custom prevailed in other government departments as well.

Also, in his 1986 report, the state comptroller noted (and denigrated) appointments made on the basis of political allegiance in a public corporation affiliated with the Department of Housing, also under the auspices of a *Likud* minister. My own research into the Israel Broadcasting Authority (1987) (a semi-independent, but rather typical Israeli bureaucracy) has shown that party-political appointments reach down to the level of heads of units. So, all in all, bureaucratic-political appointments have still remained rampant in Israel.

This has been evident also in the area of education. Not only the educational institutions, but the Departments of Education and of Religious Affairs have been politicized as well: they have long been affiliated with the religious parties. However, the situation has been complicated by the fact that recently the Department of Education has come under the auspices of the Labor Party and a Labor minister. On taking over the department, he found it to be filled with his predecessor's NRP appointees—down to the level of heads of units and even below that. Those appointees have been the people who, in actual practice, have been in charge of making the allocations to educational institutions, or have been in key positions which enabled them to apply pressure to those who had been in charge of the allocations.

The new minister introduced a small group of his own party-faithfuls as his personal advisers. But besides having a soft spot for religious education himself, he was not able to shift the (tenured) NRP faithfuls from their key positions in the department. Upon the recent retirement of the department's director general, the minister appointed a man sympathetic to Labor to succeed him. The new director general has been attempting to introduce structural changes that would increase the power of Labor supporters at the expense of NRP supporters in the department. For instance, he succeeded in subordinating a unit headed by a religious supporter to a unit headed by a Labor faithful. But all in all, at the time of this study, he had not been able, as yet, to introduce major changes into the department's political power structure.

Moreover, because allocation of funds by political criteria has been so widely entrenched in Israel, and because the political elites are united in promoting it, even when bureaucrats attempt to oppose it, they are not successful in doing so. Thus, when grants are to be distributed to *Likud*–affiliated institutions, both NRP and Labor supporters amongst the department's bureaucrats attempt to stall and procrastinate. But then the ministers with whose party the institutions are affiliated complain to the minister of education (with whom they are connected through coalition agreements) and an instruction comes down from the minister to execute the payments promptly. Whether they like it or not, the civil servants are then forced to obey.

Relatively Independent Elites

In Israel, too, there have been some relatively more independent elites, and they have given evidence of this independence in dealing with the cases at hand. One of these has been the judiciary, which in Israel has been much more independent from politics than its counterpart in the United States. This is not to say that political or quasi-political considerations have never played a role in Israeli judicial appointments. But if such considerations have intruded, they have been low–key and subdued.

This may be explained by the fact that the Israeli Judiciary has been greatly influenced by the (politically relatively independent) British one. For while the pre-state Jewish Community under British Mandatory rule had been allowed to develop its own internally autonomous governmental structures, it had not been allowed to set up its own judiciary. The judicial functions were carried out by a court and legal system devised and run by the British Mandatory authorities themselves. This system and its traditions were then inherited, lock, stock, and barrel, by the state of Israel, although new staff had to be appointed and variations were subsequently introduced. Thus, two diverse and largely incongruous traditions were inherited and perpetuated by the state of Israel, which explains the dual pattern, combining a politicized and relatively less independent bureaucracy with a relatively nonpoliticized and more independent judiciary in Israel today. In the case at hand, this independence has been manifested in particular by the High Court of Justice, as further explained below.

Relatively independent elites have also included the attorney general at that time, and the state comptroller, as well as the elite of the media, that have done much to expose and criticize the allocation of educational funds by political criteria. But, as in New York City, the efforts of all these people were more successful in exposing the practice and castigating the perpetrators, than they were in preventing or eliminating it.

Unclear Rules

Up until a few years ago, there were no clear-cut rules on the criteria by which political allocations to educational institutions were to be made, and in practice the only criterion was the strength of the political pressures applied. In 1983, Parliament passed the following decisions:

- All allocations to educational institutions are to be made by clear-cut, objective criteria.

- The department concerned must keep full records of all allocations and supervise the use made of the sums distributed by it.

Consequently, the Department of Religious Affairs drew up some rules including the following:

- An institution must have at least 25 students (15 in development towns) enrolled in it before it becomes eligible for funding.

- Absence of 25 percent of the students when inspection is carried out will result in the discontinuation of funding.

However, according to the State Comptroller's Report (1985), these rules were not followed. In its verdict of 29 May 1984, the High Court of Justice declared that no payments to educational institutions should be made on the basis of coalition agreements, and that payments should be made solely in accordance with clear, objective criteria. This verdict, too, was not heeded, and monies continued to be distributed by political rather than by objective criteria.

In 1985 the Department of Education set up a departmental committee that was charged with drawing up clear-cut criteria for the allocation of funds to educational institutions. By August 1985 such criteria had, in fact, been drawn up, and they were subsequently ratified by the state attorney general. Nonetheless, as seen before, allocations of funds lacking clear, objective criteria continued to be made.

The most likely interpretation for this state of affairs is the following: first, political allocations to educational institutions lacking clear–cut, objective criteria of need and entitlement had become an established practice, and thus created a precedent or a well-entrenched tradition which could not be abolished offhand by simply drawing up such a set of formal criteria later on. This was the case, especially, as there were powerful vested interests in perpetuating this previous tradition. Second, Parliament, which passed the resolution calling for objective criteria in allocations, was the self-same one whose members were also in charge of drawing up the coalition agreements and pressuring the departments involved to execute payments by political, rather than by objective criteria. Parliament was thereby sending a conflicting message to the departments, which put them in a double bind. This conflicting message, coming in conjunction with powerful pressures based on entrenched political interests, thus led to the perpetuation of the practice.

Conclusion

This chapter has focused on two cases of political corruption involving the exchange of benefits for political support or for resources which (through election campaigns) could be converted into political support. It has been shown that in both cases this type of corruption was encouraged by relative interdependence between elites and fractions of elites, in particular by the relative dependence of certain central elites—the economic, bureaucratic, and some judicial elites—on the governing political elite, and by relative interdependence within the political elite and the bureaucratic elite, as well as by unclear rules pertaining to those relations.

With respect to the New York City corruption scandals it has been shown that the interdependence between politicians, business people, administrators and judges, and the unclear codes—in particular with respect to city contracts—have created an atmosphere in which people who do good things unto others may expect good things to be done unto them, even when this mutual generosity is in transgression of the law and of commonly accepted standards of behavior, or falls into the "twilight zone" of what is neither clearly condoned nor clearly condemned.

It may be concluded that the U.S. political system, which has put so much emphasis on the separation and independence of the federal legislature (Congress) from the federal executive (the presidency) has not put similar stress on the separation between and within other elites on the municipal level. In the case of New York City, it may be said that by providing for a relatively close, mutual dependence, or a cozy togetherness, where there might have been independence or even hostility, the system has fertilized the soil on which political corruption has flourished.

With respect to political allocations to educational institutions in Israel, it could be seen that the practice was encouraged by the relative interdependence of the various groups within the political elite (forged by the broadly based coalition government), and by the consequent effective absence of an independent opposition. It was also encouraged by the long-standing politicization of the bureaucracy and the consequent, relative dependence of the bureaucratic elite on the governing political elite. Third, it was encouraged by the interconnection between the two: because the political elite was drawn together by common interests and mutually beneficial coalition agreements, its strength vis-à-vis the bureaucratic elite was increased. Thereby, the dependence of the bureaucratic elite on the political elite was enhanced and its ability to counter corruption (even when it was motivated to do so) was underminded. Finally, it was encouraged by the conflicting messages concerning these allocations that emanated from the political establishment.

In both cases there were some relatively independent elites, or components of elites, that attempted to stem the tide of political corruption: officers of the Department of Investigation, the prosecutors, the attorney general and his staff, commissions of inquiry, and some of the judiciary in New York City, and the High Court of Justice, the then attorney general, and the state comptroller in Israel, as well as the media in both countries. Some of these elites' or elite people's reputations (a major symbolic resource) depended on their ability to publicly reveal such corruption, and create adverse publicity for it, and in this they were relatively successful. But the rules of conduct prescribing the behavior appropriate in these circumstances were unclear or ambiguous. Also, the balance of power seemed to be tipped in favor of the governing political elite, which has had an interest in the perpetuation of the practice, or in favor of elites that have had some dependence on the political elite. Hence, so far, the effect of the independent elites in countervailing the political corruption here analyzed has been conspicuously limited.

All in all, this chapter has provided illustrative support for the general contention that in democratic regimes the extent of political manipulation and corruption, their pervasiveness, or conversely their curbing and limitation, are directly connected to the relations among elites: where the various elites are relatively dependent for their resources on the governing political elite, and where there is also a general, relative interdependence between and within elites, manipulation and corruption are likely to be pervasive.

This conclusion also ties in with the previous analysis: the same point that has been illustrated in Chapter 4 (especially with respect to the bureaucratic elite) in an historical perspective, has now been illustrated—though from the negative side—in a contemporary setting: the relative autonomy of elites, even nonelected elites—although it creates a contradiction—is of prime importance for the elimination and prevention of corrupt political practices, that obviate the democratic process, and thus for the institutionalization and actual realization in practice of proper democratic procedures. This relative autonomy of elites—despite the dilemma it creates—is important from another viewpoint as well: it sustains the ability of democratic regimes to generate change; this will be explained in the next, and final chapter.

Notes

1. During the first ten months of 1986, state and federal grand juries have returned indictments alleging corrupt behavior by public officials in five municipal agencies: the Parking Violations Bureau, the Taxi and Limousine commission, the Health and Hospitals Corporation, the New York City Housing Authority, and the New York City Board of Education.
2. Since 1977, Court of Appeal and Court of Claim judges are gubernatorial appointments in accordance with merit selection systems. At the city level, only Family Court and criminal judges are appointed by the mayor pursuant to a merit selection system. All other judges are elected.
3. Literally: The Association of Israel.
4. Literally: Cohesion.

9

The Prospects for Change

Introduction

Working within the framework of a demo-elite perspective, this book has attempted to present a more balanced view of the uses and abuses of elite power in Western-style democracies than either pluralist theories on the one hand and Marxist or elitist theories on the other hand have been able to offer. It has presented the argument that Western-style democracy is beset by several shortcomings, including tendencies of the governing elite to exert power through manipulation and corruption. Yet, it is worth preserving, because of the relative autonomy or countervailing power of other elites, which limits the power of the governing elite, and puts certain (though not always effective) breaks on its tendencies to abuse power. It is worth preserving because of the relatively greater weight given in it to public preferences (as mediated through the electoral process and through social movements) as compared to the weight given to the public in other regimes. It is also worth preserving because it forms a relatively effective arena of struggle for change. The concluding chapter completes the argument by elaborating on this last point.

Since its inception, Western democracy has been inextricably interlinked with struggles, or conflict, and change. It was brought about by struggles, it has created further struggles, and once it eventuated, has continued to change. So it would be very odd indeed if this inherently dynamic system now suddenly ceased to change and were to become ossified in its present form. Thus, any theory of democracy must necessarily also be a theory of change in a democracy. The task at hand, therefore, is to develop at least some preliminary ideas on how the most distinctive features of democracy—and particularly the relative autonomy of elites—are related to democracy's potential for struggle, or conflict, and change.

Conflict and Contradiction in a Democracy

The relative autonomy, or countervailing power, of elites is of great importance in this respect, for it is both directly and indirectly related to conflict which, in turn, is closely connected to change. Conflict (as is self-evident) springs from divergent interests. And, in all regimes there are divergent interests between elites, classes, or other groups in society. However, in a democracy the relative autonomy of elites in the control of resources exacerbates the divergent interests between them and enhances the ability of such divergent interests to make themselves felt on the political scene. Thus, the relative autonomy of elites is important for democracy not only because it entails the ability of other elites to counter, or partly counter, the uses and abuses of power of the governing elite, but also because of its tendency to enhance conflict between elites, and to bring such conflict out into the open.

Apart from this direct relationship to conflict, the relative autonomy of elites is also indirectly related to conflict, because of the contradiction it creates for democracy: as previously explained in great detail, this relative autonomy of elites is part of the very essence of democracy, yet also obviates that essence. This contradiction, in turn, like the relative autonomy of elites itself, does not create conflict (which derives from opposing interests). But it has a tendency to exacerbate conflict because of the ambivalent and controversial "rules of the game" on elite relations that it calls forth.

As also noted before, it has become one of the stocks-in-trade of the social sciences that while there is conflict in a democracy, there is consensus over the rules by which that conflict is waged. In other words, it is a widely accepted tenet that conflict in a democracy is largely institutionalized. But if, as has been argued and shown, the contradiction of democracy spells some unclear and controversial rules on the relations between elites then (by definition) democratic conflict cannot be fully institutionalized. This also implies that conflict in a democracy is deeper and more ruthless than would otherwise be the case. For such lack of clarity of rules leads the various elites to interpret the rules to suit their own interests, and thus to clash in wider areas, and more vigorously, than would otherwise be the case.

The elites' diverging interests could have led them into conflict even if the rules governing their relations had been crystal-clear, and even if there had been general consensus over these rules. But then, given that the conflict would have been fully institutionalized, it would have been more sedate, and it also would have been held in check by sanctions applied to the transgressors of the rules. As it is, the unclear rules, which in many areas govern the relations between elites, and the lack of consensus over many of them, has made it possible for the various elites to use, manipulate, and exploit such rules to enhance their own stature and power to the detriment of their rivals—and thus to exacerbate conflict—without fully effective checks and restraints being imposed on such practices and conflicts.

Empirical support for this argument (as for some of the previous arguments) has come from my study of bureaucracy (1985a) and from my study of national broadcasting (1987). These have illustrated the conflicts between governing political elites on the one hand, and bureaucratic and broadcasting elites on the other hand, and the manner in which such conflicts were, in fact, exacerbated by the lack of clarity of, and lack of consensus over, the rules that supposedly were to govern the relations between them. Like the relative autonomy of elites, the ambivalent and contentious nature of the rules governing many aspects of their relations thus may not cause sociopolitical conflict, but it certainly renders it less regulated, and more severe, than would otherwise be the case.

Conflict, Contradiction, and Change in a Democracy

The countervailing power, or the relative autonomy of elites, is thus related to both contradiction and conflict, two sets of phenomena, the analysis of which has long been of strategic importance in the social sciences in connection with the analysis of social changes. As Lipset (1985) has recently reminded us, Marx's and Marxist theories have included as a central element the idea that all hitherto existing social formations contain inherent contradictions which, together with (class) conflict push for major social transformations. And structural-functionalism has shared with Marxism the idea that the inherent contradictions in social systems press for social change.

However, the contradiction of democracy, dealt with here, differs from the contradiction dealt with in Marxist and functionalist theory, in that it has no such clear-cut, direct relationship to social change. For the contradictions dealt with by both Marxists and functionalists are of a specific kind: they are incompatibilities between different social structures, or between different aspects of the social system, which push towards its restructuring. The inherent contradiction in the exercise of power in a democracy—dealt with here—is somewhat different: it is not an outright incompatibility, but a compatibility coupled with an incompatibility.

Therefore, the contradiction highlighted here is more in the nature of a paradox, and as such it resembles the social paradox highlighted in Simmel's theory more than it resembles the "fetters" or "strains" called to our attention in Marxist and functionalist theory, respectively. And just as Simmel's paradox does not necessarily cause change, neither does the contradiction here reviewed. But this contradiction is still indirectly related to change through its tendency to exacerbate conflict. For in the wake of Marx and Marxist theory, it is now generally accepted in the social sciences that (besides contradiction) conflict, too, leads to change.

Conflict, of course, being the result of the opposing interests of different people, groups, or elites, is not a generic cause of change. But by pitting these opposing interests against each other, by making it possible for the interests of hitherto dominant groups or elites—including the elites of privileged classes defending the status quo—to be confronted by the interests of hitherto subdued groups or elites—including elites of disadvantaged classes clamoring for change—conflict may mediate between opposing interests and the actual process of change. It may thus be argued that the relative autonomy of elites, coupled with the contradiction of democracy and the ambiguous rules it generates—by enhancing conflict between elites—also enhances the chances for sociopolitical change.

This is so especially since the contradiction of democracy, and the unclear rules it creates, generate less than fully institutionalized conflict. For if (as has been widely argued) conflict in a democracy were indeed waged by generally clear and mutually acceptable rules or in other words, were totally institutionalized, it might well have become ritualized, and might have amounted to little more than a distinct pattern of elite rotation in power. Certainly it could not have served as an effective mediator of democratic change. Hence, it is precisely the fact that the rules of democracy are *not* wholly clear and consensual, and that conflict in a democracy is *not* entirely institutionalized, which enhances the prospects of it leading to change.

A certain qualification to this argument, however, is in order. For, obviously, conflict leads to change only when there is a clash between groups or elites of which at least one side pushes for change, and when the power of those pushing for change outweighs the power of those who resist it, or at least is formidable enough to force the latter into concessions and compromises.

In light of this, there are several factors which, in Western-style democracies, as they exist today, hamper the prospects of conflict leading to change. First, the major, established elites, whose relative autonomy and divergent interests lead them into conflict, derive their positions from the existing system. Hence—despite divergent interests—they have a common, underlying interest in its perpetuation. Consequently, the conflict between them frequently consists of a jockeying for position within the existing power structure, and lacks a push for significant change. Second, those parts of the public which have an interest in perpetuating the status quo wield more power and influence than those parts of the public which have an interest in change. Third, the governing political elite uses a variety of incentives, *inter alia* through manipulation and corruption, to induce other elites and the public to accept its power, and thus, to perpetuate the status quo. It might seem, then, that generally, in Western-style democracy, the cards are stacked against conflict leading to major transformations in the distribution of power and material rewards.

Despite all this—and leaving aside change initiated by the governing elite itself—democracy and democratic conflict still offer better prospects for change in these respects than do other regimes. For, first, while the relatively advantaged have disproportionate power and influence, the relatively disadvantaged have the numbers. And, in a democracy, because of the electoral principle, sheer numbers count for more than they do in other regimes. Second, while the manipulation and corruption engaged in by the governing elite is designed to perpetuate the status quo under certain circumstances, and because of the countervailing power of other elites, it may be at least partly demystified and neutralized. Third, while most established elites, and certainly the central and most powerful elites, have an interest in the maintenance of the status quo, there are other, non- or less established elites, which have an unmistakable interest in change. These, of course, are mainly the elites of the less advantaged classes and of social-protest movements, whose raison d'être is, and whose very position as elites thus depends on their ability to "deliver" at least some of the changes in the distribution of resources demanded by their supporters.

The Elites of Social Movements and Change in a Democracy

Indeed, as was seen before, it was precisely the conflict between established and non–established elites which mediated the manner in which democracy came into being and developed in the first place, and in which a variety of socioeconomic reforms eventuated. So, by the same token, there is no reason to surmise that present and future conflict between established and initially non-established elites, may not be capable of leading to further changes in the power structure and in the allocation of resources in Western, democratic regimes.

And since non-established elites (whatever their own socioeconomic background) frequently represent disadvantaged classes or groups in society, whose interest lies in a more egalitarian distribution of resources, and since they can maintain their position only if they can demonstrate at least some achievements to their supporters, there is always a certain likelihood in a democracy that non-established elites will push for, and will achieve changes towards a more egalitarian distribution of resources. To a certain extent this was, in fact, the case with the elites of the disadvantaged in the nineteenth and the beginning of the twentieth century. It has continued (though to a lesser extent) into the late twentieth century and, in principle, there is no reason why it should not continue to be so in the future.

It is true that the achievements non-established elites provide for their supporters—in terms of redistribution of resources—frequently are smaller than those their supporters had expected and those the elites themselves had initially envisaged. This was shown to have been the case in the nineteenth century and, even more so, with respect to the recent social movements. For it was seen before that although these elites have made some headway (for instance in the distribution of resources between men and women), they have not had major achievements in leading to a restructuring of resources in Western societies of the late twentieth century.

As Robert Michels has perceptively pointed out long ago (1915) this has been so because the then initially non-established elites of the labor unions and parties in the late nineteenth, and the beginning of the twentieth century, have come to share power within the existing establishment. And as they became incorporated into the establishment, the very establishment they had previously opposed, they became increasingly willing to accept the status quo.

But while Michels was correct in his factual analysis, he nevertheless missed an important point, which now, with the hindsight of close to a century, of course, becomes much clearer. The point being that, before they were incorporated into the establishment, in the very process of becoming incorporated, or even after their incorporation, the elites of the labor movement have still managed to achieve important changes in the allocation of resources in favor of their supporters. In the very process of accepting the status quo, they still managed to change it. While they were being accused of betraying the cause of the disadvantaged, and while many of them were probably doing just that in the process of becoming part of the establishment, they nonetheless led to certain redistributions of resources.

Thus, not only have these elites been instrumental in having the franchise extended to include the working class, but—partly in response to their demands and actions—economic inequalities in Western societies have decreased substantially from the second half of the nineteenth century up to the 1950s and marginally up to the beginning of the 1970s, and only since then are there signs that such inequalities have increased once again (see, e.g., Etzioni-Halevy, 1985b, ch. 4).

As had been the case in Michels's time, recently, too, some initially non-established elites have been subsequently incorporated into the establishment. Above, this phenomenon has been analyzed under the heading of the absorption of protest; it has been shown to include the device of co-opting the movement's elites into existing power and reward structures, without letting them disrupt those structures, and without their being allowed to lead to basic redistributions of resources.

The redistributive achievements of the most recent movements and their elites have been modest not only because some of their elites have been co-opted, but also because many of them have not been representing the particular interests of the most disadvantaged groups and classes to begin with. For that reason they have not been concerned chiefly with the redistribution of resources in a more egalitarian fashion, but rather with "post-materialist" issues. Hence, the redistribution that has occurred in their wake has been less impressive even than the redistribution brought about by their predecessors in the nineteenth and beginning of the twentieth centuries. But, as could be seen, this is not to say that no movements have been concerned with inequalities, and that no changes at all have resulted from their activities. The Black Rights Movements and the Feminist Movements have not followed the post-materialist pattern and the, albeit limited, changes they have helped bring about may be cumulative, and thus result in more substantial changes as time goes on.

Moreover, while several recent movements and their elites have not given high priority to rectifying inequities and inequalities, there is nothing logically inevitable or divinely preordained about this situation. Just as Marxist theory envisages revolutionary class consciousness, democratic theory (including the present one) envisages at least the possibility of democratic public consciousness. Elites that originate from disadvantaged groups or classes or that, for other reasons, identify their interests with those of the disadvantaged, may well arouse such consciousness amongst them, or give expression to such consciousness when it arises, and may well lead popular movements aimed at abolishing inequities and inequalities.

Like the past and present movements' elites, the elites of whatever new movements for greater equality may come upon the scene in the future, may well be co-opted and may eventually become part of the establishment and staunch defenders of the status quo. But in the process, they may nonetheless have substantial achievements in leading Western societies onto the path towards greater equality, as their earlier predecessors have had before them. And if, or when, they get co-opted, others may well come to take their place.

Conclusion

In conclusion, then, it may be said that—in a democracy—change frequently comes about through the countervailing power of non-established elites as against that of the governing elite, the only partly institutionalized conflict or struggle thus created, and the absorption of this conflict or protest, via the eventual incorporation of counter-elites into the establishment. In other words, the recurring cycles of the generation of non-established elites championing the interests of the disadvantaged, their conflict with the established elites, their subsequent manipulation, the according of some achievements to them, but without letting them effect major transformations in existing structures of power and resources allocations, the subsequent co-optation and absorption of several of them into the establishment and their consequent acceptance of the status quo, and finally the generation of yet other non-established elites to take their place, may be seen as a major pattern in which change in the allocation of resources in Western democracies takes place.

The reallocation of resources that occurs through this pattern at any particular point in time may not seem large or impressive. But looked at over longer time spans, the changes may be seen to be incremental and cumulative. This pattern of change has already involved major reallocations and redistributions of resources over the last centuries; and although in recent years the redistribution may have been even less impressive than before, and although inequalities have still remained great, it is not inconceivable that greater redistributions may occur in the future.

Some Options for the Future

Two possible directions which change towards a more egalitarian distribution of power and material resources in democratic regimes may take, are those toward greater democratization and lessening inequalities in political life through referenda and initiatives, and those towards greater democratization and lessening inequalities in economic life through workers' co-operatives. Both have been tried on relatively larger scales already, and their success has not been negligible. Referenda and initiatives have become institutionalized in Switzerland and seem to be working reasonably well (see Butler and Ranney, 1978). Worker cooperatives have been established on various scales in various Western countries, and they, too, have had a measure of success (see, e.g., Roy, 1976). Of course, the fact that they have had some success in some cases in the past does not ensure that they will be as successful elsewhere and in the future. But past success renders the possibility of success in the future sufficiently feasible to make at least experimental emulation of past attempts eminently worthwhile.

Neither referenda and initiatives nor cooperatives hold out the promise of abolishing elites. Indeed, to come about on a larger scale, they would themselves have to be championed by elites (most likely, by non-established or counter-elites). Also, they do not hold out the promise of abolishing economic inequalities altogether. But they are here highlighted because both hold out the promise of curbing the power of elites, of mitigating inequalities, of modifying and perhaps gradually abolishing capitalism, without bringing about state control of the economy. They hold out the promise of leading to change in democracy, and of doing so by democratic means and thus of enhancing, and creating a more equitable, and a more democratic democracy.

It is evidently possible that other forces, the nature of which cannot now be foreseen, might enter the sociopolitical arena of Western democracies. Since—as the previous analysis has shown—the present, admittedly imperfect democratic processes are fragile, it can only be hoped that if, and when, new forces of change eventuate, they will handle those democratic processes with care, lest their disruption give rise to an even more politically and economically unequal society in the framework of an authoritarian or a totalitarian regime.

References

Abraham, Henry J.
1980 *The Judicial Process*, New York: Oxford University Press. (4th edition).
Alford, Robert R. and Roger Friedland
1985 *Powers of Theory*, Cambridge: Cambridge University Press.
Ancker, D.
1982 "A Definition of Democracy," *Scandinavian Political Studies*, Vol. 15, pp. 217–35.
Anderson, Robert D.
1977 *France, 1870–1914*, London: Routledge & Kegan Paul.
Aron, Raymond
1950 "Social Structure and the Ruling Class," *The British Journal of Sociology*, Part 1—March; Part 2—June.
Aron, Raymond
1968 *Progress and Disillusion*, London: Pall Mall Press.
Aron, Raymond
1978 *Politics and History*, (trans. M. Bernheim-Conant), New York: Free Press.
Aron, Raymond (Franciszek Draus ed.)
1985 *History, Truth, Liberty: Selected Writings of Raymond Aron*, Chicago: University of Chicago Press.
Avakian, Bob
1986 *Democracy: Can't We do Better than That?*, Chicago: Banner Press.
Bachrach, Peter
1967 *The Theory of Democratic Elitism: A Critique*, Boston: Little Brown.
Barbalet, J.M.
1988 "Social Organization and Group Processes in Power Relations," Canberra: (unpublished).
Barber, Benjamin R.
1971 *Superman and Common Men*, New York: Praeger.
Barber, Benjamin R.
1984 *Strong Democracy*, Berkeley: University of California Press.
Bell, Daniel
1961 *The End of Ideology*, New York: Collier MacMillan.
Berelson, Bernard R., Paul F. Lazarsfeld and W.M McPhee
1954 *Voting*, Chicago: University of Chicago Press.
Berns, Walter
1984 *In Defense of Liberal Democracy*, Chicago: Gateway Editions.
Birch, A.H.
1975 *The British System of Government*, London: Allen & Unwin, (revised edition).

Birnbaum, Pierre and B. Badie
1983 *The Sociology of the State,* (trans. A. Goldhammer), Chicago: University of Chicago Press.

Block, Fred
1987 *Revising State Theory,* Philadelphia: Temple University Press.

Bottomore, Tom
1979 *Political Sociology,* London: Hutchinson.

Bridges, E.
1971 "Portrait of a Profession," in Chapman, R.A. and A. Dunsire, (eds.), *Style in Administration,* London: Allen & Unwin, pp. 46–60.

Brinton, Crane
1957 *The Anatomy of Revolution,* New York: Vintage Books.

Bürklin, Wilhelm P.
1985 "The Post-Industrial Non-Established and the Party System," *International Political Science Review,* Vol. 6, pp. 463–82.

Burton, Michael G. and John Higley
1987a "Elite Settlements," *American Sociological Review,* Vol 52, pp. 295–307.

Burton Michael G. and Higley, John
1987b "Invitation to Elite Theory," in G. William Domhoff and Thomas R. Dye (eds.), *Power Elites and Organizations,* Newbury Park, CA: Sage.

Butler, David and Austin Ranney (eds.)
1978 *Referendums,* Washington, D.C.: American Enterprise Institute for Public Policy Research.

Carter, April
1973 *Direct Action and Liberal Democracy,* London: Routledge & Kegan Paul.

Cawson, A.
1978 "Pluralism, Corporatism and the Role of the State," *Government and Opposition,* Vol. 13, pp. 178–98.

Cawson, A.
1983 "Functional Representation and Democratic Politics," in G. Duncan (ed.), *Democratic Theory and Practice,* New York: Cambridge University Press, pp. 173–84.

Cawson, A.
1986 "Policy Networks and Power Dependence," paper presented to the International Sociological Association Conference, Delhi, India.

Conboy, Kenneth and Joseph Hutchinson
1986 "An Assessment of the New York City Inspector General System as an Instrument for the Identification and Reduction of Corruption in Municipal Government," New York: Department of Investigation of the City of New York (Unpublished).

Cook, A.H.
1975 "Equal Pay: Where Is It?" *Industrial Relations,* Vol. 14, pp. 158–88.

Corcoran, M. and G.J. Duncan
1979 "Work History, Labor Force Attachment and Earnings Differences Between Races and Sexes," *Journal of Human Resources,* Vol. 14, pp. 3–20.

Costain, Anne N. and W. Douglas Costain
1985 "Movements and Gatekeepers: Congressional Response to Women's Movement Issues 1900-1982," *Congress and the Presidency,* Vol. 12, pp. 21–42.

Crouch, C.
1979 "The State, Capital and Liberal Democracy," in C. Couch (ed.), *State and Economy in Contemporary Capitalism*, London: Croom Helm, pp. 13–54.

Dahl, Robert A.
1956 *A Preface to Democratic Theory*, Chicago: University of Chicago Press.

Dahl, Robert A.
1967 *Pluralist Democracy in the United States*, Chicago: Rand McNally.

Dahl, Robert A
1969 "Stability, Change and the Democratic Creed," in C.F. Cnudde and D.E. Neubauer (eds.), *Empirical Democratic Theory*, Chicago: Markham Publishing Co., pp. 253–67.

Dahl, Robert A.
1970 *Modern Political Analysis*, Englewood Cliffs NJ: Prentice Hall (2nd edition).

Dahl, Robert A.
1971 *Polyarchy*, New Haven: Yale University Press.

Dahl, Robert A.
1982 *Dilemmas of Pluralist Democracy*, New Haven: Yale University Press.

Dahl, Robert A.
1985 *A Preface to Economic Democracy*, Berkeley: University of California Press.

Dahl, Robert A. and Charles E. Lindblom
1953 *Politics, Economics and Welfare*, New York: Harper.

Desai, Uday
1985 "Citizen Participation and Environmental Policy Implementation," paper prepared for the XIII World Congress of the International Political Science Association, Paris, July.

Dix, H.M.
1981 *Environmental Pollution*, Chichester: John Wiley and Sons.

Djilas, M.
1981 *The Story from the Inside*, London: Weidenfeld and Nicholson.

Domhoff, G. William
1967 *Who Rules America?*, Englewood Cliffs, N.J.: Prentice Hall.

Domhoff, G. William
1970 *The Higher Circles*, New York: Random House.

Domhoff, G. William
1974 *The Bohemia Grove and Other Retreats*, New York: Harper and Row.

Domhoff, G. William
1978 *The Powers that Be*, New York: Random House.

Domhoff, G. William
1983 *Who Rules America Now?*, Englewood Cliffs: N.J. Prentice Hall.

Dowse, Robert E. and John A. Hughes
1986 *Political Sociology*, Chichester: John Wiley & Sons (2nd edition).

Duverger, Maurice
1958 *The French Political System* (trans. B. and R. North), Chicago: University of Chicago Press.

Duverger, Maurice
1964 *Political Parties* (trans. B. & R. North), London: Methuen, (3rd Edition).

Dye, Thomas R.
1976 *Who's Running America?*, Englewood Cliffs, N.J.: Prentice Hall.
Dye, Thomas, R.
1979 *Who's Running America? The Carter Years*, Englewood Cliffs, N.J.: Prentice Hall.
Dye, Thomas R.
1983 *Who's Running America? The Reagan Years*, Englewood Cliffs, N.J.: Prentice Hall.
Dye, Thomas R.
1985 *Who's Running America? The Conservative Years*, Englewood Cliffs, N.J.: Prentice Hall.
Dye, Thomas R. and L. Harmon Zeigler
1987 *The Irony of Democracy*, Monterey, Cal.: Brooks/Cole Publishing, (7th edition).
Edelman, Murray J.
1971 *Politics as Symbolic Action*, New York: Academic Press.
Ehrlich, Eyal
1987 "Moshe Kazav's Backyard," *Ha'aretz Supplement*, 2 January, pp. 4–6.
Eisenstadt, Shmuel N.
1967 *Israeli Society*, London: Weidenfeld & Nicolson.
Ellul, J.
1965 *The Technological Society*, (tr. J. Wilkinson), London: Jonathan Cape.
Elseworth, Steve
1984 *Acid Rain*, London: Pluto Press.
England, P. and D.S. McLaughlin
1979 "Sex Segregation of Jobs and Male-Female Income Differentials," in Rodolfo Alvarez, Kenneth G. Lutterman and Associates (eds.), *Discrimination in Organizations*, San Francisco: Jossey Bass.
Etzioni, Amitai
1961 *A Comparative Analysis of Complex Organizations*, Glencoe: The Free Press.
Etzioni, Amitai
1984 *Capital Corruption*, San Diego: Harcourt, Brace Jovanovich.
Etzioni-Halevy, Eva
1979 *Political Manipulation and Administrative Power*, London: Routledge & Kegan Paul.
Etzioni-Halevy, Eva
1985a *Bureaucracy and Democracy: A Political Dilemma*, London: Routledge and Kegan Paul, (revised edition).
Etzioni-Halevy, Eva
1985b *The Knowledge Elite and the Failure of Prophecy*, London: George Allen and Unwin.
Etzioni-Halevy, Eva
1987 *National Broadcasting Under Siege*, London: Macmillan.
Etzioni-Halevy, Eva with Rina Shapira
1977 *Political Culture in Israel*, New York: Praeger.
Etzioni-Halevy, Eva and Ann Illy
1986 "Women in Legislatures: Israel in a Comparative Perspective," *Contemporary Jewry*, vol. 7, pp. 65–77.

Evans, Peter, Dietrich Rueschemeyer and Theda Skocpol (eds.)
1985 *Bringing the State Back In*, Cambridge: Cambridge University Press.

Field, G. Lowell and John Higley
1980 *Elitism*, London: Routledge and Kegan Paul.

French, D. and E. French
1975 *Working Communally*, New York: Russell Sage Foundation.

Fromm, Erich
1960 *The Fear of Freedom*, London: Routledge & Kegan Paul.

Giddens, Anthony
1977 *Studies in Social and Political Theory*, London: Hutchinson.

Giddens, Anthony
1981 *A Contemporary Critique of Historical Materialism*, London: Macmillan.

Giddens, Anthony
1982 *Profiles and Critiques in Social Theory*, London: Macmillan.

Gladden, E. N.
1972 *A History of Public Administration*, London: Frank Cass.

Goldenberg, E.N.
1984 "The Permanent Government in an Era of Retrenchment and Redirection," in L.S. Salmon and M.S. Lund (eds.), *The Reagan Administration and the Governing of America*, Washington D.C.: The Urban Institute Press.

Great Britain Central Statistical Office
1985 *Social Trends*, No. 15, London: Her Majesty's Stationary Office.

Gross, B.M. and J.F. Kraus
1982 "The Political Machine Is Alive and Well," *Social Policy*, Vol. 12, pp. 38–46.

Habermas, Jurgen
1975 *Legitimation Crisis*, (trans. T. McCarthy), Boston: Beacon Press.

Harmel, Robert
1985 "On the Study of New Parties," *International Political Science Review*, Vol. 6, pp. 403–18.

Heilbroner, R.L
1962 *The Making of Economic Society*, New York: Macmillan.

Held, David
1987 *Models of Democracy*, Cambridge: Polity Press.

Higley, John, Desley Decon and Don Smart
1979 *Elites in Australia*, London: Routledge and Kegan Paul.

Hindess, Barry
1980 "Marxism and Parliamentary Democracy," in Alan Hunt (ed.), *Marxism and Democracy*, London: Lawrence and Wishart, pp. 21–54.

Hobsbawm, E.J.
1962 *The Age of Revolution 1789-1848*, New York: Mentor Books.

Hobsbawm, E.J.
1968 *Labouring Men*, London: Weidenfeld & Nicolson (2nd edition).

Hobsbawm, E.J.
1972 *Labouring Men: Studies in the History of Labour*, London: Weidenfeld & Nicolson.

Hobsbawm, E.J.
1975 *The Age of Capital 1848–1875*, London: Weidenfeld & Nicolson.

Holgate, Martin. W
1979 *A Perspective on Environmental Pollution*, Cambridge: Cambridge University Press.
Horowitz, Irving L.
1984 *Winners and Losers*, Durham, N.C.: Duke University Press.
Huntington, Samuel P.
1968 *Political Order in Changing Societies, New Haven: Yale University Press.*
International Institute for Strategic Studies
1970-71,
1986-87 *The Military Balance*, London: Arms & Armour Press.
Ippolito, Dennis S.
1976 *Public Opinion and Responsible Democracy*, Hempstead, Herts: Prentice-Hall International.
Israel State Comptroller
1984 *Report for the Financial Year of 1984, and for the Financial Reports of 1983* (35).
Israel State Comptroller
1985 *Report for the Financial Year of 1985, and for the Financial Reports of 1984* (36).
Jacoby, H.
1973 *The Bureaucratization of the World*, (tr. E.L. Kanes), Berkeley: University of California Press.
James, J.L.
1974 *American Political Parties in Transition*, New York: Harper & Row.
Jessop, Bob
1978 "Capitalism and Democracy," in G. Littlejohn, G. Smart, B. Wakeford, and N. Yuval-Davis (eds.), *Power and the State*, Croom Helm: London, pp. 10–15.
Jessop, Bob
1979 "Corporatism, Parliamentarism and Social Democracy," in p.C. Schmitter and G. Lehmbruch (eds.), *Trends Toward Corporatist Intermediation*, Beverly Hills: Sage Publications, pp. 185–212.
Johnston, Michael
1982 *Political Corruption and Public Policy in America*, Monterey: Brooks/Cole.
Jones, Frank L.
1983 "Sources of Gender Inequality in Income," *Social Forces*, Vol. 12, pp. 134–52.
Jones, Frank L.
1984 "Income Inequality," In Dorothy H. Broom (ed.), *Unfinished Business: Social Justice for Women*, Sydney: George Allen & Unwin, pp. 101–15.
Kariel, H.S.
1970 *Frontiers of Democratic Theory*, New York: Random House.
Keller, S.
1963 *Beyond the Ruling Class*, New York: Random House.
Kitschelt, Herbert P.
1985 "Political Opportunity Structure and Political Protest," *British Journal of Political Science*, Vol. 16, pp 57–85.
Knoke, David
1981 "Power Structures," in S.L Long (ed.), *The Handbook of Political Behavior*, New York: Plenum, pp. 275–326.

Knowles, L.C.A.
1932 *Economic Development in the Nineteenth Century,* London: Routledge & Kegan Paul.

Kornhauser, A.W.
1959 *Problems of Power in American Democracy,* Detroit: Wayne State University Press.

Langrod, J.S.
1967 "General Problems of the French Civil Service," in N. Raphaeli (ed.), *Readings in Comparative Public Administration,* Boston: Allyn & Beacon.

Lefebvre, Georges
1947 *The Coming of the French Revolution, 1789,* (trans. R.R. Palmer), Princeton, N.J.: Princeton University Press.

Lefebvre, Georges
1962-64 *The French Revolution,* London: Routledge & Kegan Paul.

Leichter, Franz
1986 "Campaign Contributions to Members of the Board of Estimate and the Democratic County Committees, 1981–86," (Unpublished).

Leonard, R.L.
1968 *Elections in Britain,* London: Van Nostrand.

Levine, A.
1981 *Liberal Democracy: A Critique of Its Theory,* New York: Columbia University Press.

Lindblom, Charles E.
1977 *Politics and Markets,* New York: Basic Books.

Lipset, Seymour M.
1965 *Sociology of Democracy,* Neuwied: H. Luchterhand.

Lipset, Seymour M.
1967 "Party Systems and the Representation of Social Groups," in R.C. Macridis (ed.), *Political Parties,* New York: Harper & Row, pp. 40–74.

Lipset, Seymour M.
1985 *Consensus and Conflict,* New Brunswick, N.J.: Transaction.

Lipset, Seymour M., Martin A. Trow, and James S. Coleman
1956 *Union Democracy,* Glencoe, Ill: The Free Press.

Lorwin, Val R.
1954 *The French Labour Movement,* Cambridge, Mass.: Harvard University Press.

Macridis, Roy C.
1967 *The Study of Comparative Government,* New York: Random House.

Mandel, Ernest
1975 *Late Capitalism,* (trans. J. De Bres), London: New Left Books (revised edition).

Mann, Michael
1984 "The Autonomous Power of the State," *Archives Européennes de Sociologie,* Vol. 25, pp. 185–213.

Marcuse, Herbert
1964 *One-Dimensional Man,* Boston: Beacon Press.

Margolis, M.
1983 "Democracy: American Style," in G. Duncan (ed.), *Democratic Theory and Practice,* Cambridge: Cambridge University Press.

Marx, Karl
1969a *The Civil War in France,* in Karl Marx and Friedrich Engels, *Selected Works* (in 3 Volumes), Moscow: Progress Publishers, Vol. 2.
Marx, Karl
1969b *The Class Struggles in France,* in Marx and Engels, *Selected Works,* Vol. 1.
May, J.D.
1978 "Defining Democracy," *Political Studies,* Vol. 26, pp. 1–14.
McClosky, H.
1969 "Consensus and Ideology in American Politics," in C.F. Cnudde and E. Neubauer (eds.), *Empirical Democratic Theory,* Chicago: Markham, pp. 268–302.
McConnell, G.
1966 *Private Power and American Democracy,* New York: Knopf.
McKenzie, R.T.
1963 *British Political Parties,* London: Heinemann (2nd edition).
Meehan, Elizabeth M.
1985 *Women's Rights at Work,* Basingstoke: Macmillan.
Meynaud, J.
1964 *Technocracy,* (tr. P. Barnes), London: Faber & Faber.
Michels, Robert
1915 *Political Parties,* (trans. E. and C. Paul), London: Jarrold.
Milbrath, Lester W. and M.L. Goel
1965 *Political Participation: How and Why Do People Get Involved in Politics,* Chicago: Rand McNally (2nd edition).
Miliband, Ralph
1973 *The State in Capitalist Society,* London: Quartet Books.
Miliband, Ralph
1977 *Marxism and Politics,* Oxford: Oxford University Press.
Miliband, Ralph
1982 *Capitalist Democracy in Britain,* Oxford: Oxford University Press.
Mills, C. Wright
1959 *The Power Elite,* London: Oxford University Press.
Moore, Barrington Jr.
1969 *Social Origins of Dictatorship and Democracy,* Harmondsworth, Middlesex: Penguin Books.
Mosca, Gaetano
1939 *The Ruling Class,* (trans. H.D. Kahn), New York: McGraw Hill.
Moss, Robert
1975 *The Collapse of Democracy,* London: Abacus, Sphere Books.
Mueller, C.
1973 *The Politics of Communication,* New York: Oxford University Press.
Müller-Rommel, Ferdinand
1985a "New Social Movements and Smaller Parties: A Comparative Perspective," *Western European Politics,* Vol. 8, pp. 41–54.
Müller-Rommel, Ferdinand
1985b "The Greens in Western Europe: Similar But Different," *International Political Science Review,* Vol. 6, pp. 483–500.
Mushaben, Joyce Marie
1985 "Cycles of Peace Protest in West Germany," *Western European Politics,* Vol. 8, pp. 24–40.

Nas, T.F., A.L. Price, and C.T. Wever
1986 "A Policy Oriented Theory of Corruption," *American Political Science Review,* Vol. 80, pp. 107–19.

Nedeleman, Brigitta
1984 "New Political Movements and Changes in Processes of Intermediation," *Social Science Information,* Vol. 23, pp. 1029–48.

O'Connor, James
1973 *The Fiscal Crisis of the State,* New York: St. Martin's Press.

O'Connor, James
1978 "The Democratic Movement in the United States," *Kapitalistate,* Vol. 7, pp. 15–26.

OECD
1980 "Women in the Labour Market," *OECD Observer,* No. 104, pp. 3–15.

Offe, Claus
1972 "Political Authority and Class Structures—An Analysis of the Late Capitalist Societies," *International Journal of Sociology,* Vol. 2, pp. 73–108.

Offe, Claus
1984 *Contradictions of the Welfare State,* Cambridge, Mass: MIT Press.

Ostrogorski, M.
1902 *Democracy and the Organization of Political Parties,* London: Macmillan.

Page, Edward C.
1985 *Political Authority and Bureaucratic Power,* Knoxville: University of Tennessee Press.

Palmer, R.R.
1964 *The Age of the Democratic Revolution,* Princeton, N.J.: Princeton University Press.

Panitch, L.
1980 "Recent Theorizations of Corporatism," *British Journal of Sociology,* Vol. 31, pp. 159–87.

Panitch, L.
1981 "Trade Unions and the Capitalist State," *New Left Review,* Vol. 125, pp. 21–43.

Parenti, M.
1980 *Democracy for the Few,* New York: St. Martin's Press.

Parris, H.
1969 *Constitutional Bureaucracy,* London: Allen & Unwin.

Pateman, Carole
1970 *Participation and Democratic Theory,* Cambridge: Cambridge University Press.

Pedersen, J.T.
1985 "The Relationship Between Democratic Values and Norms in the Danish Electorate," *Scandinavian Political Studies,* pp. 23–43.

Perkin, Harold
1969 *The Origins of Modern British Society 1780–1880,* London: Routledge & Kegan Paul.

Peters, B.G.
1978 *The Politics of Bureaucracy,* New York: Longman.

Peters, J.G. and S. Welch
1978 "Political Corruption in America," *American Political Science Review,* Vol. 72, pp. 974–84.
Pierson, Christopher
1984 "New Theories of the State and Civil Society: Recent Developments in Post Marxist Analysis of the State," *Sociology,* Vol. 18, pp. 563–71.
Plotke, David, Ernesto Laclau, and Chantal Mouffe
1982 "Recasting Marxism," *Socialist Review,* Vol. 66, pp. 92–113.
Poggi, Gianfranco.
1978 *The Development of the Modern State,* London: Hutchinson.
Polsby, N.W.
1985 "Prospects for Pluralism," *Society,* Vol. 22, pp. 30–34.
Poulantzas, Nicos
1975 *Political Power and Social Classes,* London: New Left Books.
Poulantzas, Nicos
1978 *State, Power, Socialism,* (trans. P. Camiller), London: New Left Books.
President's (the) Commission on the Status of Women
1963 *Women in America,* Washington D.C.
President's (the) Commission on Campus Unrest
1970 *Report of the President's Commission on Campus Unrest,* Washington, D.C.
President's (the) Task Force on Women's Rights and Responsibilities
1970 *A Matter of Simple Justice,* Washington, D.C.
Prewitt, Kenneth and Alan Stone
1973 *The Ruling Elites,* New York: Harper & Row.
Price, Roger (ed.)
1975 *1848—Revolution and Reaction,* London: Croom Helm.
Qualter, T.H.
1985 *Opinion Control in the Democracies,* London: Macmillan in association with the London School of Economics and Political Science.
Rich, Wilbur C.
1982 *The Politics of Urban Personnel Policy,* Port Washington, N.Y.: Kennikat Press.
Richards, P.G.
1963 *Patronage in British Government,* London: Allen & Unwin.
Ridley, F. and J. Blondel
1964 *Public Administration in France,* London: Routledge & Kegan Paul.
Riesman, David
1961 *The Lonely Crowd,* New Haven: Yale University Press.
Riker, W.
1986 *The Art of Political Manipulation,* New Haven: Yale University Press.
Rotstein, Maurice
1983 *The Democratic Myth,* Florham Park, N.J.: The Florham Park Press.
Roy, E.P.
1976 *Co-operatives: Development, Principles, and Management,* Danville, Ill: Interstate Printers and Publishers (3rd edition).
Sartori, Giovanni
1962 *Democratic Theory,* Detroit: Wayne State University Press.
Sartori, Giovanni
1987 *The Theory of Democracy Revisited,* Chatham N.J.: Chatham House Publishers.

Scanlon, J.
1986 "A Root of Municipal Scandals," *The New York Times,* 9 June, p. A23.
Schattschneider, E.E.
1960 *The Semi-Sovereign People,* New York: Holt, Rinehart & Winston.
Schmitter, P.C. and G. Lehmbruch (eds.)
1979 *Trends toward Corporatist Intermediation,* Beverly Hills: Sage Publications.
Schonfeld, W.R.
1981 "The 'Closed' Worlds of Socialist and Gaullist Elites," in J. Horworth and P.G. Cerny (eds.), *Elites in France,* London: Frances Pinter, pp. 196–215.
Schumpeter, Joseph A.
1976 *Capitalism, Socialism and Democracy,* New York: Harper & Row (5th edition).
Scott, Hilda
1984 *Working Your Way to the Bottom,* London: Pandora Press.
Searls, E.
1981 "Ministerial Cabinets and Elite Theory," in Horworth and Cerny (eds.), *Elites in France.*
Selznick, Philip
1949 *TVA and the Grass Roots: A Study in the Sociology of Formal Organization,* Berkley, Cal.: University of California Press.
Sharkansky, Ira
1986 "Distinguishing 'Corruption' from 'Flexibility' in the Israeli Public Sector," paper prepared for delivery at the 1986 Annual Meeting of the American Political Science Association, Washington, D.C.
Skocpol, Theda
1979 *States and Social Revolutions,* Cambridge: Cambridge University Press.
Small, Melvin
1984 "The Impact of the Antiwar Movement on Lyndon Johnson, 1965–1968: A Preliminary Report," *Peace and Change,* Vol. 10, pp. 1–22.
Soboul, Albert
1977 *A Short History of the French Revolution 1789–1799,* (trans. G. Symcox), Berkeley, Cal.: University of California Press.
Sovern, Michael I., Chairman, State-City Commission on Integrity in Government
1986a "Report and Recommendations on Conflict of Interest and Financial Disclosure Requirements" (Unpublished).
Sovern, Michael I., Chairman, State-City Commission on Integrity in Government
1986b "Report and Recommendations Relating to City Procurement and Contracts" (Unpublished).
Sovern, Michael I., Chairman, State-City Commission on Integrity in Government
1986c "Report on a Bill on Campaign Financing and Public Funding of Election Campaigns" (Unpublished).
Sovern, Michael I., Chairman, State-City Commission on Integrity in Government
1986d "Report on the Merit Selection System for New York Judges" (Unpublished).
Sovern, Michael I., Chairman, State-City Commission on Integrity in Government
1986e "The Quest for an Ethical Environment" (Unpublished).
Sowerwine, Charles
1982 *Sisters or Citizens?,* Cambridge: Cambridge University Press.

Stone, Clarence N.
1987 "Elite Distemper Versus the Promise of Democracy," In Domhoff and Dye (eds.), *Power Elites and Organizations*, pp. 239–65.
Suleiman, Ezra N.
1974 *Politics, Power and Bureaucracy in France*, Princeton: Princeton University Press.
Therborn, Goran
1977 "The Rule of Capital and the Rise of Democracy," *New Left Review*, Vol. 103, pp. 3–41.
Therborn, Goran
1978 *What Does the Ruling Class Do When It Rules?* London: New Left Books.
Thompson, E.P.
1980 *The Making of the English Working Class*, London: Victor Gollancz.
Thompson, Elaine
1983 "Democracy, Bureaucracy and Mythology," in Alexander Kouzmin (ed.), *Public Sector Administration*, Melbourne: Longman Cheshire, pp. 517–77.
Thomson, David
1966 *Europe Since Napoleon*, Harmondsworth, Middlesex: Penguin (Revised Edition).
Tilly, Charles
1981 *As Sociology Meets History*, New York: Academic Press.
Trager, David G., Chairman, State of New York Commission of Investigation
1986 "An Investigation of the New York City Taxi and Limousine Commission: Findings and Recommendations," (Unpublished).
Truman, David
1971 *The Governmental Process*, New York: Knopf (2nd edition).
United States Bureau of the Census
1986;
1987 *Statistical Abstract of the United States*, Washington, D.C.: Government Printing Office.
United States Commission on Civil Rights
1970 *The Federal Civil Rights Enforcement Effort: A Report*, Washington, D.C.: U.S. Government Printing Office.
United States Commission on Civil Rights
1971 *The Federal Civil Rights Enforcement Effort: One Year Later*, Washington, D.C.: U.S. Government Printing Office.
United States Commission on Civil Rights
1973 *The Federal Civil Rights Enforcement Effort: A Reassessment Report*, Washington, D.C.: U.S. Government Printing Office.
United States Commission on Civil Rights
1975 *The Federal Civil Rights Enforcement Effort—1974*, Washington, D.C.: U.S. Government Printing Office.
United States Commission on Civil Rights
1978 *Social Indicators of Equality for Minorities and Women: A Report*, Washington, D.C.: U.S. Government Printing Office.
Useem, Michael
1984 *The Inner Circle*, New York: Oxford University Press.

Walker, J.L.
1966 "A Critique of the Elitist Theory of Democracy," *The American Political Science Review,* Vol. LX, pp. 285–95.

Wass, D.
1985 "The Civil Service at the Crossroads," *Political Quarterly,* Vol. 56, pp. 227–41.

Weber, Max
1947 *The Theory of Social and Economic Organization,* (trans. A.M. Henderson and T. Parsons), New York: Free Press.

Weber, Max (H.H. Gerth and C. Wright Mills eds. and trans.)
1958 *From Max Weber Essays in Sociology,* New York: Oxford University Press.

Weber, Max
1968 *Economy and Society,* (trans. G. Roth and L. Wittich), New York: Bedminster Press.

Werner, Simcha B.
1983 "New Directions in the Study of Administrative Corruption," *Public Administration Review,* Vol. 43, pp. 146–54.

Williams, P.M.
1954 *Politics in Post-War France,* London: Longmans Green.

Williams, P.M.
1964 *Crisis and Compromise,* London: Longmans, Green & Company (3rd edition).

Wilson, H.T.
1984 *Political Management,* Berlin: Walter de Gruyter.

Zeitlin, Maurice
1980 "On Classes, Class Conflict and the State: An Introductory Note," in *Classes, Class Conflict and the State,* Cambridge, Mass.: Winthrop Publishers, pp. 1–37.

Name Index

Subject Index